Advanced Creative Nonfiction

Online resources to accompany this book are available at http://www.
bloomsburyonlineresources.com/advanced-creative-nonfiction. Please
type the URL into your web browser and follow the instruction to access
the Companion Website. If you experience any problems, please contact
Bloomsbury at: companionwebsites@bloombury.com

BLOOMSBURY WRITER'S GUIDES AND ANTHOLOGIES

Bloomsbury Writer's Guides and Anthologies offer established and aspiring creative writers an introduction to the art and craft of writing in a variety of forms, from poetry to environmental and nature writing. Each book is part craft-guide, with writing prompts and exercises, and part anthology, with relevant works by major authors.

Series Editors:

Sean Prentiss, Norwich University, USA

Joe Wilkins, Linfield College, USA

Titles in the Series:

Environmental and Nature Writing, Sean Prentiss and Joe Wilkins

Poetry, Amorak Huey and W. Todd Kaneko

Short-Form Creative Writing, H. K. Hummel and Stephanie Lennox

Creating Comics, Chris Gavaler and Leigh Ann Beavers

Forthcoming Titles:

The Art and Craft of Stories from Asia, Xu Xi and Robin Hemley

Fantasy Fiction, Jennifer Pullen

Advanced Fiction, Amy E. Weldon

Advanced Creative Nonfiction

A Writer's Guide and Anthology

Sean Prentiss and Jessica Hendry Nelson

BLOOMSBURY ACADEMIC

LONDON • NEW YORK • OXFORD • NEW DELHI • SYDNEY

BLOOMSBURY ACADEMIC
Bloomsbury Publishing Plc
50 Bedford Square, London, WC1B 3DP, UK
1385 Broadway, New York, NY 10018, USA
29 Earlsfort Terrace, Dublin 2, Ireland

BLOOMSBURY, BLOOMSBURY ACADEMIC and the Diana logo are
trademarks of Bloomsbury Publishing Plc

First published in Great Britain 2021

Cover design: Namkwan Cho
Cover image: 'Open Mind' by Johson Tsang

A catalogue record for this book is available from the British Library.

Library of Congress Cataloging-in-Publication Data
Names: Prentiss, Sean, 1972- author. | Nelson, Jessica Hendry, author.
Title: Advanced creative nonfiction : a writer's and illustrator's guide
and anthology / Sean Prentiss and Jessica Hendry Nelson.
Description: London ; New York : Bloomsbury Academic, 2021. |
Series: Bloomsbury writers' guides and anthologies | Includes
bibliographical references and index. |
Identifiers: LCCN 2020040932 (print) | LCCN 2020040933 (ebook)
| ISBN 9781350067806 (paperback) | ISBN 9781350067813 (hardback) |
ISBN 9781350067820 (epub) | ISBN 9781350067837 (ebook)
Subjects: LCSH: Creative nonfiction–Authorship. | Essay–Authorship. |
Creation (Literary, artistic, etc.)
Classification: LCC PN145 .P626 2021 (print) |
LCC PN145 (ebook) | DDC 808.02–dc23
LC record available at https://lccn.loc.gov/2020040932
LC ebook record available at https://lccn.loc.gov/2020040933

ISBN: HB: 978-1-3500-6781-3
         PB: 978-1-3500-6780-6
         ePDF: 978-1-3500-6783-7
         eBook: 978-1-3500-6782-0

Series: Bloomsbury Writer's Guides and Anthologies

Typeset by Integra Software Services
Printed and bound in India

To find out more about our authors and books visit www.bloomsbury.com
and sign up for our newsletters.

To Sean's mentors: Kim Barnes, Mary Clearman Blew, and Joy Passanante. To Jess's mentors: Andrew Merton and Vijay Seshadri. To our beloved students, for your courage, curiosity, and wild hearts. To Lindsay Gacad and Paul Acciavatti for reading every chapter, offering suggestions, big and small, and for joining us on this journey. To the authors in our anthology. Your work insists on the vitality of creative nonfiction, and why we must continue to write. Thank you.

—Sean and Jess

Contents

Illustrations

Credits and Permissions

Credits

"Basement Story" by Austin Bunn. Originally published in *Third Coast Magazine*, Spring 2010.

"Women These Days" by Amy Butcher. Originally published in *Brevity* Magazine, Issue 58, May 2018.

"A Refuge for Jae-in Doe: Fugues in the Key of English Major" by Seo-Young Chu. Originally published in *Entropy*, November 2017.

"Leave Marks" by Melissa Febos. Originally published in *Abandon Me*, Bloomsbury 2017.

"Collective Nouns for Humans in the Wild" by Kathy Fish. Originally published in *Jellyfish Review*, October 2017.

"Open Season" by Harrison Candelaria Fletcher. Originally published in *Brevity* Magazine, Issue 53, Fall 2016.

"Loitering Is Delightful" by Ross Gay. Originally published in *The Book of Delights* © 2019 by Ross Gay. Reprinted with the permission of Algonquin Books of Chapel Hill. All rights reserved.

"What I Do on My Terrace Is None of Your Business" by Och Gonzalez. Originally published in *Brevity* Magazine, Issue 61, May 2019.

"Loyalty" by Peter Grandbois. Originally published in *Word Riot*, August 2016.

"Mighty Pawns" by Major Jackson. Originally published in *Roll Deep*, W. W. Norton and Company 2015.

"A Log Cabin Quilt" by Sarah Minor. Originally published in *Diagram*, 18.2. Reprinted in *Best American Experimental Writing 2019*, Wesleyan University Press.

"Buying a House" by Sean Prentiss. Originally published in *Sou'wester*, Spring 2010.

"The Funambulists" by Jonathan Rovner. Originally published in *Mud Season Review*, Issue 23, September 2016.

Part 1

Craft

1

History of Creative Nonfiction

As Francis Bacon wrote, "The word for [the essay] is new, but the thing itself is ancient." From the earliest **Neanderthal cave paintings**, red hands stenciled approximately 64,000 years ago in Spain, humans have used symbols to signify experience, to essay. We cannot be sure what these red hands signify (if anything), but they may be Neanderthals saying, *I am here.* Later, 35,000 years ago in Indonesia, a human draws an image of a pig on a cave wall. Five thousand years later in France and Romania, humans draw images of animals in caves. Are they saying, *These are offerings to our god(s)*? Or do they tell others about the dangers in the area (cave lions, panthers, bears, and volcanoes)? Or do they attempt to explain the larger, more complex world (birth, death, war)?

In 3400 BCE, the **Sumerians of Mesopotamia** (Mesopotamia is often referred to as the "cradle of civilization") invent the first system of writing in the form of notches in clay, called cuneiform. The symbols serve as a rudimentary accounting system and help Sumerians survive the rapid changes that ensue from their prosperity—the degree of which had never before been achieved by humans—and their many inventions, including agriculture, the wheel, the first means of transportation in the chariot and the sailboat, the concept of time, astronomy and astrology, maps, cities, and mathematics. Writing, for the ancient Sumerians, is a system of accounting. Cuneiform evolves, but its function does not. It is a strict nonfiction, a matter of facts. *I gave you this much, and you paid me this much*, it says. It helps Sumerians grow their markets and account for commerce, and in this way the Sumerians flourish for almost five centuries. Their downfall, when it comes, is swift, ruthless, and irreversible.

When the waters of destruction recede, a story emerges, our first written myth, which comes from **Ziusudra, the last king of Sumer,** prior to the great flood. Here for the first time, in 2700 BCE, is written language for a purpose beyond accounting. Amidst the desolation of destruction and loss, Ziusudra writes to the future of humanity, in hopes that his advice might help us flourish once again. In this moment, Ziusudra's new aims reshape written storytelling forever as he recounts the flood that destroyed the Sumerian cities while adding a series of practical yet heartfelt instructions to future generations.

"Friends," Ziusudra writes, "let me share with you the advice that those wise ones tried to offer. Let me give you these instructions, and please don't neglect them. Lessons from the past can still be useful for today, for any path that we may take in life is one that is treading the earth." In this simple missive, we recognize the roots of the essay, that fundamental form of creative nonfiction, an attempt to make sense out of chaos and the will to survive it.

"Knowledge is not intelligence," writes **Heraclitus of Ephesus**, around 500 BCE in Greece. It is a time of burgeoning governments, discovery, and unrest. Greece is fragmented by its motley landscape—steep mountains, valleys, and many islands—out of which hundreds of city-states have formed. Amidst the violence of feuding city-states, Heraclitus embraces instability, as both a constant and a mode of dialectical composition. "Change alone unchanges," he writes, two centuries before Aristotle famously asserts that "time is the measure of change." The conversational quality of creative nonfiction—sometimes in voice but always in aim—is reflected profoundly in Heraclitus's work, (which exist only in fragments today):

> The stuff of the psyche is a smoke-like substance of fine particles that give rise to all other things, particles of less mass than any other substance and constantly in motion: only movement can know movement.
> The psyche rises as a mist from things that are wet.
> A dry psyche is most skilled in intelligence and is brightest in virtue.
> [...]
> A psyche lusts to be wet.

In these exchanges, we bear witness to an internal debate, a quest for more than mere knowledge. It is an attempt to put order to the mystification of the world and give shape to the amorphousness of ideas. And there is salvation here, too, in the ways that Heraclitus makes a kind of sense out of the raw materials of observation. It is a fine example of an essay mirroring the movements of the mind and, wrested from the context of antiquity, as prescient today as it was during its time of composition. This is the timeless quality of creative nonfiction, which while structurally variable always attempts to give physical form to consciousness.

And, here, Heraclitus shows that creative nonfiction, more than other literary forms, functions as a dialogue in conversation with itself, other essays, and the world. Creative nonfiction replicates the movements of the mind, those digressive, dialectical exchanges between the narrator and themselves and the narrator and the wider world. The essay aspires toward relationships, a whispered intimacy, like the hushed exchanges between lovers at night.

Plutarch, of first-century CE Greece, understands intimately the link between narrative and identity. Outside of his roles as an administrative priest (interpreting the auguries of an oracle who presides over the Temple of Apollo at Delphi), mayor, magistrate, and ambassador, he hosts lavish dinner parties for guests from all over the Empire. He oversees dialogues with his guests that are recorded and collected, along with seventy-eight essays and other compositions, in *Moralia*. Individual essays in the collection range from "On the Fortune or the Virtue of Alexander the Great"—about whom he also writes in his famous collection of biographies, *Parallel Lives*— to "Odysseus and Gryllus," a humorous dialogue between Homer's Odysseus and one of Circe's pigs. But Plutarch is not a staunch historian and often writes different interpretations of the same events, changes that he deems "expansions," "abridgments," and "transpositions." For example, in several places in *Parallel Lives*, he recounts different versions of the conference at Lucca in 56 BCE, a last-ditch effort by Caesar to save the crumbling Triumvirate. The inconsistencies illustrate a common and persistent question about veracity and creative nonfiction. Plutarch resolves the contradictions by insisting that he writes lives, not history, and while this may not satisfy historians, it speaks to an essential difference between history and memory, between facts and lived experience. Human lives are not a sum of facts but a creation—mutable, fallible, and artificial. They are, to use Plutarch's own words, expansions, an amalgamation of materials and imagination.

Plutarch is revolutionary in other ways, too. His essays are radical in form and if published today would likely be categorized amidst the "new" forms of creative nonfiction, those highlighted by digressions, anecdotes, and spare prose. His essay "Some Information about the Spartans," for example, could be called a collage essay. Plutarch presents his subject through a series of stories, anecdotes, jokes, and asides stripped of explanations or expository analysis. In other words, he lets the material speak for itself, and like contemporary collage essays, short fragmented sections accrete in meaning as the essay progresses. Here are two such sections, which in juxtaposition and without exposition resonate across the white space:

> Another mother in Sparta once said to her son: "I send you off to battle with this shield your father made. Through many years and many battles he kept this weapon safe. Let me suggest that you also keep it safe, for the terrors of the battlefield won't be anything compared to what will happen if you lose it."
>
> *
>
> There is the story of the Spartan boy who complained to his mother that the sword she had given him was too small for battle.
> His mother replied sternly: "A real man doesn't need a sword."

This aphoristic, anecdotal style also shows up in the work of **Sei Shōnagon**, a courtesan to Empress Teishi during the Heian period in Japan, around 1000 CE. This does not demonstrate a direct lineage between Plutarch and Shōnagon but a form natural to patterns of human thought. Shonogan's *Pillow Book* follows a long tradition in Japan of nightly journaling, called *makura no soshi*—"notes of the pillow"—which are kept in the drawer in the wooden pillows used by well-to-do women.

Shōnagon is well versed in Japanese and Chinese poetry, and the book contains witty, poetic observations about court life in tenth-century Kyoto. She adheres to the philosophy of *mono no aware*—"beauty is precious because it is brief"—and composes her *Pillow Book* in short, flash-like stories, anecdotes, lists, and images. Together, these disparate pieces create a prismatic portrait of the writer and the world she inhabits. In tone, Shonogan is astute, ruthless, funny, and direct. One entry reads simply: "Things people despise: A crumbling earth wall. People who have a reputation for being exceptionally good-natured." Other entries are cultural commentaries, arguments on such far-flung subjects as religious piety and male flutists.

Her work foreshadows the insights of some twentieth-century female creative nonfiction writers, whose cultural observations and keenly rendered arguments forge space for women to more actively shape the cultural and creative landscapes of their day—Virginia Woolf, Maya Angelou, and Joan Didion, for example. In her time, however, Shonogan's work was suppressed and only printed for the first time in the seventeenth century, more than six hundred years after her death. We might explain this stretch of time as Shōnagon's longest white space, an extended pause in which her voice is suspended, only to reassert itself all those centuries later.

With this perspective, we see the performative quality of creative nonfiction, how it contributes to conversations past, present, and future. We might, for example, be able to imagine an exchange between Shōnagon and Didion, as when Shōnagon writes, "How ever did I pass the time before I knew you? I think of that past time as now I pass each passing day in lonely sorrow, lacking you," and Didion responds, "A single person is missing for you, and the whole world is empty."

Still more conversations traverse time and space until we reach **Michel de Montaigne**, who coins the term *essai*, which comes from Middle French and is translated as "a test," "a trial," or "an experiment," to refer to his personal writing, and who quotes Plutarch so frequently it is as if he is in attendance at one of Plutarch's famed dinner parties. Montaigne's work marks a distinct and irreversible shift in the development of creative nonfiction writing, and many consider this the formal beginning of creative nonfiction. In 1571, at the ripe old age of thirty-eight, Montaigne retires from his legal and administrative career to spend the remainder of his days in prolific pursuit of wonder and self-knowledge: "Know thyself," he etches into his ceiling. From the tower library in the family estate in the south of France, Montaigne breaks with the conventions of scholasticism with his bold use of the first person—a transgressive move in a culture dominated by doctrinal thought—and his embrace of skepticism, doubt, and confession.

In his essay "Of Cripples," he writes, "We become habituated to anything strange by use and time; but the more I frequent myself and know myself, the more my deformity astonishes me, and the less I understand myself," which can also be read as a metaphor for creative nonfiction itself. In Montaigne's radical approach, the essay is a drama, an active pursuit toward knowledge. And yet, Montaigne doesn't reach conclusions in his essays, only better-refined questions. "If my mind could gain a firm footing," he writes in "On Repentance," "I would not make essays, I would make decisions; but it is always in apprenticeship and on trial." Here, Montaigne realizes that the human mind is more adept at asking questions than finding answers.

Montaigne's writing style calls into question the authoritative practices of his day, particularly the dogmatic religious disputes of sixteenth-century France—he loathes the cruelties and hypocrisies of the religious wars. This is a profound shift in narrative prose, to boldly assert one's own life and mind as significant and worthy subject matter. "I am myself the matter of my book," he proclaims in the preface of the first edition of his *Essais*—which earns him a massive readership for his day. "You would be unreasonable to spend your leisure on so frivolous and vain a subject," he continues in the preface. It's a ploy, of course, and one that crumbles under the weight of his ambition and literary success. Indeed, even mighty Shakespeare is one of Montaigne's devoted readers, and many believe that Hamlet (that most introspective of characters) would not exist without the inspiration of Montaigne's muscular, meandering mind.

Only a few decades after Montaigne's death in 1592, the Protestant Reformation in England under Elizabeth I gives way to a spike in literary culture. This creates space for English writers to explore creative nonfiction writing in a variety of forms, though the term "creative nonfiction" does not yet exist. During this time, **Francis Bacon** adopts a more formal and emotionally withholding style than Montaigne's, although the French writer was one of Bacon's literary inspirations. Both writers recognize the ancient origins of creative nonfiction, as well as the paradox surrounding it. "The word for it is new," writes Bacon, acknowledging Montaigne's coinage of the term *essai*, "but the thing itself is ancient." As if in direct opposition to the volatility of life under Elizabeth I, Bacon's signature style is controlled, aphoristic, and methodical. His work shares none of the whimsy and flourish of Montaigne's work, and yet his style is marked by the fiery energy of his clear, decisive, and definitive sentences. It is not surprising that Bacon also formalizes the scientific method in Europe, as his essays are formal, process-based arguments, typically an accretion of carefully spun aphorisms, which Bacon finds to be fundamentally sensical and comforting.

Bacon's aphorisms include: "Youth is the seedbed of repentance"; "Old men are afraid of everything, except the Gods"; "Pride is the ivy that winds about all virtues and all good things"; and "We think according to our nature, speak as we have been taught, but act as we have been accustomed." We see in these reflections a mind desirous of control amidst a country besieged by prejudice and violence—a near police-state in which Bacon, a Catholic, is vulnerable. Bacon desires provable truths, and so his creative nonfiction takes on a form that can contain them—a stark contrast to the more free-wheeling, digressive style of Montaigne, who had more leisure (and the voracious curiosity) to indulge it. "What do I know?" Montaigne asks, whereas Bacon's tight, decisive voice reflects confidence in knowledge. And this is one of the beauties and powers of creative nonfiction. It is a tangible reflection of the creator's consciousness, the vessel through which writers make sense of the cultural and spiritual elements of their time as they either lean into or push against the culture they are writing from within.

And yet Bacon's withholding style is, in many ways, the antithesis of true creative nonfiction. It leaves little room for surprise, digression, change, or discovery—hallmarks of creative nonfiction, which is inherently dialectical.

During this time, writers begin to intuitively recognize that creative nonfiction doesn't even need to be in prose form, even if this isn't articulated. The shape of creative nonfiction, in other words, is not one of its defining characteristics. We'll talk about this in much more detail soon, but the most important characteristic of creative nonfiction is an engagement with "real" life. In 1700s England, the poet **Christopher Smart** composes wildly imaginative poems like "My Cat Jeoffrey," "A Song to David," and "Jubilate Agno." While in poetic form, these works are also decidedly creative nonfiction—in engagement with the real world and in search of meaning through experimentation with form. Smart possesses a religious zeal so profound he is occasionally confined to a mental institution for "religious mania," which is where his most famous works are composed. "A Song to David" is written during one such stay and seeks to combine aspects of the life of King David with Christianity:

Beauteous, yea beauteous more than these,
The shepherd king upon his knees,
For his momentous trust;
With wish of infinite conceit,
For man, beast, mute, the small and great,
And prostrate dust to dust.

Likewise, the work of **William Blake**, often a mix of poetry, prose, and illustration, is often creative nonfiction. "The Marriage of Heaven and Hell" is one such example, a text so deeply dialectical and formally explosive that it defies definition, simultaneously exemplifying the structural freedom of creative nonfiction. Some sections are in verse, while others take the form of lists, prose, or proverbs. What unifies these sections as creative nonfiction is the focus on "true" experience and Blake's efforts across the sections to refine profound ethical and religious quandaries.

And in 1700s Ireland, **Jonathan Swift** composes satire that might easily be labeled fiction were it not for the soundness of its implicit rhetorical arguments. His famous essay, "A Modest Proposal for Preventing the Children of Poor People in Ireland from Being a Burden to Their Parents or Country, and for Making Them Beneficial to the Public," makes an earnest argument under the guise of metaphor and hyperbole: "[A] young healthy child well nursed is at a year old a most delicious, nourishing, and wholesome food, whether stewed, roasted, baked, or oiled; and I make no doubt that it will equally serve in a fricassee or a ragout."

Blake and Swift's examples reflect the shapeshifter quality of creative nonfiction, the ways in which it is not "unto itself" but instead able to take on features of other genres like masks—not to hide its true nature but to point to some larger nature. Forms are born of necessity, as reflections of the culture, and not superimposed on content with abandon. Forms contribute to meaning. Swift understands that such egregious treatment of the poor necessitates satire to point out its hypocrisies. No other form will do.

The nineteenth century—as the far corners of the world are brought together by trains and steamboats, which usher in the Industrial Revolution—brings a surge of performative, self-reflective, and wildly lyrical creative nonfiction. In France, **Charles Baudelaire** imagines a prose style with the expressiveness of poetry. "Who among us," he asks, "has not dreamt, in moments of ambition, of the miracle of a poetic prose, musical without rhythm and rhyme, supple and staccato enough to adapt to the lyrical stirrings of the soul, the undulations of dreams, and sudden leaps of consciousness?" In other words, he seeks to pattern his prose after the movements of the mind and in the process breaks with the strict conventions of French poetry. The result is "free verse" or "lyric poetry," a style as associative as the human thought process—unrestricted and unconventional. "Be drunk," Baudelaire commands in his famous prose poem of the same name. "Wine, poetry, or virtue—as you wish. But be drunk."

In England during the nineteenth century, writers are similarly harkening to Montaigne's expressiveness and self-portraiture. "C'est moy que je peins"—*It is myself that I paint*—inspires highly performative and personal creative nonfiction from a generation of writers, including William Hazlitt, Stendhal, Charles and Mary Lamb, William Wordsworth, and John Keats. Many of these writers experiment with prose poetry and futurism, inspired by the Industrial Revolution and its implicit drama. Anything imaginable is newly possible. Fact and fantasy comingle, and in some cases cease to be distinguishable—for example, **William Hazlitt's** "other self," his bombastic narrator and literary persona. In contrast to his gentle, benign real-life personality, Hazlitt's literary doppelganger is angry, vehement, and flamboyant. He makes bold, opinionated declarations in his writing, including in "On the Pleasure of Hating," in which he asserts hatred to be both intrinsic to human nature, as well as corruptive and detrimental: "Love and friendship melt in their own fires. We hate old friends: we hate old books: we hate old opinions; and last we come to hate ourselves." Like Montaigne,

Hazlitt lets his mind wander. He embraces discrepancies and contradictions. He uses creative nonfiction as a place not only to rail against utilitarianism and systems but also to argue with himself. Creative nonfiction is a place for Hazlitt to set ideas aflame, then grow new ones from the fertile ashes of the old. Hazlitt's agile, combustive approach highlights a key feature of the human thought process—its antagonism—and like Montaigne, he finds a form to replicate and animate that process.

In Italy, **Dino Campana** pens "The Night," creative nonfiction published as poetry in 1914 in *Orphic Songs*, his only published collection. In his incandescent prose, Campana blurs the line between reality and fantasy, submitting to its muddy borders: "Evening: in the empty chapel, in the shadows of the modest nave, I held Her, the rose-pale flesh and the burning fugitive eyes: years and years and years melted together in the triumphal sweet taste of memory."

"I write because I don't know," writes **Fernando Pessoa** in *The Book of Disquiet*, "and I use whatever abstract and lofty terms for Truth a given emotion requires." It is Portugal, and we're solidly inside the nineteenth century. Pessoa seeks "Truth" in fervent, kaleidoscopic bursts. In *The Book of Disquiet*, his masterpiece, he writes from the perspective of Bernardo Soares (a self-proclaimed *flâneur*), one of the seventy-odd literary personas Pessoa adopts over his lifetime. The book is theory, fantasy, monologue, anecdote, and history. It shatters and recomposes itself a thousand times. This is creative nonfiction in collage form, and in its search for identity through the embrace of multiplicity, it calls the whole charade of "self" and "truth" into question. It's a hallmark of a new generation of creative nonfiction in which the notion of a distinct and "true" "self" is circumspect—subject to endless reworkings and experimentations.

Other similar examples include **Virginia Woolf's** 1928 novel *Orlando: A Biography*, in which a fictional narrator inspired by Woolf's lover, Vita Sackville-West, herself a poet, changes sex from male to female at the age of thirty and goes on to live for another three hundred years without aging perceptibly, all the while recounting a very real (and satirical) history of English literature. This is creative nonfiction in the form of a love letter under the guise of fiction. On October 5, 1927, Woolf notes in her diary the inspiration for *Orlando*: "[A] biography beginning in the year 1500 and continuing to the present day, called *Orlando*: Vita; only with a change about from one sex to the other."

Or take **Gertrude Stein's** similar experiment, *The Autobiography of Alice B. Toklas*, written in 1933 in the voice of her life partner, Alice B. Toklas.

The book "is in every way except actual authorship Alice Toklas's book," writes a friend of Stein and Toklas, the composer and critic Virgil Thomson. Thomson goes on to write, "It reflects her mind, her language, her private view of Gertrude, also her unique narrative powers. Every story in it is told as Alice herself had always told it.... Every story that ever came into the house eventually got told in Alice's way, and this was its definitive version."

Back in Lisbon in the mid-1900s, the sculptor **Ana Hatherly** writes in a style she calls *tisanes*, named after a French herbal tea infusion. This style of creative nonfiction mixes the observational with the fantastic. It is yet another example of creative nonfiction so uncontainable that it is relegated to publication as "fiction"—seemingly the catch all term for anything that doesn't fit neatly in another category. But calling Hatherly's *tisanes* fiction, as so many other hybrid creative nonfictions get labeled, ignores the importance of its source material, the "true to experience" wellspring that lends the work much of its meaning. Hatherly's braided narratives move between myth—"Once upon a time there was a landscape where there were never any clouds. To make it rain it was necessary to wash the horizon with feathers"—and short personal narratives—"I was quickly crossing the lobby when I felt very dizzy to support myself I put out my hand to the big table that was there when I closed my eyes the table disappeared." In Hatherly's dialectical creative nonfictions, myths are as fundamental to reality as lived experience.

At the same time, in Mexico, **Octavio Paz** creates essay collections that befuddle critics who can't seem to decide if his work is fiction, nonfiction, or poetry. Paz writes poetry and prose and takes a keen interest in dualities of all kinds, but still critics struggle to understand nonfiction that aims to convey more than just information.

Around this time, creative nonfiction begins to find settings beyond the narrator's own mind. Until now, the site and setting of the narrator's meditations have not been nearly as important as the clarity of consciousness and the soundness of rhetorical argument. But just as many late-nineteenth and early-twentieth-century painters move from portraiture and religious reenactments to *plein air* ("open air") painting and Impressionism—which seeks to capture a feeling or experience rather than an accurate depiction—so too are writers looking out to the wider world. Scene and setting become integral to meaning-making, as if creative nonfiction can no longer bear the containment and decides to go out and have a look around. This focus on scene and setting might be in direct response to the writers' ability to learn about the larger world as news travels across continents in weeks, and then days, and soon enough in moments, and from the writers' ability to travel the world themselves in trains and automobiles and planes.

Scene and scenery offer essayists a newly vivid stage. They offer a new way of contextualizing personal material, but also new opportunities for metaphor. In "Death of a Moth," published in 1942, **Virginia Woolf** observes a moth fighting death upon her windowsill and interacts with this curious scene to make bold metaphorical claims about the nature of life and death. "Watching him," Woolf writes, "it seemed as if a fibre, very thin but pure, of the enormous energy of the world had been thrust into his frail and diminutive body. As often as he crossed the pane, I could fancy that a thread of vital light became visible. He was little or nothing but life."

Other writers during this time also write from a specific place in the world. **E.B. White** makes similarly momentous discoveries along the shores of his childhood vacation spot on a lake in Maine. **James Baldwin** enacts astute social critiques on the streets of Harlem. **George Orwell** writes about his disillusionment with British imperialism by recounting his time spent in Burma as an imperial policeman.

In the late twentieth century, **Annie Dillard** writes her Pulitzer-Prize-winning book *Pilgrim at Tinker Creek*, which merges nature and memoir writing, and **Gretel Ehrlich** pens *The Solace of Open Spaces*, which memorializes the American West. In each text, the authors move lucidly between nature and mediation, observation and metaphor, to create forms as expansive and dynamic as the landscapes they render.

In the 1960s, creative nonfiction undergoes another renaissance, both conceptually and commercially. It's a tumultuous time. John F. Kennedy is elected and then assassinated three years later. The Vietnam War rages. There are marches, protests, and the fight for civil rights. Malcolm X pens his autobiography and is later assassinated. Martin Luther King Jr. fights, triumphs, and is murdered. There are bellbottoms, communes, and rivers on fire. There is free love, Nixon, the Equal Pay Act, and the *Feminine Mystique*.

Such tremulous times demand a new approach to media. The emergence of **"New Journalism"**—longform reporting notable for its emphasis on "truth" over "fact," immersive reporting, and a subjective, literary style—garners a mainstream audience. New Journalism is a departure from conventional reporting, which sticks to facts and attempts to remain objective. Pioneers include **Hunter S. Thompson, Tom Wolfe, Joan Didion, Norman Mailer, Terry Southern, Gay Talese**, and others. Their work is featured in some of the most prominent magazines, including *The New Yorker, Harper's*, the *Atlantic Monthly*, and *Rolling Stone*, as well as in books.

Amidst radical cultural shifts, these journalists mix investigative reportage with memoir, fiction, cultural criticism, and ethnography, earning both critical and commercial interest. The journalist Marc Weingarten notes that these new journalists "recognized [...] one salient fact of life in the sixties: the traditional tools of reporting would be inadequate to chronicle the tremendous cultural and social changes of the era." This is a time of wildly new forms of creative nonfiction—playfulness and curiosity grounded in literary ambition and intellectual daring.

True crime narratives, like **Truman Capote's** *In Cold Blood* (which the author calls a "nonfiction novel"), stir an American fascination with violence and redemption narratives, which might be in response to the heightened media attention on violence, including the Vietnam War. Though *In Cold Blood* might be the most famous, this category of writing could be traced back to the Puritan execution sermon and it continues today with the proliferation of true crime memoirs, documentaries, and podcasts.

Memoirs (which typically offer a glimpse into a particular period of a writer's life), rather than **autobiographies** (considered more exhaustive accounts of the writer's life), grow more popular. **Elie Weisel** publishes *Night* in 1960, a memoir about his time spent in the Auschwitz concentration camp during the Holocaust; it soon becomes a staple of high school English curriculums across the United States. In 1969, **Maya Angelou** publishes *I Know Why the Caged Bird Sings*—a memoir mixing cultural criticism with personal experience that demonstrates the full force of her poetic prowess. We, as readers and members of society, seek ever more ways to make sense of rapid social, cultural, and technological shifts, and memoirs help us do that.

Creative nonfiction soon becomes a popular format for writers to explore **illness and disability narratives** amidst increasing frustrations with the health care system and what Arthur Kleinman, professor of medical anthropology, describes as "the alienation of the chronically ill from their professional care givers and, paradoxically, to the relinquishment by the practitioner of that aspect of the healer's art that is most ancient."

William Styron's *Darkness Visible*, published in 1990, explores his debilitating depression. **Philip Roth** publishes *Patrimony: A True Story* in 1991, about his father's terminal brain cancer and the ensuing family trauma. In 1994, **Elizabeth Wurtzel** brings attention to illness narratives with *Prozac Nation*, a memoir about her experiences with atypical depression. The book is reminiscent of **Sylvia Plath's** 1963 semiautobiographical novel, *The Bell Jar*, in its raw and personal account of mental illness. Reviews of *The Bell Jar* are similarly mixed and focus on its relative veracity to Plath's life, a reading that distracts from the literary merit of the text. In response, critic Elizabeth Hardwick urges readers to distinguish between Plath as a writer and Plath as an "event," foreshadowing decades of memoir scandals and debates about their relative veracity. The most famous example, perhaps, is **James Frey's** 2003 memoir *A Million Little Pieces*, which is discovered to be largely contrived and is famously condemned by Oprah Winfrey.

Today, creative nonfiction continues to soar in popularity even as the form remains increasingly hybrid and hard to categorize. We turn to creative nonfiction to enact the strangeness of experience, to wrestle chaos from the world around us into a shape that might offer new insights. Sometimes, as in the essays of **David Foster Wallace**, that shape is highly digressive, marked by an abundance of footnotes. Or it is brief and elliptical, like **Diane Seuss's** prose poems. Or it is sprawling and windy, like **Cheryl Strayed's** *Wild*. Or elegant and rhetorically sound, like the essay collection by **Ta-Nehisi Coates**, *Between the World and Me*. Or quirky and satirical, like the personal essays by **David Sedaris**.

In contemporary culture, creative nonfiction is a ubiquitous art form. We see creative nonfiction not only in our books, magazines, and journals but also in podcasts, documentaries, television shows, and on social media. When we craft our Instagram and TikTok stories, we construct a cultivated and curated **social media** *story of self*.

Podcasts like *This American Life*, *Radiolab*, *The Moth Podcast*, and *True Crime Garage* are all examples of creative nonfiction. Indeed, most of our podcasts today are creative nonfiction, telling true stories in audio form. Sometimes these stories are first-person narratives, like *The Moth* Podcast, where storytellers share personal stories, recorded at live events, which are then collected into podcast episodes. Others present a variety of human interest stories, including subjects like true crime, science, politics, art, and social commentary.

Documentaries abound, including a host of serialized TV documentaries, and reality TV shows (even if only loosely tied to truth) continue to dominate programming. *Hoop Dreams* examines inner city basketball; *Super Size Me* lives the fast-food lifestyle; *Bowling for Columbine* reflects on school shootings; and *An Inconvenient Truth* delves into climate change.

Daily, we are inundated with **news narratives**, as a seemingly endless cascade of political, scientific, and social changes integrate with our sense of identity and place in the world. Because of this, today's readers relish opportunities for intimacy and reflection, a trusted narrator to guide us through the anxieties of daily life. We seek refuge in the minds of others and derive deep pleasure out of the dialectical movements of a writer's quest for meaning. And there is a voyeuristic appeal, too, peering inside the emotional and intellectual concerns of others. It is here where we find recognition, where we learn *how we live now*. In our desire to understand one another, we also seek to better understand ourselves.

2

Genre and Veracity

II: VIGNETTE

Back in the late 1990s, I got a job building trails in the Pacific Northwest with the Northwest Youth Corps. Each day I'd take my crew—a group of ten youths—into some remote wild area and build trails or saw trees or remove noxious weeds. Then we'd stumble back, nine hours later, to our tent camp. We'd sharpen tools, cook dinner, and then fall off into sleep, exhausted from hours of manual labor. The work was hard, the food terrible, and the sense of accomplishment incredible. The job and the youths taught me more about life than almost anything else. And in some strange way, this job led me to becoming a professor.

Fast forward to 2011. My wife Sarah and I were at a writing retreat in one of the exact spots where I had built trails. Each day, I'd work on my memoir, Finding Abbey: The Search for Edward Abbey and His Hidden Desert Grave. *Each day, Sarah would hike the La Plata Mountains, do yoga in Colorado wildflowers, play guitar, and cook. And each day, Sarah would tell me to write something different than my memoir. She wanted me to not only revise but create.*

Since I was within steps of the trails my crew had built, I decided to write about my time as a crew leader. Every time I put fingers to keyboard, the material came out not as an essay, which was what I normally wrote, but as poems. That week in southwestern Colorado, I wrote poem after poem about building trails, my crew members, and these and other mountains. Soon, I had an entire collection, an entire memoir-in-verse.

This was one of my first lessons that creative nonfiction is more than one thing. It can be the essay. It can be the memoir. It can be environmental writing. It can be immersion writing. It can be speculative writing. It can be poetry. Or, like this collection of poetry about building trails, it can be all of those things, all at once. Just like the La Plata Mountains, creative nonfiction is massive, stunning, and beautiful with its own diverse ecosystems.

—Sean

III: OVERVIEW

According to most people, there are four genres in creative writing: poetry, drama, fiction, and creative nonfiction. The oldest genre is poetry. The term **poetry** originates from the Latin word for "poet," which means "maker" or "author." The original term *poiétria* refers to all creative writing. So, in the beginning, all creative writing was poetry. Why? Because poetry was born from our need to remember oral narratives. Poetic techniques—including rhythm, rhyming, and meter—helped poets commit poems to memory. The key that makes poetry unique from its sibling genres is the use of the line break. The shape of the poem is one that employs line breaks.

Next-oldest is drama. Drama uses stage directions and dialogue to tell a narrative. The term **drama** originates from the Greek word for "to take action" and means either a "theatrical act" or a "play." The shape of a drama on the page is a script.

Most people consider the next genre to be fiction. **Fiction** includes all invented narratives. The key here is that these narratives are invented by the writer. And then the newest genre would be creative nonfiction. But, as we saw in "History of Creative Nonfiction," creative nonfiction (and fiction) has been around since, at least, dramas.

Along with the issue of the age of each genre, we have a larger issue, and that is that two of the genres—poetry and drama—are categorized one way (by focusing on shape) and two others—fiction and creative nonfiction— are categorized in another way (by focusing mostly on their reliance/lack of reliance on truth).

To explore this further, we might look to the definition of genre, but most definitions of genre are not terribly useful because they assert that genres can be defined by style, form, or content. For example, music genres include rock (style) and ballads (form) and love songs (content). All of these terms are related to music, but these "genres" aren't related to each other. The other way genre is defined is as "a kind," which is so vague as to make it not useful at all. Genre traces itself back to the word for "gender," which almost offers a bit more clarity until you trace "gender" back to its archaic roots and see that it means "a kind, sort, or class."

For the purposes of this book, we propose a clearer and simpler definition for genre. In creative writing, we argue, the shape of a work determines its **genre**. Or, genres are differentiated by shape. Why did we choose this definition? Because the two oldest genres, poetry and drama, are defined by their shape. Poetry uses the line break. Drama uses the script. Truth is left out of the equation. So we look to history to help us unravel the best way to understand a single, clear definition for genre.

But this definition of genre does not work for fiction and creative nonfiction. These two are defined by their relationship to truth. Fiction and creative nonfiction don't follow the same rules concerning genre that poetry and drama do. Instead, fiction and creative nonfiction are something separate from poetry and drama, defined by a different measuring stick. Most people define creative nonfiction by this simple formula: Truth + Prose = Creative Nonfiction. For fiction, we could merely replace "Truth" with "Invention." But if fiction and creative nonfiction have a different definition for genre (one based on truth or invention), how can we clarify this confusion?

We propose that there are only three genres. We have poetry, drama, and **prose**—writing shaped by paragraphs. The term **prose** is birthed from the Latin word for "straightforward," since most prose is more linear than poetry. Prose uses paragraphs, sentences, and (usually) traditional uses of punctuation. Prose doesn't care if things are invented or true. That is outside the domain of prose (and genre). Prose only cares if the writer uses paragraphs.

There are just three genres: poetry, drama, and prose, and each one of these is clearly defined by its shape.

Literary Genre	Defining Feature
Poetry	Writing that uses line breaks.
Drama	Writing that uses stage settings and dialogue.
Prose	Writing that uses paragraphs.
Hybrid Genre	Writing that uses two or more of the above genres.

A: But What Is Creative Nonfiction If It Is Not a Genre?

If we agree that creative nonfiction is not a genre—since it is not defined by its shape—then what is it? To help us figure this out, we can contrast it with fiction. If fiction uses invented characters, settings, dialogue, and/or action to tell a narrative, then creative nonfiction is the opposite: telling true narratives about real characters in a real place who say real things and perform real actions. The difference is simply invention versus truth. Or, to return to our formula above, Truth + ~~Prose~~ = Creative Nonfiction. In other words, **creative nonfiction** is a true narrative told in any genre (poetry, drama, and/or prose) that uses creative or literary elements. Rather than concerning itself with shape (genre), creative nonfiction engages veracity. **Veracity** comes from the Latin word *vērāx*, which means "to speak truthfully." Creative nonfiction is also, therefore, writing that lives on the "truth" side of the veracity scale while fiction lives on the "invention" side. And yet, as we'll discuss at length later on, veracity is not black or white, but a spectrum with plenty of gray.

While we acknowledge the problematic definitions of "truth" and the ways in which memory and experience fail to live up to the verifiability of facts, we fundamentally believe that truth in creative nonfiction relies on the writer's instincts to be as honest as possible. We will address this further in "Phenomenal Truths". Creative nonfiction is also, therefore, writing that lives on the "truth" side of the veracity scale, while fiction lives on the "invention" side. By nature, many creative nonfiction pieces straddle the line between truth and invention and live the in the gray area.

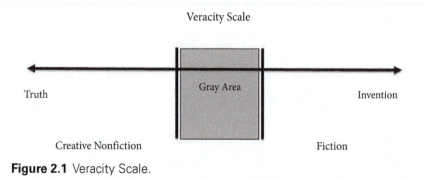

Figure 2.1 Veracity Scale.

One narrative from the anthology that embraces this ambiguity is Austin Bunn's "Basement Story." When we were putting together the anthology, we asked every writer if their essay was true. Bunn responded:

> "Basement Story" is a stew of fact and fiction: that record of death sounds is real and I loved it, and the game my brother, Colin, and I played is real, my parents' divorce and my mom's disease and her lover moving on from her, all real. But the mental issues are invented. To answer your question, Colin reads "Basement Story" and laughs. He knows it is about 60 percent false. This essay, which is also a solo theater performance, resides in the gray zone of creative nonfiction.

Amy Butcher's "Women These Days" highlights its own veracity. To begin, Butcher writes, "*[Compiled and arranged by searching 'woman + [verb]'* (walking) *in national news outlets over the past twelve months],*" alerting the reader that what follows in "Women These Days" is taken verbatim from national news outlets. The essay lives on the truth side of the veracity spectrum. It is engaging with facts, although they are artfully arranged by the writer in order to create an emotional truth, too.

B: But Why Go to All This Work?

Rather than labeling their work as either poetry, drama, fiction, or creative nonfiction, writers would instead make two labels, one for the work's veracity [true/invented/hybrid] and one for the genre [poetry/drama/prose/hybrid].

The most important reason for this change is that it gives writers permission to play with form and opens them up to a broader range of craft strategies without their work being deemed "experimental" or "subversive." All writing is intrinsically experimental, and experimentation should not marginalize or exclude work from the realm of creative nonfiction. Historically, creative nonfiction that plays with genre or veracity is automatically deemed 'poetry' or 'fiction,' which alters the way the work is experienced by the reader. It commonly constrains creative nonfiction to prose, and mistakenly insists that the work stick wholly to facts, rather than emotional truths.

As a result, poetry and drama classes often ignore veracity. Veracity, the current system insists, is only the purview of prose. That's confusing for the writer and the reader.

This new system argues that shape (genre: poetry, drama, and prose) is less defining than veracity, and that shape is more useful as a meaning-making tool within a range of veracities. This system gives creative nonfiction writers permission to write in other genres than just prose because we've separated veracity from genre. Now a writer need only choose a genre, a veracity, and then create art.

Finally, this new system clearly instructs the reader as to the nature of the work. In "Phenomenal Truths," we look at the contract between the creative nonfiction writer and reader in more detail. But this view of creative nonfiction as writing from true, lived experience—the writer's and/or their subjects'—makes the contract between writer and reader clearer. When we label our narratives as creative nonfiction, rather than fiction or hybrid, we signal to our reader our intentions. Regardless of the shape of the narrative, the writer is striving to tell the truth.

Now, Reader, you know exactly what you are reading when you delve into our anthology. Every piece, whether it looks like drama (as with Bunn's essay) or poetry (as with Major Jackson's "Mighty Pawns") or some other shape (like Brooke Juliet Wonders's "Self Erasure," which is an erasure/blackout piece created from Wonders's boyfriend's suicide note), is true to the best of the writer's ability and intentions unless, as Bunn does, the writer lets us know otherwise.

IV: READING AS A WRITER

The following exercises will help you practice the concepts learned in this chapter.

A: Veracity in Poetry
In poetry, the writer doesn't often tell the reader if a collection of poems or an individual poem is true or invented. Look at some of your favorite collections of poems. Can you tell what veracity they are? Do some poems in the collection "feel" as if they are true? If so, why? Do you want to know if the poem or collection of poems is true? Why or why not?

B: Veracity in Drama
Often in drama, just like in poetry, the screenwriter or playwright doesn't tell the reader if a screenplay or play is true or invented.

Watch or read a few of your favorite pieces of drama. Can you tell what veracity they are? Do some plays, television shows, and movies feel more true, while others feel more invented? If so, why? Do you want to know if a play, television show, or a movie is true? Why or why not?

C: Studying Genre and Veracity in the Anthology
Look at any three pieces from our anthology. Explore how they use genre and veracity. Which piece is closest to prose? Which piece leans into those other genres? Which piece is closest to fact? Which explores hybrid veracities more?

    Piece 1:
            Genre:
            Veracity:
    Piece 2:
            Genre:
            Veracity:
    Piece 3:
            Genre:
            Veracity:

V: PROMPTS

The following prompts will help put to practice the concepts learned in this chapter.

A: Playing with Genre

Write a piece of flash creative nonfiction heavy in dialogue. Now, re-write this piece as a poem. Next, re-write this piece as a drama. Then re-write the piece using two or more genres at the same time. Explore how this one piece of writing transforms merely by re-conceiving its genre.

B: Playing with Veracity

Take the same piece of flash creative nonfiction that you wrote for Exercise A. Now play with veracity. Add some elements of invention. What happens as we create a hybrid veracity? Then add another element of invention. And another. How does the piece change as it moves from creative nonfiction to hybrid to fiction? And when do you feel that the piece has left the realm of creative nonfiction for hybrid veracity, and when has it left hybrid veracity for fiction?

C: Playing with Unfamiliar Genres

Rank the three genres in terms of how comfortable you are with them. Once you've determined the genre with which you feel least comfortable, write a flash piece in that genre. Make sure you are focusing on truth. Have fun with this new (to you) genre.

3

The Central Question

II: VIGNETTE

One evening last summer, as the sky began to darken around nine o'clock, my husband and I heard a loud and persistent knocking on the front door. I got up to answer it, pulled back the curtain on the window, and saw an unfamiliar man swaying under the porch light. His hair was blue and his eyes were black. He looked to be in his mid-twenties and probably drunk. He wore a pair of black, leather, unlaced combat boots. For a moment, we stared at one another through the glass.

"Where's Jane?" he demanded.

I told him I was sorry but I didn't know a Jane; she wasn't here. Either he didn't hear me or didn't believe me because he began to yell for her and jiggle the locked door handle. My husband came to the door and told the man to leave.

"Jane!" the man said. "Jane, I need to talk to you!"

He banged on the glass of the door so hard I thought it might shatter. I felt not so much afraid as curious. The man looked too drunk and slight to cause much harm, even while his banging shook the windows and neighboring porch lights began to click on one by one across the street.

Today had been a lovely day. I'd driven to Craftsbury, Vermont, from my home in Winooski, Vermont—about an hour each way—to meet with my writer's group and then give a short reading of my work at the public library. The crowd had been small but interested, and after the reading we gathered on the library's patio for cheese, fruit, and wine. In the distance, mountains ribbed the horizon. When I got home from the event, my husband had been in the garden tending to his plants while the two young boys who lived next door pestered him for tomatoes and cucumbers, which he doled out generously.

And yet, all day I'd felt uneasy. Beneath the day's placid veneer, my husband's recent confession—"I don't think I want children after all"— conflicted with the lush landscape, my friends' tender faces, and the inviting atmosphere at the library. So much beauty and possibility, but the sudden realization that I would not be able to have a child with the man I loved and had recently married grated against the contours of my consciousness. Memories from our decade as a couple beat inside me as I drove. As I'd crested the hill in Craftsbury, the landscape splayed in front of me like a lover. Terror and awe collided. I thought about the nonfiction book I was reading, Stendhal's Naples and Florence: A Journey from Milan to Reggio, *published in 1817, in which the author—who'd been enamored with the city of Florence for years before finally arriving to kneel before Giotto's frescoes in the Basilica of Santa Croce—writes, "As I emerged from the porch of Santa Croce, I was seized with a fierce palpitation of the heart; the wellspring of life was dried up within me, and I walked in constant fear of falling to the ground." In the two centuries since the publication of Stendhal's travelogue, countless others have reported similar reactions to art. And it's not always art, necessarily, but some other physical evidence of profound personal meaning. A temple in ruins, say, or Mother Theresa's profile on a piece of burnt toast. A Plath poem or the distant cry of a beluga whale off of the Aleutian coast. Reports consistently mention rapid heartbeat, fainting, even hallucinations. Some people lose their breath, consciousness, or common sense. Loved ones are called and hospital visits are common. There are follow-ups with the shrink. Prescriptions for Xanax. These days, this sort of experience has a name: Stendhal Syndrome. It suggests that there are consequences for sneaking a peek up Creation's billowing skirt. For fingering the tenuous threads of metaphor. By the time this drunken man came banging on our door, he seemed to me like the embodiment of the day's wonder. By the time the cops arrived and escorted the man off our front porch, I was already starting to formulate an essay in my mind.*

—Jess

III: OVERVIEW

Almost daily, we hit on an issue, idea, or question that we can't let go. Or we recall a complicated image and obsess over it. We linger over what confounds us, examining it, naming and re-naming it, unraveling it. These obsessions compel us toward creating a story to explain this riddle we are trying to solve, since narratives are our primary tool for understanding. It is how we make sense of chaos; find order out of disorder; seek (though we may not find) answers to questions. We explore obsessions not because we are experts with a point to argue but because our voracious curiosity compels us to give form to wonder.

Creative nonfiction, just like the issues we struggle with in our everyday lives, is compelled by what we do not know or understand. The writing process for creative nonfiction, therefore, is motivated by examining obsessions, which are articulated on the page as a central question. In other words, what and why do we want to know about this image/idea/discovery/memory?

Our first job as creative nonfiction writers, therefore, is to find questions that obsess and haunt us, and that don't have an easy answer. The **central question** is the curiosity (or a set of curiosities) that serves as a writer's motivation, inspiration, and compositional directive. Some might call it a creative nonfiction writer's hypothesis. In Jess's vignette above, she wants to understand the emotional and intellectual relationships between her day in Craftsbury, the ideas she was reading about in Stendhal's work, her desire to have a child (and the fear that she never will), and the strange blue-haired man who had shown up unbidden on her doorstep, pining for someone who was not there. Her intuition, her meaning-making mind, suggested that they had intrinsic value and that together they worked in symphony to create meaning.

But how?

That was what Jess needed to discover in order to answer to discover her central question.

This is how the writing process begins: with charged moments in which we intuit deeper emotional and universal truths, even if we don't understand these moments completely. We start from a place of not knowing and understand that the writing process will be one of discovery—an attempt to articulate our questions clearly—rather than one of definitive answers.

Kristen Millares Young's central question is explicit in her essay "A Few Thoughts while Shaving," which is about the creative imperative to both have children and write books. "Will I have time to write or won't I?" she asks early in the essay, while her toddler son plays nearby while she showers, pregnant with her second child. While academic writers often cover their tracks, erecting an argument like a set of logical proofs, creative nonfiction writers understand that the tracks *are* the story—the journey to discovery *is* the narrative. Young works through her question in a series of scenes from her past, experiences that ultimately reassure her of her own resilience. In the end, she can't answer her original question with any certainty, but she is able to refine it. "Over time, I have come to understand that there is no deserving of happiness, only the great fortune of receiving it," she writes. "By this measure, I am rich, given a vocation and years to see it through, granted one son and pledged another, gifted promise that lives within, kicking and kicking and kicking." That final image complicates what might otherwise be a simple conclusion. Instead of reaching a simple "yes" or "no" answer, Young reframes the question. What matters is the art of receiving, not earning, joy, but even this is a struggle—"kicking and kicking and kicking."

And that is what makes central questions different from an academic text's thesis, because rather than proving a thesis through evidence, in creative nonfiction the writer works as an explorer, a map-maker, a diver into deep waters of memory and experience. We write to refine the central question, to ask it with greater clarity, feeling, and precision, but we don't often find answers.

A: Drafting toward Discovery

The best creative nonfiction narratives contain genuine surprises for the writer and, therefore, the reader. Think of our first drafts as mounds of clay; as we draft, form begins to emerge. At first, not much more than a vague outline is discernible. Often, we don't yet know what our central question will be, and we don't know how it will become meaningful, either to us or to a reader.

In this part of the writing process, no material is wrong or irrelevant. Discovery lives in the spaces between the movements of a writer's mind. As we continue to draft—or to return to the sculpture analogy, *mold the clay*—notice what is taking shape. Do we see the shadows of metaphor, perhaps? Any connective tissue? Do we sense any through-line or patterns?

We may discover our central question while writing the first draft or it may take many drafts before the central question becomes evident. But whenever and however we discover the central question, let it point us toward the material that feels most relevant, even if we don't yet understand *how* it is relevant. That becomes the writer's job, the writer's intention, aiming everything toward the central question. As metaphors and connections begin to emerge, bring them into high relief by focusing on them. In Jess's case, she started to notice how she often returned to a particular definition of *wonder*: the conflation of terror and awe. Her hazy sense of motherhood (motherhood in her imagination, anyway) was both terrible and awesome, the most radical creative act. In Jess's imagination, motherhood had come to symbolize the ultimate creative imperative—inaccessible to her in any other way. Slowly and incrementally, this became Jess's central question: *Is motherhood the most radical creative act for a woman (for me, in particular), or can art sustain me as a creative person if I must forgo motherhood in order to keep my marriage?*

During this process of writing toward the central question, it is important to do two things: (1) slowly focusing the direction the narrative is headed in, while (2) keeping ourselves open to the unknown, letting the language, images, and scenes propel our curiosity. This is how we write toward discovery. As we begin the writing process, everything may seem interesting and relevant, but as we continue to draft, notice the ways in which certain stories, ideas, facts, philosophies, or images are more relevant to our central question than others. Incorporate those that seem most aligned with the central question and discard the rest—or save them for another narrative.

Below, we'll explore ways to keep ourselves open to the unknown by looking at creative memory (see Section B below) and creative research (see Section C below). But for now, we will focus on ways to discover which direction our central question might be leading us. Initially, we'll often have two or three or four potential central questions competing for space. In the end, we'll have to decide which one will control the narrative. We'll have to decide which question best encompasses our deepest curiosity and concerns. What do we most want to understand about a particular memory or set of experiences? Where are certain relationships and metaphors surfacing?

"It's not what happened," says Sean's mentor, the memoirist Kim Barnes, "but why. It's not what you remember, but why you remember what you do. It's not what you're telling us, but why you are telling us." *What* happened is not enough to drive creative nonfiction. Creative nonfiction is always most powerful when it examines Barnes's *why* (*why* do we remember what we do and *why* are we telling this all to the reader).

One way to begin focusing in on a single central question is to notice if certain images (for Jess it was images of fertile Vermont) keep reappearing. Or if a particular metaphor (the Vermont landscape as a body, for example) feels true to the material. Or if the places of friction or trouble (Jess's husband saying he doesn't want a child and the blue-haired man banging on the door) seem to relate. These are a writer's signposts. Pay attention to them! Let these signs guide us toward discovering our central question. Keep asking *why*. Why do we remember what we remember; why do we remember those experiences as we do? Why have our memories shifted over time? Why have certain subsequent experiences changed the nature of the memories? Why do we understand something anew because of later experiences or because of new discoveries? Why do we need to tell this particular narrative? Why can't we let it go?

In Young's essay, the narrator recounts an experience from her childhood in which her mother underwent treatment for cancer. Despite her attempts to keep her mother's illness a secret from her peers, she's accused of using her mother's illness to delay her school deadlines, which she admits was true. Young was tired and weak from watching her mother endure. And yet, "[that] may be why I'm so productive while pregnant," she muses. After all, "Nothing sharpens the mind like a deadline." The connection between her mother's illness and her own persistence was only clarified through the process of writing it.

B: Creative Memory

Memory doesn't work like some sort of file cabinet in the brain. Memories aren't stored as if on a hard drive, just waiting to be opened. They aren't preserved in paraffin like the useless organs of long-dead primates. Memories are mutable, science tells us, an act of creation, infused with imagination and viewed through an ever-changing set of lenses. Each time we call upon a certain memory, we re-invent it. Further, the more often we call upon a certain memory, the more it is altered. We re-create our memory to fit our sense of self, the world as we see it now... and now... and now. Essentially, this means humans are not merely a sum of our memories, the way many of us have come to understand our sense of self—instead, we are each of us artists, forever in the process of re-creating our identity anew. Karim Nader, an associate professor who studies memory at McGill University, confirms: "When you are remembering something, the memory is unstable. It's being re-built, re-created." Our brains re-create (as a function of self-defense or self-sabotage maybe) a slightly larger hand, a slightly longer hug, a steeper walk, a harder ache, a toothier smile, a smaller child. The memories most susceptible to changes are the ones we call upon the most, since every time we re-remember them they change. Novelist Toni Morrison writes, "Memory (the deliberate act of remembering) is a form of willed creation. It is not an effort to find out the way it really was— that is research. The point is to dwell on the way it appeared and why it appeared in that particular way."

We've already discussed how creative nonfiction should have a single central question and how writers can draft toward that central question. Here, we'll examine another way to help discover the central question: by analyzing memories. Often, the memories that return to us most are those we do not understand. These memories contain an implicit sense of mystery, which is a signal that they are meaningful—only through exploring what we don't know, change becomes possible. These memories, by virtue of repetition, are part of the narrative we tell ourselves about ourselves—in other words, our personal mythology. This is how humans create meaning out of chaos by stringing together memories into a cohesive narrative that tells us who we are, what we care about, and where we're headed. We call this process **creative memory**, plumbing our complicated memories to try to make sense of them by fitting them into our personal mythologies. This is the creative memory at work—discovering who we are by mining where we've been.

In the days, weeks, and months after Jess's reading in Craftsbury, the boys crying for tomatoes, and the blue-haired stranger swaying under the porch light, Jess could not stop wondering about those experiences. Did these moments relate in ways beyond the coincidence of having happened on the same day? How was Jess remembering them through the lens of her desire to have a child? And why did Stendhal's awe seem inexplicably tied up in these memories? These events haunted Jess, and her linking of them is her creative memory at work.

It reminds us, too, that the memories most worth writing about are not always the most sensational or dramatic. Instead, pay attention to the memories that haunt you anyway, the small but pivotal and nuanced experiences in which nothing and everything seems to have happened. It is here that discovery is possible—in the memories and experiences that seem to defy logic, that charge through your complacency unbidden, and that stay with you despite, at first, not understanding why.

C: Creative Research

Though memories steer us toward a central question, they're not the only way we find material to write about. Creative nonfiction writers are almost always involved in research, whether we're conscious of it or not. Some of this research is specific, focused, and working directly toward refining a central question, much like an academic writer. This is especially true in literary journalism, science writing, profile writing, biography, and other topics in creative nonfiction that rely on subject matter outside our personal experiences.

But we are always researching merely by actively observing the world around us and discovering connections between it and our own lives. This work, making connections between our private selves and the world around us, is not frivolity; it is the central business of living. Humans make these connections all the time as we move through our days: what we read, see, hear, experience, and learn become parts of the great web of consciousness and connection that help us navigate our lives. Actively observing and researching the world around us (and this includes everything from remembering to researching to interviewing to reviewing maps and photos) and connecting it to our central questions is called **creative research**.

The key to creative research is to allow it to be a fluid process. We may or may not always be specialists on our writing topics. More often, we are collectors: of stories and words, science and myths, jokes and images, and ideas and history. Writers are not oracles but explorers. Our job is to unearth material from diverse and strange places and meld it into meaningful experiences for ourselves and our readers. To make the strange familiar. Or to make the familiar strange.

The best creative nonfiction writers are Renaissance people, fueled by curiosity, tenacity, and a hunger to learn, ask questions, see where those questions lead, and work toward welding diverse ideas together. We are not merely witnesses but players and creators. Think of Darwin, who while studying the wild creatures of the Galapagos Islands, was not content to merely observe but insisted on interacting with his subjects. In *The Voyage of the Beagle* (1839), Darwin recounts attempting to ride on the backs of giant tortoises and picking up lizards by their tails, just to see what would happen. "I threw [a lizard] several times as far as I could, into a deep pool left by the retiring tide; but it invariably returned in a direct line to the spot where I stood." While Darwin's creative research may have been an imperfect science, it speaks to the kind of exuberant energy with which the best writers engage with their world.

As creative nonfiction writers, we have an opportunity (some may even say a responsibility) to translate facts and ideas to a general readership, to bring narrative structure to bear on disparate topics, and to present "information" in a way that excites and inspires the reader. "A Log Cabin Square" by Sarah Minor, for example, activates information about quilts, cloth, and the "log cabin" quilt pattern with meditations on the narrator's ambivalent feelings about her home and the nature of home more generally. Our interpretations/observations of the world become maps or guides for readers who, like us, seek to find meaning in the experience of everyday life.

D: Bodies in Time and Place

No human is a self-contained vessel floating in darkness. We are bodies in time and space. Each of us exists in a private and public way. We are a man named Sean who lives on a lake with his wife and new daughter and their wild dog and who, each winter day, skis into the woods. We are a woman named Jess who is moving to a new city in Ohio to start a new job and who teaches creative writing to students of all ages and backgrounds. But we are also pieces of history. We understand that our lives signify, and our stories contain, deep ethical implications. Our stories matter. The French memoirist and novelist George Sand writes, "Everyone has his own story, and everyone could arouse interest in the romance of his life if he but comprehended it." With proper perspective, writers can create meaningful narratives out of the most seemingly mundane experiences: walking to school in Philadelphia; learning to swim in the Delaware River; falling in love on the edge of a cornfield; cooking soup one December afternoon. With perspective and engagement, these ostensibly benign experiences can shimmer with resonance.

But first, we must learn to see beyond the tunnel vision of our own lives and into the web of time and space in which we live. We cannot take for granted the elements of ourselves that govern our societal interactions in ways that are unique to our moment in history: gender, race, religion, class, ethnicity, sexual orientation, etc. We must bear witness to the social and cultural shifts that take place during our lifetimes and write from the experiences in our own lives that intersect with these shifts. The same holds true for the historical moment we are living in. Think of the larger issues swirling around you. Think about what historical events have recently occurred or appear about ready to occur.

We see this happening in Harrison Candelaria Fletcher's "Open Season," where he ties his experiences to so many of the pop culture experiences of his youth:

> Here they come coyote, the Speedy Gonzalez cartoons, the Frito Bandito erasers, the Ricky Ricardo's "got some splainin' to do," the Chico and the Man's, "it's not my job, man," the Ricardo Mantalban's "Corinthian leather," the Telly Savalas Pancho Villa, the Marlon Brando Zapata, the West Side Story switchblade, the wolf in Zoot Suit clothing, the low-rider steering wheel made from chrome chains.

We call this the **social self**. To look at what it means to be human—and who we are as a species—we must look at history, art, religion, politics. We must let these threads enter and alter the body through which we write, and conversely, we must let the idiosyncratic "I" shape the voice of history. Novelist Milan Kundera writes, "History is nothing more than a thin thread of what is remembered stretched out over an ocean of what has been forgotten." Creative nonfiction is a lighthouse amidst a dark ocean of forgetfulness, helping us navigate the future.

To consider who our social selves are, consider the cultural artifacts that we take for granted. How do these aspects of our world impact our point of view? Jess assumed, for example, that because she was raised without formal religion, her sense of the world was not rooted in spirituality. She did not realize, before she started down the rabbit hole of her maternity/wonder research, how much of her layman's sense of life and death and the collective unconscious—to which we all belong and return—could be informed and deepened by Jung and Stendhal and the portraits of Chuck Close and intentional rotational grazing and Catholicism and Pixar and Madonna. Jess didn't quite know how many layers of history were woven into her understanding of maternal choice until she started diving in.

Facts are all around us: in newspapers and scientific journals, in books and textbooks, on the internet, in magazines, and on the news and radio, and in conversations, lectures, podcasts, an so on. Creative nonfiction writers must make a habit of collecting them like so many seashells on our windowsills. Look for a human story (your own or someone else's) that seems to be informed, changed, or influenced by these facts. Interweave the human story with these facts. Let each influence the other. Let them speak to one another. Let them contradict one another.

Or we can do creative research by having a new experience, immersing ourselves in a new environment, learning interviewing skills, reading broadly, harnessing our inner wonder, and being the Renaissance writer our culture so desperately needs. Albert Einstein wrote, "The most beautiful experience we can have is the mysterious. It is the fundamental emotion that stands at the cradle of true art and true science. Whoever does not know it and can no longer wonder, no longer marvel, is as good as dead, and his eyes are dimmed."

E: Situating the Reader

As we think about creative memory and creative research, we must remember, since our bodies are situated in a specific time and place, that we must also situate our reader in specific times and places. And this leads us to the second half of the central question equation. If the central question is why we are exploring an idea or event, the **situation** is what is being explored: *who* (the characters), *what* (the plot), *where* (the setting), and *when* (the time period).

The situation is often simpler to discover and share with the reader than the central question, but it is just as vital. If the reader isn't grounded in the situation, they won't be able to follow our narratives long enough to unravel the central question. Imagine if Jess's vignette was not occurring in bucolic Vermont but in, well, nowhere. Imagine if there was not a blue-haired man at the door but, merely, someone. And that door he was pounding on led to who-knows-where. Imagine if Jess's vignette had no husband. Just someone beside her on the couch. Man? Woman? We don't know. Imagine if Jess didn't tie this all together by letting the reader know her desire to have a child. Though the central question *might* linger in Jess's mind, the reader would be lost in time and place and action and character.

Also, notice how quickly Jess, in this chapter's vignette, grounds the reader in the situation. The reader gets who ("my husband and I"), where ("on the couch"), and when ("last summer") all in the opening line. Less than half a page later, the reader gets another location: Craftsbury, Vermont. The reader also understands what is occurring. Jess is taking the reader through "a lovely day." So within half a page, the reader knows almost all of the situation. Generally, the sooner the writer can give the reader the situation, the better, often on the first page. And as new characters or locations are added, it is often best to share the who or where with our reader. This allows the reader to feel grounded in the situation, to feel confident in what is occurring as they work to uncover the central question that drives the narrative. With the grounding details, the reader is equipped to enter our narrative, to move confidently into an adventure of discovery.

F: The Knot of Meaning

Throughout this chapter, we've been focusing on finding, exploring, and writing toward a central question. But ultimately, by the end of the exploration of a central question (or any quest, really), an explorer must find *something*. It may not be the answer we were looking for, or any answer at all, really, but we will have discovered some new idea or perspective. A change must take place; we must have a new way of considering the central question. The meaning that emerges should not be prescriptive or reductive, nor a finely honed or provable argument, as in most academic writing. When we write toward, wrestle with, and examine our central question from a multitude of perspectives, we discover not a single meaning but a **knot of meaning**. If, as mentioned above, the central question might be considered the creative nonfiction writer's hypothesis, then the knot of meaning might be considered the (subtly stated) thesis that proves, disproves, or complicates the writer's hypothesis. This proving, disproving, or complicating arises from creative memory and creative research and is creative in nature.

The knot of meaning contains nuance and contradiction, just like life. It is not easy to articulate in a few words. If it were, we wouldn't need to write the narrative, wouldn't feel compelled to wrestle with the questions for days and weeks and months and years. Often, the knot of meaning asks the reader to see two opposing truths as equally true. Or it is like a crystal that shatters a truth of light across the room. Or it is a dense knot of rope, unraveling thread by thread.

This knot should almost never tell us exactly what to think. Instead, it should allow readers to think on their own, to take our knot and bring it into their own world. Minor's "A Log Cabin Square" progresses in the shape of the pattern it describes, accruing pieces of imagery, anecdote, reflection, and research like swaths of cloth. In the final searing image, Minor reasserts her knot, which is an embrace and a fear of home. Retelling her grandfather's story of working at a racetrack as a kid in Virginia, she recounts his story of the time the barn burned and the untethered horses kept running back to their stalls, their "bright home—in other words, they were compelled back to a place of both origin and certain danger.

IV: READING AS A WRITER

The following exercises will help you practice the techniques learned in this chapter.

A: Reading Like a Writer (Articulating the "Knot of Meaning")
Choose any three narratives from our anthology. Write down what you think the knot of meaning is. How is the writer asking the reader to hold opposing truths in the same hand? Pick three scenes from each narrative and write down how each one contributes to some aspect of the knot.

B: Working Backward
Now, working backward, using those same three narratives, start to jot down the questions that seem to drive the narrative. Can you articulate a central question? How did the central question lead to the knot?

C: Considering Alternatives
One of the most useful ways to begin to make deliberate choices in our narratives is to consider how a particular narrative would have a different knot if it were written differently. Consider three scenes, meditations, or other distinct elements of a narrative in our anthology, and think about why the writer composed them as they did. Is a particular scene especially lyrical? Is the first paragraph reflective or active? Is the flashback in the second-person point of view? Why did the author make those particular decisions, and how do they help elucidate the knot? What if the writer had composed these elements differently? How would that change the knot?

D: Complicated Memories
Examine your memories. Do particular memories feel especially charged with meaning? Do you sense mystery that you can't articulate? Pick one memory that feels especially confusing, charged, or nuanced. What baffles you about it? What don't you understand?

For each of these questions, consider sources outside yourself that may help you discover new ways of thinking about them. Don't limit yourself. Think broadly. You never know what you will discover that will change the way you understand experiences.

E: Social Self and the Situation

Examine any narrative from our anthology. First, examine how the writer is showing their social self. Try to explain how the writer highlights their social self.

Next, examine how quickly you can find the situation (who, what, where, and when). What can we learn from how long it takes to receive a situation?

Now do the same thing for a narrative you are working on. See how quickly you can find your social self and your situation.

V: PROMPTS

The following prompts will help put to practice the techniques learned in this chapter.

A: Being a Collector

For the rest of the week (or your life), keep a notebook where you jot down odd or interesting facts, stories about others, and news items. Let it grow large and unwieldy. Draw from news stories, conversations, books and articles, podcasts, radio broadcasts: the often-overwhelming onslaught of information that forms the backdrop of our days.

At the end of the week, circle five facts at random and list out personal experiences/memories that relate to that bit of information. Don't censor and don't be choosy. Let the notebook material spark your memory without judgment.

Then freewrite one of these memories into a complete and detailed scene. Write toward connection: literal or metaphorical. See if you can use the notebook material in your scene to reframe the personal material and elucidate the connections.

After you've completed the freewrite, reread it while jotting down a list of questions for more ways to explore creative research.

B: Playing with Time and Place

Open an existing draft of a narrative you are working on. Jot down the time and place in which the experiences rendered occurred. What cultural, technological, or historical shifts define that time and place? Do some research. Look for places of connection or intersection. How does the cultural, technological, historical moment impact the personal story? Let your research cast new light on the material. Try incorporating the research and spend time unpacking the literal or metaphorical connections.

C: The Situation

Take a flash narrative you are working on and write it in two different ways. In one, hide the situation (who, what, where, and when) for as long as possible. Then write that same flash narrative with the situation stated as quickly as possible. Discern the pros and cons of each approach.

4

Form and Topic Interplay

I: RELEVANT READINGS

Austin Bunn, "Basement Story"
Seo-Young Chu, "A Refuge for Jae-in Doe: Fugues in the Key of English Major"
Vivek Shraya, "Trisha"
Ira Sukrungruang, "Invisible Partners"
Jill Talbot, "The Professor of Longing"
Elissa Washuta, "Incompressible Flow"
Xu Xi, "Godspeed"

II: VIGNETTE

I recently spent two years trying to find the perfect home to buy in Vermont. My search was tireless—hours spent on websites and real estate apps, multiple daily drive-bys, countless phone calls and appointments with my realtor. Nothing I found felt right. I had a specific vision for my future home, not just of the house itself but the life that house would enable me to live. I wanted nature and quiet, but also easy access to the wider world. In my new home, my new life, I would become the best version of myself: creative, domestic, capable of throwing lavish dinner parties, but also peaceful and studious. The house would always be perfectly clean and beautifully appointed. I'd only eat organic food in my new house, and every soap would smell delicious.

When that vision failed to manifest in the perfect home, I grew frantic. How could I become this perfect version of myself if I could not find the perfect space in which to become her? Of course, while I did eventually find and purchase a lovely home, none of my fantasies came to fruition. I was still, sadly, myself: messy, anxious, and a terrible cook.

When I decided to write about this experience, I sensed that it was more than just a story about real estate. Real estate was merely the lens through which I had failed to become someone other than myself, someone better. Why did real estate loom so large in my imagination, I wondered? What were the connections between my domestic ambitions and my sense of failure as a woman, especially since I had never put much conscious stock in, nor had any role models of prescribed feminine roles? With these burgeoning central questions in mind, I began to draft an essay. I tried to write it as a braided narrative, moving back and forth between my house-hunting experiences and research into contemporary concepts of domesticity. While I had some interesting material, the essay wasn't coming together. I wasn't discovering the threads of connection that would lead me to a knot of meaning. I tried writing it as a lyric essay next, sinking into language and sentence structure, attempting to uncover some profound metaphor that would translate the emotional truth. I failed there, too.

Finally, I had an idea. What if I wrote the essay in a hybrid form, using the format of Zillow listings—the website I'd spent so much time on during the hunt? I could dig back into my search history and pull out the listings for each home I had toured, but instead of the traditional house descriptions, I would recall the way the space felt when I'd toured it, the various fantasies that had played out in my imagination, and the many nightmares I had envisioned as more and more homes failed to fulfill my outsized longings. The form itself—those many Zillow listings—reinforced the fallacies of marketing, and the language of them (which I borrowed) pointed to the ways that an astute marketer can manipulate emotions. "Sweeping views" suggest peaceful, meditative afternoons; "meticulously maintained gardens" project a connection to nature through ownership; "fully refurbished hardwood floors" convey gleaming, barefoot mornings, the sun reflecting in the high-gloss finish.

The final "found" form worked with my content in more than one way to create meaning, and in the interplay between the two was the tension of impossible longing that seemed so fundamental to what I was trying to convey. But those early drafts were not a waste; each one brought me closer to the form that would ultimately best scaffold the material.

—Jess

III: OVERVIEW

As we saw in "The Central Question," working toward a knot of meaning is the writer's most important job. One of the ways to do that is to consider the ways that forms and topics intersect to create energy and help the reader understand the knot of meaning.

A: Form in Creative Nonfiction

Form—the ways in which we choose to organize our content via images, scenes, flashbacks, research, and other techniques—is how writers fashion situations into central questions, knots of meaning, and, ultimately, art. At its most basic, form is about containing or holding. In Latin, the verb *continere* means "to hold together, enclose." Form gives our content shape, and shape is what distinguishes raw material from masterpiece, the chaos of experience from artifact, similar to how a ceramicist molds clay.

Consider the architecture of a house. We might have two houses that use the exact same types and amounts of materials. But in the end, it is less the materials that make that house and more how the architect lays out the rooms that impacts the way we move, think, and feel inside those spaces. Similarly, the way homeowners organize the content of those rooms gives meaning to the way we experience those materials. An oversized sofa in the middle of a space disrupts flow, perhaps, but it also emphasizes the primacy of relaxation and togetherness. A large landscape painting will feel different if it's centered on a large, blank wall than if it is tucked down a dark hallway.

The same holds true for creative nonfiction. Situation matters. But what matters more, by far, is how we arrange those real situations from our lives. Where and how and why we put our spaces (or our situations) together reveals what we value, how we value it, who we are, and how we understand ourselves in relationship to the universe. It also affects which central questions we explore and the meanings we derive from them.

There are eight primary creative nonfiction forms: traditional, braided, collage, flash, lyric, graphic, found, and hybrid. Though it appears that we offer this as a definitive list, we see it as merely the beginning of a potentially endless list of forms—the same way that we might list seven types of houses (ranch, bungalow, A-frame, Craftsman, colonial, and the more unique tree and tiny) while recognizing that there are many other architectural forms.

Also, if it seems that we offer each form as distinctive with its own boundaries, this is not the case. These forms often bleed into and influence each other. It might be more difficult to write in a single form than to write across two or more forms. These forms are merely guides for organizing material. They are not formulas. What is most important is to use form in ways that best reveal a narrative's meaning, because narratives breathe, expanding and contracting against their own walls.

Finally, before moving on, let's talk quickly about the differences between form and genre since they both seem, by definition, to be so similar. Both are about shape. But think of genre as the largest shapes (poetry, drama, prose) while forms are sub categories of those larger shapes. Some forms go across multiple genres (found pieces are often in prose or poetry while flash pieces are often in prose or drama), while some are normally found in only a single genre. To go along with that, since most creative nonfiction is written in prose, we highlight the forms that are most associated with prose.

B: The Eight Forms

The most widely used form is the **traditional** form, in which the writer has a beginning, middle, and ending and typically uses standard chronology. The beginning often focuses on a question or an issue. The middle is where the writer mucks around with that question or issue. And the ending brings us toward some sort of conclusion concerning that question or issue, even if no answer is achieved. As mentioned above, this is the most standard form, which means that the reader is most used to this form. Often, the traditional form relies on cause and effect to show meaning or depends on a clear sense of the order of events or experiences to show change. In "Godspeed" by Xu Xi, the narrator investigates the effects of income inequality between her family in Hong Kong and the "servants" they hired in the sixties to care for them. The traditional essay begins in the narrator's childhood, using past tense to explore her experiences with Ah Siu, her one-time caregiver, and concludes in the narrator's adulthood, in which she has recently hired caregivers to help care for her elderly mother. The difference, the narrator reflects, is that she refuses to treat her employees as servants. The "cause" includes the ways in which the narrator witnessed the mistreatment of Ah Siu, and the "effect" is the more equitable relationship she has with her mother's caregivers. The thorough exploration of the "cause" leads to the discovery of the "effect."

Unlike the traditional form, the **braided** form weaves together two or more ideas, experiences, and/or images, eschewing chronology as its organizing principle. The braided form slowly intertwines questions, ideas, and/or moments, bit by bit, until by the end, the reader cannot help but see these ostensibly separate strands as naturally linked. One of the components that comes along with this weaving is that the ideas being explored are revealed to the reader slowly.

The braided form suggests the ways in which our experiences color other experiences, the inextricably woven shape of human consciousness. The past informs the present. Ideologies intersect with emotions. Science reveals motive. All is implicated and inextricable. For example, the way that Jess relates to her brother's addiction (a common topic in her writing) is informed not just by her personal experiences with his addiction but also by her father's death from alcoholism; the mass incarceration of addicts in America; that time her college roommate overdosed inside a fraternity bathroom; the etymology of certain euphemisms for addicts; the sounds and conversations she heard growing up visiting her father's favorite bar; and the history of the working-class neighborhood where she spent her early years. And much else besides.

By braiding various threads together and returning again and again to look at them anew—especially when the threads are disparate ideas—we can see how the braided form itself asserts independence. And that contributes to a knot of meaning about the ways in which addiction is not just a personal disease but also a cultural, social, and familial condition.

Similar to the braided form is the collage. The **collage**, rather than braiding ideas together, juxtaposes multiple and often seemingly unrelated images or ideas side by side. Thoughtful juxtaposition is key to this form. How two or more images or ideas bounce off each other is where the collage gathers its strength. Rather than working chronologically or neatly tying things together, as in the braided narrative, the writer is after the effect that comes from putting together a range of startling or striking images or ideas. An example of a collage essay is Seo-Young Chu's "A Refuge for Jae-in Doe: Fugues in the Key of English Major," which collates a variety of narrative elements—prose, poetry, Q&A, image, etc.—to create her knot.

But Chu cannot simply juxtapose images and ideas willy-nilly. The juxtapositions must evoke meaning in the intersections. Chu's first section recounts a phone call from a current student calling to collect donations for the alumni association at the university where Chu was once sexually assaulted by a professor when she was a student there. Initially Chu believes the call is heralding the apology she's waited twenty years to receive. The next section, subtitled "Discuss the Following Quotation," includes only a single newspaper quote from her assailant, concerning his love for teaching: "'There's a great pleasure in teaching freshmen because you're sort of being folded into their lives at a particular, powerful moment in which you can make a difference,' he said. 'And to some degree, you can "convert" them to English. It becomes a way of trawling for majors.'" By virtue of the juxtaposition there, the reader feels the emotional impact of the irony of the quote. Chu does not need to reemphasize the double meaning implicit in words like "pleasure," "convert," and "trawling" in reference to freshman students; the reader feels it keenly through the lens of the preceding section. Meaningful juxtaposition reduces the risk of sentimental language by implying powerful emotions, rather than insisting on them.

The form itself, devoid of content even, suggests an expansiveness of vision, an effort to *take it all in*. Much of the energy is derived from the tension between the fractured content and the points of fusion. In other words, these narratives are simultaneously pulling apart and coming together, and propulsion is a result of the writer's efforts to reconcile these opposing forces. In the white space that follows that first section in Chu's essay, the tension between the narrator's point of view and her former professor's is irreconcilable, propelling the reader on.

The **flash** form is less defined by what it is and more defined by the size it is. For the flash form, there is a strict word count, which leads to a compression of ideas and images. Some consider flash to be anything under five hundred words. Others set the word count higher or lower. Regardless, it's the use of compression that sets flash apart.

Consider what a short, compressed form like flash means, even devoid of content. The reader brings certain connotations about brevity when they hear "flash." The flash form suggests a certain audaciousness and wonder, like a model town made of matchsticks. Flash, much like a poem, often works best when the content is focused on a single scene or image, allowing the writer to zoom in close to a subject. Often, the flash form begins *in medias res* and relies on a single image to suggest both character and narrative arc, wherein the beginning and ending are implied by a provocative middle. The flash form might also end in a moment of suspense, which propels the narrative energy forward. Examine the last sentences in Ira Sukrungruang's "Invisible Partners" and notice how the suspenseful final image provokes volatile imagined futures for the "three dressed-up girls," the narrator's former dates, who are ignorant even as "a pair of scissors come down to sever them," wielded by the narrator's mother, who ruthlessly cuts them out of old photographs. Flash narratives often conclude in image, rather than reflection, which is a strategy that helps the writer reinforce a complicated knot without spoon-feeding it to the reader.

Another form is the **lyric,** which poets call the prose poem. Whereas most of the above forms focus on narratives based around an idea, the lyric form leans into poetic elements to create meaning: language, rhythm, sound, alliteration, torque, repetition, cadence, and musicality. Indeed, the root of the word lyric is *lyre*, a musical instrument that accompanied ancient song. The lyric form is songlike; it hinges on the inherent rhythms of language and sound, both to create shape and to reveal meaning. Lyric narratives are artful, but with purpose, provoking meditation and requiring the reader to complete the meaning.

The lyric often uses white space as an invitation to pause and rest: an invitation for response from the reader. That same white space also brings together disparate ideas and images, similar to the braided and collage. Also, although the lyric is in search of answers, often the reader is left the task of assembling an answer from the disconnected and/or fragmented ideas and images. How does this reading task apply to Elissa Washuta's lyric essay "Incompressible Flow," which eschews easy meaning for more nuanced connotations? Consider the white space between the following two paragraphs, for example:

> *In spite of these obvious differences, these two flows are governed by the same laws, and their fluid dynamics are very similar. The purpose of the wing is to lift the airplane, while the purpose of the propeller is to*

> produce the thrust on the boat. I begged us forward, into our second winter, into seriousness as our friends put on suits and gowns and got serious adult marriages. He poured water on my cat and picked her up by her neck. In secret, I started smoking again.

The former, excerpted from the textbook *Incompressible Flow* by Ronald Lee Panton, as Washuta tells us in a footnote, mentions "two flows governed by the same laws," an idea picked up in the latter paragraph, after the white space, in which we might imagine these two flows as the narrator and her ex-lover. What does that suggest to us about other connections between these two paragraphs?

The **graphic** form is rapidly gaining popularity. This form pairs visual images with words. These images might be pen and ink, photographs, paintings, etc. These images establish tone, setting, and other vital details. The writer relies less on words, especially because there is less space on the page for words, and more on the intersections and combinations of words and images. Further, because the reader receives information from words and images, the brain is engaged in multiple ways. Another power of graphic forms comes from the compression of words, which makes it act, in some ways, like the flash form.

Vivek Shraya's "Trisha" explores the narrator's identity by juxtaposing photos of Shraya's mother with re-creations of those same photos with Shraya as the subject. Because Shraya is a transgender woman, the recaptured photos provoke a series of complicated questions about gender, identity, and inheritance, especially in conjunction with an interspersed written narrative.

Rather than taking on their own shape, **found** forms adopt a structure from other structures. For example, a writer might create a narrative that looks like a take-out menu, a website for a pet adoption facility, a how-to guide, a playlist, an address book, a field guide, a set of directions for building something, an email, a map, an interview, a math problem, a test, or a multitude of other forms. The only limitation of found forms is the writer's imagination.

Whichever form is taken, the writer should lean into this form and use the "rules" and "norms" of this form. This found form should also deeply inform the knot, so there must be a reason that the writer writes within a found form. The found form must help the writer and reader move toward the knot of meaning.

In "The Professor of Longing," Jill Talbot recounts her separation from her daughter's father and her struggles through heartbreak, money trouble, and moves across state lines. "The Professor of Longing" looks exactly like a syllabus, with readings and assignments that reveal Talbot's personal pain and preoccupations, while also offering a personal narrative about Talbot's experiences as a single mother and adjunct professor. The syllabus form suggests something particular about the way Talbot moves through, and understands, her own experiences. By organizing intimate life stories into a syllabus structure, Talbot suggests that even the most well-intentioned educators are ultimately unable to separate their professional and personal lives, that each of us bear our grief, joys, and anxieties in our every day. The syllabus serves as visual and metaphoric scaffolding for Talbot's intimate revelations and works to contain what might otherwise feel uncontainable: her profound sense of loss. Talbot armors especially fraught or potentially sentimental content with the protective covering of the appropriated form. She writes:

> **Texts:** We're not going to read anything beyond my own proclivities. We'll discuss stories, essays, and poems that remind me of my most recent misgivings, the lingerings I'm unable to yield, the words underlining my

past. Our study will include recurring images, my own, of course, as well as the themes of my disposition. The text in this class is me.

Attendance: It's strange to think I'm even here. Years from now, I will feel as though these weeks were nothing more than an interruption, a curve in the story's road.

Disclaimer: While these aren't the texts I really used that semester, they most accurately reflect who I was during those weeks when I kept my eyes to the sidewalk.

Talbot names her stakes early in the front matter of her faux syllabus, suggesting that the narrative will also be a critique of the form itself, questioning the objectivity of any given syllabus and the image of academia as the stalwart, stoic purveyor of knowledge—unaffected by personal pain.

Found forms point directly to their own construction-ness. When we read found forms, we should consider what parts of the original forms are preserved, what aspects are lost or transformed, and what these decisions say about the knot of meaning.

Though these are some of the major forms in creative nonfiction, there are many other forms that might be discussed. What we hope you take away from this section is the breadth and depth of creative nonfiction, and an understanding that creative nonfiction can take any form imaginable as long as it helps heighten the central question. And remember that forms are never formulas. They are malleable, adaptable, and changeable.

And that leads to our final way to consider form: the **hybrid** form, which encompasses narratives that employ more than one form. Like found forms, hybrid forms point to their own artifice. A hybrid (the verb: *to hybridize*) juxtaposes, usually without transitions, two or more unlike elements. Consider mules, for example, the offspring of a horse and a donkey, which possesses the thick head, long ears, thin limbs, small narrow hooves, and short mane of the donkey and the height and body, shape of neck and rump, uniformity of coat, and teeth of the horse, in order to optimize their performance as working animals; they are reputed to be of higher intelligence than either of its parent breeds. Charles Darwin wrote: "The mule always appears to me a most surprising animal. That a hybrid should possess more reason, memory, obstinacy, social affection, powers of muscular endurance, and length of life, than either of its parents, seems to indicate that art has here outdone nature." The same assessment might apply to hybrid forms, which capitalize on the energy and logic with which the writer moves between forms.

When reading hybrid forms, it is important to consider how the hybridization itself changes the content and how the original (pre-hybridized) forms are both persevered and altered. How does the writer control the reader's attention in this process, and how does the process emphasize certain ideas, images, and/or scenes? Where does the hybrid form point to its own hybridization and where does it attempt to conceal it? Why and how?

An example of the hybrid is Austin Bunn's "Basement Story," which some might classify as a poem. Others might call it a screenplay. Bunn himself calls it multiple things, including an essay and a solo theater performance.

Regardless of what form is chosen, the knot of meaning is the intuitive essence of emotion, metaphor, image, and idea that makes creative nonfiction more than just a collection of scenes or observations, something greater than the sum of its parts.

C: Topics in Creative Nonfiction

Along with forms, we also have a variety of topics that writers can write about or within. Often, topics are mistaken for genres or forms. They are neither; **topics** are simply the situation, especially *what* is occurring. We can write about any given topic in any genre, using any degree of veracity, and within any form. Below, we focus on a few of the many topics available.

Autobiography is a chronology of the writer's entire life. It begins at the beginning and ends whenever the writer stops writing. It focuses on all the major details of a writer's life. The autobiography is shaped to reveal the impact of seminal events and/or shifts on the subject's emotional, physical, and/or intellectual development—or the subject's impact on other people.

Environmental and nature writing focuses on how humans interact with or affect the world around us. These pieces often focus on a place.

Immersion is where the writer tries on a new life, experience, or activity. This is either something the writer has never done before or something the writer hasn't done in many, many years. The newness of the activity is what the writer is exploring.

Literary journalism is the intersection between journalism (factual reporting) and creative nonfiction. Here, writers focus on reporting, but they also lean more into heightened language and scene work.

Meditation is more philosophical and often works to unpack ideas of profound personal importance to the writer. Meditation tie back to

Montaigne's *Essais*. Often meditation don't aim to prove a point but rather to explore a question in depth and with precision. These narratives are often not structured chronologically but instead follow the movements of the mind.

Memoir is one of the most popular topics of creative nonfiction. The memoir examines a period of a writer's life, especially as related to a single question or idea, and particularly related to past moments, which is why the memoir takes its name from "memory." This is a major focus of the memoir: probing our memories in order to reveal complex meaning.

The **Personal Essay** is similar to memoir. Some writers highlight page length as the difference between these two topics (personal essay is often considered short, say under twenty pages, while memoir is book-length), but we argue that the personal is determined not by length but by a focus on more immediate events than memoir. Whereas memoir looks backward, the personal examines the immediately lived life. In some ways, the distinctions between the two are negligible and indefinable but they are worth offering here as a launching point for discussion.

Portrait writing examines someone or something other than the writer themselves. The writer turns their gaze from their own life and instead focuses on a person, event, or place.

Persuasive writing focuses its attention on proving a point. Here, the writer, rather than exploring a question—as seen in the meditation—stares right at the issue and tries to convert the reader to a new point of view.

Science and math Essays deal with explaining or highlighting key new discoveries. This topic often works to "translate" a complex scientific or mathematical idea into language an average reader can understand.

Speculative writing focuses on situations where the writer uses hypothesis, deduction, and extrapolation to write about something they do not fully know. Often, the speculative looks forward or backward in time to make an educated guess on how an event might have turned out differently.

Sports writing zeroes in on an event or athlete and focuses on the game or activity being played. These can, overlap with the profile.

Travel writing focuses on giving the reader an inside look at another place. The travel topic often examines insiders and outsiders.

D: Finding the Right Form for a Topic

How do we find the most useful form for our topics? Depending on our audience, publication venue, and especially our goals for the piece, any topic of human interest can be adapted to any form, or more specifically, *revealed through any form.* A story about the Philadelphia Eagles's triumphant 2018 Superbowl win for *Sports Illustrated* might not be the place to use a found form, for example. On the other hand, this same topic might adapt beautifully to a braided narrative on community bonding for a literary journal. This same topic can be utilized to reveal two very different knots of meaning, and therefore potentially work with different forms. Similarly, a literary journalism piece about Syrian refugees in Turkey for *The New Yorker* is probably best composed in a traditional form, whereas a portrait of a Syrian refugee's journey for *The Threepenny Review* could be more lyrical.

As we draft and revise, let these questions guide us. What is gained by writing creative nonfiction as a series of lyric narratives, for example, as opposed to a chronological memoir? What is lost? How might we mitigate those losses while retaining our chosen form? Don't take form for granted, but scrutinize it as a meaning-making tool. Think imaginatively about form and broadly about the possibilities each form offers. Do not be afraid to draft in myriad forms or even a hybrid form. Often, both Jess and Sean try multiple forms before finding the one that feels most like home for the topic at hand.

IV: READING AS A WRITER

The following exercises will help you practice the techniques learned in this chapter.

A: Form and Your Writing
Look at three of your own narratives. Examine what form(s) you use. Do you typically rely on one form? If so, why? Do you explore a variety of forms? How so? Make a list of the forms you would most like to try and next to each one, list possible experiences and/or ideas that fit that form well.

B: Examining Form
Choose any three narratives from our anthology. Examine their form and explore why the writer might have chosen that form. How does this form contribute to the knot of meaning?

        Piece 1:
        Form:
    Reason:

Piece 2:
Form:
Reason:

Piece 3:
Form:
Reason:

C: Hybrids

Look for three narratives in our anthology that use more than one form or more than one topic. Name their forms/topics. Briefly, argue how these narratives fit into multiple forms/topics.

V: PROMPTS

The following prompts will help put to practice the techniques learned in this chapter.

A: Uncomfortable Forms

Look at our list of forms. Order them in terms of the ones you feel most comfortable using to least comfortable. Once you have that list, write a narrative that uses one of the forms you are most uncomfortable with.

B: Taboo Topics

Make a list of ten subjects that were forbidden, taboo, or discouraged as topics of conversation in your childhood. Circle the one that feels most troublesome or fraught. Now, make a list of five experiences with that subject, either personal experiences or experiences of people someone close to you. Again, circle the one that feels most troubling, confusing, vivid, and/or fraught. What's the image that stands out the most in this memory?

Without providing context, write the image in one paragraph only, being as specific as possible. Go back to your original list of subjects and repeat this process, letting your image paragraphs accumulate on the page. Repeat this process five times. Title this collage "Taboo." Look for recurring ideas, details, and metaphors. Revise with an eye toward making these connections clearer. What do they suggest about a knot of meaning?

C: Forms and Topics

Write a list of three forms you want to explore. Then write a list of three topics you want to explore. Pair them up, each of the three forms receiving a topic. Now choose one, two, or all three of these to turn into new drafts.

5

Meaningful Imagery

I: RELEVANT READINGS

Melissa Febos, "Leave Marks"
Ryan Van Meter, "First"
Christian Wiman, "The Limit"

II: VIGNETTE

This image has haunted me for years. I was seven years old and sitting in a tide pool on a beach in New Jersey, the warm, stagnant water just covering my thighs while I traced vanishing lines through the wet sand between my legs. I don't know if it was the hum of my family's voices in the distance, or the undulant smack and shush of the waves, or the heat of the sun on my neck, or the evaporating marks I made in the sand, but suddenly I understood— violently, viscerally—that my life would end. I sensed the blankness, the black, and I slid onto my back in the belly of the salt-spunked water and let myself feel it. If the sands had parted then, if the universe had opened its maw and invited me in, I would have gone willingly, joyfully.

But the universe did not take me.

In the distance, a new universe sounded—the ocean waves, the wailing gulls, the scratch of hermit crab claws against the sand, my brother's voice pleading for ice cream. I woke to it slowly.

It was my first shock of death: the realization that death exists, that I will die. I've wanted to write about that moment for years but struggled to discern the larger meaning in that image. Not what happened—I knew that, but why it happened. Why did that moment reveal to me such a sudden and morbid epiphany? Why did I remember it so vividly? How does it connect to other moments in my life—many of which have been more intimately related to death? What's the narrative?

It wasn't until a few months ago, twenty-six years later, that I glimpsed how that image of my child-self on the beach might be more meaningfully interwoven in my psyche, my personal mythology. I was thirty-three years old, and I'd been running through the woods near my house when I came across a squirrel in the middle of the path in front of me, splayed and dead, his white belly to the heavens, his four legs cast out in opposing directions, a near-perfect simulacrum of death's preferred posture—wholly supplicant at the last—with his front right paw curling back over his heart; it was as if he had deposited himself there deliberately like a set prop. Black flies poured in and out of the squirrel's gaping mouth and paced across his round, glassine eyes. They congregated near his nostrils and occasionally dipped a foot into the chasm. I noticed the dead squirrel's tiny, white teeth, aligned perfectly along his lower, distended jaw. I had the urge to run my finger along his downy throat and over the swell of his stomach, still warm, a siren of energy radiating out from his expired heart.

And then the dead squirrel shuddered, gasped, and heaved. The flies knocked their heads together in a frenzy to escape. I screamed, seized with wonder, and grabbed the nearest sizeable rock.

These two very different images were far apart in time and space, and yet, as I thought about the not-quite-dead squirrel in the hours and days after discovering it, I kept returning to that first image too—my child-self on the beach. I sensed that they were connected in some deeply universal, emotional, and metaphorically significant way. I set out to write an essay that could contain and connect those images and through that process clarified my central question: How does one's recognition and understanding of death change over time? The images were my cornerstones, the knots of meaning I needed to untangle. Through a process of drafting and revising those images—and a few more—and conducting and incorporating research about the limits of our cognitive understanding of death, I was able to clarify the central question, which until then had been ineffable. This is often how the process of writing creative nonfiction unfolds.

—Jess

III: OVERVIEW

Writing instructors encourage newer writers to construct images on the page, to create a picture in the mind of the reader, but scientists still debate the nature of images in the brain: Are these "images" more like pictures or more like language? And while actual pictures can't be found in most of our writing (graphic forms notwithstanding, like Vivek Shraya's "Trisha"), the reader's desire for images built out of language reflects a hunger for immediacy and to feel as if they are experiencing the writer's world. After all, images, like Jess's image of the dead squirrel, are more solid than ideas or abstract emotions, like a vague idea of death, and these images ground our writing in the material world in immediately recognizable ways.

But the word "immediacy" means to bring one into "direct and instant involvement with something," which ultimately creative writing cannot produce, since it is filtered through the veil of language. Writers, no matter how hard we try, are unable to render anything, like Jess's squirrel, in any real way. Instead, we all must employ a cache of artistic techniques in order to get as close to the sensation of immediacy as possible. This means drawing on lessons from the visual arts as well as poetry and learning how to use significant, sensory details in order to evoke an emotionally and intellectually engaging image.

In this chapter, we'll explore these craft techniques in detail, as well as ways to create a web of meaning using imagery and metaphor. We'll also discover ways to create an imagistic or metaphoric organization by following our own associative logic.

A: Significant Sensory Details

If a primary goal of our creative nonfiction is to close the gap between the writer's actual experience and the reader's literary experience, it's only logical that our work on the page should be grounded in the visceral, corporeal realities we inhabit. This requires a deep engagement with sensory details as a way of replicating the symphony of sensations that comprise our time on Earth. This is how we engage our readers with our experiential and emotional realities: by embodying memory. In this way, we avoid the fixed meanings of symbols and allow our reader to become an active participant in the meaning-making process.

Most creative writing books mention our five senses—sight, hearing, taste, touch, and smell. But contrary to popular belief, there are many more senses than just those five. We also have pressure, itch, temperature, pain, thirst, hunger, bowel movements, directions, time, balance, muscle tension, and more. And these senses, and all the rest, provide the details that help us create **sensory images**. We should use as many of these senses as possible on the page so that the reader literally (and they do, *literally*) feels as if they are seeing what the writer shares, smelling what the writer shares, and feeling the itches, the pressures, the pains that the writer shares.

But sensory details are only half of the equation. Jess could share tens or hundreds or thousands of details about her dying squirrel, but that would overwhelm the reader with detail. Sensory details must be carefully chosen to serve more than one purpose. The best sensory details evoke an emotional or aesthetic mood, cultivate setting or character, create or extend a metaphor, or in some other way convey multiple levels of meaning. These are **significant sensory details**: sensory details that work on multiple levels to reflect emotional truth and teach the reader how to experience the image.

Consider the following image from Ryan Van Meter's "First," which contains significant sensory details:

> In the car, Ben and I hold hands. There is something sticky on his fingers, probably the strawberry syrup from the ice cream sundaes we ate for dessert. We have never held hands before; I have simply reached for his in the dark and held him while he holds me. I want to see our hands on the rough floor, but they are only visible every block or so when the car passes beneath a streetlight, and then, for only a flash.

The image renders details that contribute to the knot of meaning: the innocence and joy of first love and, equally, the pain of realizing that his love is not acceptable to the adults around him. The strawberry syrup conveys the youth and sweetness implicit to the knot. There's innocence implied in all the sibilance, too: a whiff of life in rhymes and repetition and all those s-sounds, like a Dr. Seuss book. The image suggests intimacy and acceptance, too. The narrator does not recoil from the stickiness but experiences it as a kind of wonder. Then, the line "We have never held hands before; I have simply reached for his in the dark and held him while he holds me" provides a physical description, yes, but it also uses repetition to insist on the tenderness implicit in the gesture. They hold one another. They are each holding and being held. Later, the "flash" of their hands illuminated by streetlights conveys the physical image, but it also functions metaphorically to suggest the fleetingness of their bond, this secret in the dark.

"First" is a curated experience—incorporating details that transcend mere reality to evoke emotional truths, too. Effective images are not transcription but the cultivation of meaningful experiences. These images point to the knot of meaning. The image above evokes innocence and love. Later images will evoke their inverse. Together, they cultivate the knot.

B: Image as Cornerstone

Newer writers often have a pile of memories that feel relevant to their creative nonfiction but have no idea where to start. When students struggle to come up with ideas for their creative nonfiction, Jess suggests beginning with the images that feel especially troubling—those that they don't understand (those fight-or-flight, novel, and altered-state moments, which will be discussed in "Expanding and Contracting Scene").

In this way, images serve as an inspiration for content and for beginning to understand our central question. Images are often the cornerstone of the rest of a narrative. Like the cornerstone of a building, the first stone set and the one to which all the rest of the stones will be set in reference, **cornerstone images** serve as the foundational images or scenes for rich creative nonfiction. These images help us discover the next image and the next. Once Jess finished writing the image of the not-dead squirrel, she recalled the experience on the beach when she was seven and first understood the finality of death. The cornerstone image of the squirrel led her to the next relevant image. Together, they began to suggest her central question: *How do I live with the fact of death, instead of despite it?*

If we are struggling to figure out where to begin, we can plumb our memories for cornerstone images. What images confound us in ways that feel significant or potentially meaningful? What images linger even if we don't understand why? Look closely at these cornerstone images. Often, they contain nuances of meaning and metaphoric possibility not only for our creative nonfiction but also for our very lives, which is exactly why we hold onto them in the first place.

C: Image and the Ecstatic

The Imagiste Movement of the early twentieth century, pioneered by Ezra Pound and others, is perhaps best represented by Pound's famous two-line poem, "In a Station at the Metro":

> The apparition of these faces in the crowd:
> Petals on a wet, black bough.

The Imagistes prized the direct treatment of "the Thing" (which we might call *the situation*) over the fixed-value system of symbolism. What this means is that by utilizing significant sensory details, the Imagistes sought to bring the reader as close as possible to the emotional and intellectual experience of the writer. The Imagistes's "Thing" can be defined as experience translated into image.

The origin story of "In a Station at the Metro" is perhaps as famous as the poem itself and speaks to how an image can, in an instant, bypass analysis en route to the ecstatic. Pound writes:

> I got out of a "metro" train at La Concorde and saw suddenly a beautiful face, and then another and another, and then a beautiful child's face, and then another beautiful woman, and I tried all that day to find the words for what this had meant to me, and I could not find any words that seemed to me worthy, or as lovely as that sudden emotion.

After thirty drafts and a year had passed, Pound had distilled the experience into the two precise lines above, which in their brevity, specificity, and musicality are far more resonant than the lengthy description he gave of them.

Pound and his fellow Imagistes developed three major tenets. By replacing their use of "the Thing" with "image," we can see how these ideas are related to image-making.

- To employ direct treatment of the [image], whether subjective or objective
- To use absolutely no word that does not contribute to the presentation of [the image]
- As regarding rhythm: to compose in sequence of the musical phrase, not in sequence of the metronome.

This final tenet refers to the ways that rhythm and cadence can be manipulated on the page to reflect emotional truth, rather than being meted out in plodding, predictable patterns.

The Imagiste philosophy eschewed unnecessary ornamentation and verbosity, valued brevity and precision, and asserted style as a means of articulating the *knot of meaning*, which they called the *ineffable*. As much as possible, Imagistes sought to pierce through the veil of language to reach "the Thing" itself by counting on the reader to add their individual experiences into the equation. In this way, a third space is created between writer and reader, inaccessible to either party alone.

The three tenets of the Imagistes are not the province of poets alone but instead good craft techniques in any writing that seeks to create an inclusive, ecstatic space of meaning.

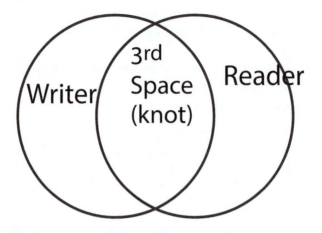

Figure 5.1 The Meaning-Making Space.

D: Image and Painting

> I learn as much from painters about how to write as from writers.
>
> —Ernest Hemingway

Now that we have seen how images must be both sensory and significant and that the most important images from our memories are often the cornerstone images to our creative nonfiction, we can explore specific ways to play with those images. One way we play with images is through the study of various art movements including realism, impressionism, and expressionism as a way to understand how one image can be painted in a variety of ways.

Each of these movements championed different methods of rendering aesthetic truths in visual art, and writers can sample these techniques in language. It is less useful, however, to apply these labels retroactively—in other words, to say that Jess's squirrel or Jess's New Jersey beach image is realist or impressionist or expressionist—since most writers employ a variety of techniques in a single image. The best way to learn from these artistic movements is to try out different techniques liberally, diversely, and deliberately. Also, keep in mind that while we'll cover these three movements in art, there are many others worth studying for their approaches to imagery.

In both literature and art, **realism** attempts to represent the physical world as objectively and accurately as possible, much like the Imagistes did. The goal is to render the world as a camera might, with as much attention to detail and as little embellishment as possible. The painter, or the writer, aims to serve as the camera's lens, leaving their own subjective perceptions out of the image. An example of a realism painting is Johannes Vermeer's *The Music Lesson*, which is so precise and detailed that art historians have suggested that Vermeer may have painted it with the aid of a camera obscura.

Like a realist painting, realist images are full, prolonged representations (or we might call them dilated moments, as we talk about in "Expanding and Contracting Scene"). **Dilated images** are slowed down and close-up, suggesting an image that has been long considered, as fight or flight and novel moments often are, or an image that has been seared into our brain. This kind of careful observation leads to an image that not only is realistic but also reflects the writer's relationship to that image. We remember it in precise detail because it *matters*.

Realist images are particularly useful when the image being conveyed is violent, disturbing, or distressing. In these instances, an objective rendering helps the writer maintain authority and control and keeps the image from becoming unnecessarily exploitative or sentimental. Such images don't need sentimental language on top of what is inherently emotional. In other words, they speak for themselves, just like Jess's squirrel.

In "The Limit" by Christian Wiman, the narrator reimagines a story about his aunt's suicide in slow, realistic precision:

> I can see my Aunt Opal, too, gathering the laundry, humming something, deciding at the last minute to wash the coats. She is not beautiful but there is something of the landscape's stark simplicity about her face, a sense of pure horizon, as if what you saw were merely the limit of your own vision, not the end of what is there. As she shakes out her husband's coat, a single forgotten shotgun shell falls out of the pocket onto the floor. I can see the dull copper where the light dies, the little puckered end of the red casing.

Here, Wiman renders not just the image of a woman contemplating suicide but also his own empathy. He watches her in his imagination, carefully resurrecting her final moments with tenderness. Most impressively, though, he controls the language. It's exacting, almost reportorial in tone, which gives the reader the opportunity to simply watch without forced judgment. This moment is dangerous, the realism implies; this is devastatingly matter-of-fact. How suddenly and simply Wiman's aunt seems to slip into suicide. It could happen to anyone, the tone suggests.

Impressionism began in the nineteenth century, with artists like Monet, Cezanne, Manet, and Pissarro. Unlike realists, these artists were not interested in objective, detailed representation but instead the sensations of the eye, that which can be glimpsed in an instant. The paintings often appear sketchy, incomplete, rendered in quick, arresting brushstrokes. Instead of showing the exact world as seen through the camera's eye, these painters show the world as being in motion, in transformation, alive and changing. Impressionists sought to capture fleeting plays of light and movement and so were drawn particularly to scenes and landscapes in transition: a drifting fog over a harbor, the falling light of dusk, the undulations of a crowd in the distance. These paintings offered the viewer an impression of how one individual, the painter, saw the world in a single moment.

Stephen Crane's dictum "You must render: never report" expresses how this carries over into creative writing and image-making in particular. An impressionist image captures what the eye sees and the beholder experiences in an instant. The idea is that if the image is rendered in such a way as to reflect the initial sensations, it will translate the emotional experience most closely without the distortion of time and reflection. The impressionist image need not explain or reflect upon the image's emotional truth; it will be clear in the way the image is manipulated on the page. We might think of Crane's "reporting versus rendering" as the difference between playing a basketball video game versus actually playing a basketball game. The former contains the idea of playing basketball, while the latter contains the *feelings* of playing basketball.

The difference between realism and impressionism is that realism suggests that which exists—the noumenal world—whereas impressionism aims to get as close to the perceived, phenomenal world as possible. Both the noumenal and phenomenal will be discussed in more detail in "Phenomenal Truths." Since the impressionists leaned into how the artist perceived an image, impressionist images often work well as in present-tense narratives, giving the narrative a sense of immediacy. These images focus on the external objects and sensory details in a way that implies (but does not explain) the internal, emotional world of the character who is witnessing them. Or, as Hemingway said: "No explanations or dissertations should be necessary."

The goal of an impressionist image is to create subtext, a way to access internal emotion via the material world. "My face is boneless, ghostly on the black screen. I'm hardly there," writes Wiman in a flashback to a time when he was eight years old and watching his father carry their kitten and a hammer outside, intent on killing it for scratching the narrator's mother. Winman suggests horror and despair in the impressionistic image of his ghostly, boneless reflection. He doesn't need to say it explicitly; it's in the subtext.

In partial revolt against impressionists, **expressionism** paintings (perhaps the most recognizable today being Edvard Munch's *The Scream*) sought to infuse objective reality with interior subjectivity. Robert Paul Lamb, author of *Art Matters*, writes: "Rather than mimetically reproducing the impressions of the scene, expressionists sought to portray the emotions these impressions evoked in the artist. Although expressionists depicted the external world, the objects of that world were not accurate representations so much as they were externalized depictions of subjective states." Such images are projections of a subjective experience onto the objective world. It's as if the objective image is inferred by the character's subjective response and may read like the literary equivalent of a photo negative. Images are created like sense impressions. Consider the descriptions in the latter half of the opening sentence in Melissa Febos's "Leave Marks": "We first made love in a hotel room in Santa Fe, where the five o'clock sun simmered on the horizon, grazing her shoulders with its fire as she knelt over my body." Notice how the gentle sibilance of "sun" and "simmered" leads into the more electric sound of "horizon" and "grazing," an aural map of the emotions, which are first soft and then afire. And, too, notice how the image of the lover is as if she is herself set aflame by the setting sun ("grazing her shoulders with its fire"), which expresses the narrator's emotions in the image itself.

E: Metaphoric Imagery and Associative Development

Another way to consider image is to study how it creates metaphors. Image and metaphor are foundational to human consciousness, intrinsic to how we make sense of chaos—how we make our way here on Earth. Humans are always in the process, consciously or subconsciously, of comparing things, just as Jess did with the ocean, her scribblings in the wet sand, and the way the saltwater washed those scribblings away. Humans often experience images as inherently metaphorical. A strong image connects us to universal truths and invokes comparisons and emotions. To compare the various elements of our experiential reality is to contain them in a knot of meaning.

Images are not themselves narrative, but they contain narrative possibility. Jess's image of the dead squirrel, for example, suggests a past (the squirrel's recent frolics through the woods followed by its sudden seizing, perhaps), present (the liminal space between life and death), and future (wherein Jess smashes the squirrel's head with a rock). The images also suggest metaphor, the ways in which we connect disparate ideas or images to create a sense of meaning. The squirrel lay "splayed and dead, his white belly to the heavens, his four legs cast out in opposing directions,"—a metaphor for the helplessness and supplication Jess (and most humans more universally) feels about mortality. The flies "knocked their heads together" before flying away, which foreshadows Jess's rash and violent attempt at mercy, but also serves as a metaphor for our often reactionary and thoughtless responses to death.

So we can see how images create metaphors on the page. But how, exactly, does a metaphoric image lead to associative development, which is how the writer makes new meaning?

In Jess's narrative about the squirrel, the metaphors revealed in the imagery got her thinking. By reimagining and drafting provocative images on the page, Jess was clued in to her own intellectual and emotional concerns. This let her follow a path of association to make decisions about where to go next. The squirrel image reminded her of that image on the beach, that split second of affinity with the universe, that first reckoning with death. It also compelled her to research child development, which led her to Freud's notions of a "life instinct" and "death instinct," which led to a memory of her brother's recent drug overdose, which led to ideas about the treatment of mental illness. The point is, the image can be a starting point for a journey of discovery. In this way, creative nonfiction can be developed out of the tenor and texture of a single cornerstone image. **Associative development** is the process through which the writer crafts and studies their own images to discover a set of implicit concerns, obsessions, or curiosities, which can then be unpacked and analyzed through a series of associative leaps both intellectual and creative.

The example above shows the ways in which imagistic associative development is a wild, often subconscious process, subject to the leaps of the imagination. But this feature of associative development keeps our creative nonfiction fresh and inventive. It mirrors the astonishment of living and the practice of meaning-making in a chaotic world. It keeps our creative nonfiction from becoming homogenous and predictable, and it facilitates discovery on the page. Without discovery, there is no change and without change, there is only stasis—which rarely makes for compelling writing.

This brings up another fundamental feature of the metaphorical image: uncertainty. It bears repeating that images are not "the Thing" they represent but re-creations constructed out of language. The image is not immutable, though it is arguably more solid than, say, an idea or abstraction. The image emerges out of the changing tides of memory and, depending on how we recall and render it, triggers different psychic movements, connecting the conscious and unconscious realms. These images are vulnerable to, and dependent upon, reader participation in order to make meaning. Each reader brings their own set of experiences to the page, and interpretations vary.

The poet Robert Bly contended that the image saves us from certainty, a staunch resistance to change. In his essay "What the Image Can Do," Bly writes, "When a poet creates a true image, he is gaining knowledge; he is bringing up into consciousness a connection that has been forgotten, perhaps for centuries... The imagination calls on logic to help it create the true image so as to recover the forgotten relationship."

The "forgotten relationship" is the province of the associative imagination, and it begins in image. "[Even] my tenderness for kittens includes an impulse to put them in my mouth," writes Febos—an image that leads her to this connection in the next paragraph: "Lust is also a desire to be consumed [...] Under my mouth, my beloved squirmed. Her hips rose, shoulders clenched, body resisted and yielded at once."

F: Image and Infrastructure

Images can create an infrastructure for creative nonfiction. An imagistic **infrastructure** in creative nonfiction is like a web of connected or resonant images that hold the work together like nexus points in a spider web. This may be especially true for creative nonfiction that eschews chronology in favor of associative development. Read Febos's "Leave Marks" again, this time noticing how many images of characters eating, chewing, and sucking you find. Notice how these moments keep the essay thematically cohesive as it develops.

Without image, creative nonfiction is little more than idea (say "death") and abstraction (say "fear"). Precisely rendered images that employ significant sensory details point to our knots of meaning. Much like painters, writers have a multitude of craft strategies at our disposal. What matters is that we use our images to create visceral and nuanced worlds within. Exploring these reimagined worlds is a rich and endlessly transformative experience.

IV: READING AS A WRITER

The following exercises will help you practice the techniques learned in this chapter.

A: Detail Hunting

Choose a selection from the anthology and underline three impactful images. For each one, circle the significant sensory details and unpack their levels of meaning, the ways in which they function on more than one level. They should all describe a physical reality. That's one level of meaning. Do they also function as metaphors? Do they foreshadow? Do they reveal character? Do they set the mood or reflect the zeitgeist? How are they details that *mean*?

B: Analyzing the "Third Space"

Using the same three images, note the idiosyncratic connotations that each one brought up for you. What did they remind you of? What are you comparing them to from your personal experience? What shades of meaning might not be available to a different reader? Now, have a partner perform the same exercise and compare your responses. Discuss the ways in which the same images have different effects on each of you.

C: The Image Reveals the Knot

Consider three different images in any particular narrative in this anthology and think about why the author composed them as they did. How do the images contribute to the knot of meaning? What do they say without saying it?

V: PROMPTS

The following prompts will help put to practice the techniques learned in this chapter.

A: Cornerstone Images

Think about your life and the images that linger with you, especially those that you don't yet understand. Then put together a list of as many of these cornerstone images as you can. Next, work to pair them up with other cornerstone images or new images. Use these pairings to start a new work of creative nonfiction.

B: Detail Plumbing

Choose any of the cornerstone images from Prompt A. Now come up with five to seven specific details related to that image. Now see which of those details relates most powerfully to the central question. Now use these details in a work of flash creative nonfiction piece.

C: Detail Re-plumbing

Take the narrative you wrote using Prompt B, but now rewrite it using a different central question. As you do, notice how your significant sensory details morph and change.

6

Dramatic Design

I: RELEVANT READINGS

Seo-Young Chu, "A Refuge for Jae-in Doe: Fugues in the Key of English Major"
Och Gonzalez, "What I Do on My Terrace Is None of Your Business"
Jessica Hendry Nelson, "When You Were a Boy in Maine"

II: VIGNETTE

As I was getting ready for work the other day, I went into the kitchen only to discover, much to my horror, that I was out of coffee. I flashed back to three days prior when I'd been grocery shopping and tried to recall whether I'd picked up the bag of coffee at all or perhaps left it in the trunk. Then I flashed back even further to the last time I'd had coffee in the house and realized that it had been nearly a week since I'd made coffee at home. In my laziness, I had chosen instead to buy coffee at the local gas station on my way to work. I checked my watch and did some quick calculations. Twenty minutes until I had to be at work, where I would undoubtedly find a student at my office door, probably Vera, who only yesterday had been crying about a grade deduction for lateness. Twenty minutes. So, I flashed forward, imagining myself running into the gas station to grab a crappy cup of coffee. I could taste its bitterness, remembering (or anticipating) its fluttering effects. I'd need the caffeine to deal with my mother, too, who'd be calling with updates from her doctor about her broken kneecap, which had been a result of a minor car accident a few weeks ago. If I could make it to noon without having a breakdown, I'd be able to take a long walk. I'd watch the white sailboats gliding in slow figure-eights across the dark surface of the lake and listen to the seagulls channel the caws of my own racing heart. These are the sorts of stories that help me survive these days.

—Jess

III: OVERVIEW

Since Aristotle, perhaps, prose writers have thought about **narrative** as a beginning, middle, and end, organized by *time*, rather than *space*. Mostly, we believe that our experience began at *this* moment, and then moved to *this* moment, before ending in *this* moment, all occurring chronologically. This makes sense since so much of our lives are dictated by doing one thing before another. We attend elementary school, junior high, and then high school. We go on a first date, we commit to a relationship, get engaged, and then get married.

While chronology has a role in all creative nonfiction, which we will discuss, this chapter explores **dramatic design**. Dramatic design includes all the ways we can intentionally choose to organize and shape our creative nonfiction—through either chronological movement or associative movement—to reinforce and contribute to the central question and knot of meaning. Dramatic design is a way to organize creative nonfiction to allow the reader to see meaning in the artful juxtapositions of focus, content, ideas, time, or imagery.

A: Chronological and Associative Movements

Before we analyze less traditional dramatic designs, we'll explore the most traditional one: chronology. All creative nonfiction narratives (or at least 99.9 percent) of them must have a temporal frame—some movement through time. Without movement through time, there can be no change in or narrator or characters—and this change is essential to the success of creative nonfiction. Without movement through time, creative nonfiction is little more than static images. But as soon as 'the writer' offers the reader some chronology, two different versions of them begin to emerge. First, we see the writer as a character in action. We also see the writer as someone reflecting on those actions; this is our narrator. All of this will be explored in greater detail in "The Human, the Writer, the Narrator."

As far as temporal frames go, the human lifespan is our most obvious, physically and psychologically, so it is no wonder we so often defer to chronology to tell our stories. We are wedded to our understanding of the human lifespan, so we perceive the past as constantly growing and the future as constantly shrinking. This movement from past (the writer-in-action), to present (narrator), to future provides inherent tension as we get nearer and nearer to our creative nonfiction's ending. But it's not actually the future that is shrinking—only our perception of it. Look at Seo-Young Chu's "A Refuge for Jae-in Doe: Fugues in the Key of English Major." She begins by reflecting on a phone call from a current student at Stanford University, her alma mater. The call takes place in the winter of 2015–16. Chu establishes this timeframe as the present. It is here, now, that the stakes are established. Chu tells the unnamed student the story of her experiences at Stanford, thereby changing from a narrator to the writer-in-action. As Chu moves in and out of present time, the reader stays wedded to it, understanding that the whole narrative is in service of understanding her present and her future. That's where the stakes live, not in the past, which is gone. *How will the narrative change* Chu's present-tense perspective? As we get nearer to the ending "A Refuge for Jae-in Doe: Fugues in the Key of English Major," the reader feels tension mounting. *Will she understand something anew by the end of this?* we wonder. *And what will it mean?*

Consider Jess's vignette above. This daily narrative, like most daily narratives, isn't particularly chronological—she flashes back and forth, considering multiple pasts and potential futures quickly—but because we become aware of a problem that *has arisen*, requiring Jess to take *present* action, to bring about a desired *future*, the narrative seems chronological. According to Nancer Ballard, a creative nonfiction writer who also studies the role and experience of time in life and creative writing:

> We continually relegate our current thoughts and actions to memory as we update sensory information and future expectations, a process that gives us the impression that we are "moving through" the present. If we didn't quickly relegate a moment ago to the past, "now" and five minutes ago would be the same "present" and we would not know where we are.

The key for creative nonfiction writers is to consider when to hold onto chronology and when to relinquish it, and why. Writers are often trained to write as if a dogged adherence to chronological time (*this happened, then this happens, then this will happen*) is the most meaningful way to organize our work. Anything that breaks with chronological organization is too often considered "experimental," outside of the boundaries of traditional meaning-making. We borrow terms from other art forms (lyric, collage, braided, which we've already discussed) to describe these **achronological narratives**, which are creative nonfiction works not arranged in chronological order.

Further, though we often expect creative nonfiction to be told chronologically, we, often do not remember our lives in sequential order. Think how many times you've tried to tell a story from the first moment to the last but kept having to say something like, "But, well, before that, x happened" or "Oh, wait, I forgot to tell you about." Or think of all the times that we tell stories that jump from year to year as we gather similar moments.

In Chu's essay, she gathers sections thematically, rather than chronologically, and thoughtfully juxtaposes them to highlight the knot of meaning, which might be distilled to the terror of sexual violence, despite her continued hope in a better world.

Our brains don't rely solely on chronology. Rather, we flash forward and backward in order to create meaning out of experience, because meaning often comes not from what occurred immediately before or after any one experience. Instead, our brains make meaning *across* time and *through* space, bringing to bear a plethora of achronological information. Often, the brain is less interested in chronology, per se, and is more invested in survival, and so it pulls relevant information from all directions to facilitate. The last two sections in Chu's essay, for example, are both assertions of the narrator's hard-won strength and autonomy— the former a letter to Stanford that shares her experiences with her abusive former mentor there, asking them to reconsider naming an award in his honor, and the latter what might be called a prose poem that enumerates her reasons for joining the Women's March in January 2017. Much of the power in these last two sections comes out of their thoughtful juxtaposition, even though they are not chronologically or even topically related. They are about wildly different experiences, and yet they make similar and escalating arguments about power and belief. Once, Chu had her agency diminished by a man in power. Now, she speaks out, persists, and fights for change.

Dramatic design can evolve through the interplay between the central question and the situation. Sometimes chronology works best. Other times, it is better to use **associative movement**, as Chu does which means tying things together not by chronology but by association. Associative movement generates energy not through "what will happen next" but through the deeper suspense of "what it all means," as the narrator compares the central question to the situation, linking together ideas not based on time on how they thematically relate to each other.

The writer sparks meditation by bringing together various ideas, images, or scenes associatively. Meditation often leads us to other memories and situations, which may be not chronological but associative. Like complementary colors, emotional or logical resonances are more vivid depending on what surrounds them. The placement of scenes drastically changes the way a reader understands the hard nugget of truth that belies our impulse to write in the first place. In Chu's piece, notice the emotional resonance in the white space between the section subtitled "Lecture, 2078" and the one that follows, "Discuss the Following Quotation," The emotional irony of the latter is greatly influenced by the hypothetical lecture. Notice how the lecture prepares the reader to understand the section that follows it more significantly.

B: Leaps and Juxtapositions

When we break from chronology, we often struggle crafting transitions. chronology reduces the power of transitions because they are expected. Achronological transitions leap across time and space in order to highlight significant moments in the narrative. The associative movement asserts that every paragraph has meaning. Nothing is included simply because 'it's what happened next,' but because it signifies something of importance to the knot of meaning. Simple transitional phrases ("A week later…" or "Once, when I was twelve and we were living in Texas…" or "Yesterday…" or "Years from now, when Max is a newlywed…") keep a reader grounded in time and space as we leap from section to section, or paragraph to paragraph.

If we stick too doggedly to the timeline, insist on holding our reader's hand through time, we are often left with a series of plodding plot points, what we might call the **toothbrush syndrome,** wherein the writer narrates a painfully slow series of uninteresting actions rather than simply skipping to the next interesting moment: *I get up to the sound of the chirping alarm. I walk to the bathroom and pick up my toothbrush. It's still wet from the night before. I put the toothpaste onto my toothbrush. I brush my teeth and my mouth tingles. A few minutes later, I finish brushing my teeth and turn around,* etc. Eventually, we get to the funeral parlor with a six-shooter and a digital camera (now it's getting interesting!), but it sure does take a while. And what was the point of that toothbrush stuff again? The "toothbrush syndrome" is the opposite of leaping. It contains too many uninteresting details, too much chronological overkill. It attempts to capture an all-encompassing experience of time. Everything is predictable and staid. Even when our creative nonfiction is more or less chronological, not everything will be connected to the knot of meaning. Cut any filler. Be ruthless about what creates energy and contributes to meaning, and what doesn't. Move from interesting image to interesting image, or complicated idea to complicated idea.

Consider the following example from Jess's essay, "When You Were a Boy in Maine." In it, she shares a complicated history about a past lover with her current lover. She tells him:

> The real boy—a man now living in New York City—is not, has never been, who I wanted him to be. Just a character in my story, and me in his, until we found one another again a few years ago and he finally told me what I'd always wanted to hear, inside that dark bar in our old neighborhood—I love you, I've always loved you—tall and tattooed and army-strong, and I knew suddenly it was not me he loved but the story of us: childhood sweethearts reunited on the other side of years and war. Broken halves who together make a whole. *You were meant to be*, the story insists. *You were always in the process of becoming.*

The original draft of that scene includes many more sensory details about the bar, the man, and the evening, and while those details work to create atmosphere, they ultimately distract from the knot: the idea that romance is not always organic but a function of narrative demands. Those details make it more difficult for the reader to understand the scene's role in the essay, what it's there to illustrate. Ultimately, cutting those details gives Jess more real estate to make associative leaps. At one point, she leaps from an image in the bar with the old lover to a story he tells her about his mother's death and cremation, which draws interesting parallels between the death of a love story and the death of a loved one.

In this way, much of the meaning in associative leaps is rendered through thoughtful **juxtaposition**, which serves as a torch of light down the dark hallway of the half-remembered and the barely-there, the signposts of emotional epiphany and the tenuous structures that keep them aloft. Juxtaposition places two "things," often unrelated, side by side to see what is created or revealed. *How* we put things together in creative nonfiction is as crucial as *what* we put together, and that is what juxtaposition is: Let's return to the juxtaposition we just noted, wherein the bar scene was juxtaposed with the anecdote that Jess's former lover told her about scattering his dead mother's ashes in the Atlantic Ocean, only to discover later that the ashes were actually his uncle's dog, and his mother had been buried against her wishes when he was serving in the Iraq War. The juxtaposition is important here. The scene from the lover's past is made starker and startling against the innocence of his confession of love. Similarly, the blow of realizing that his feelings for Jess have been, in large part, a story he's told himself strikes the reader as quaint when compared with the horror that follows it. The two scenes work in tandem to create new shades of meaning in each. Light is brighter when contrasted with dark. Pain is more acute beside beauty. Thoughtful juxtapositions are one way the writer can point to what's interesting and focus the reader's attention there.

Another way to cultivate associative movement is through flashbacks and flash forwards. **Flashbacks** are when a character or narrator re-experiences an earlier event. Flashbacks are different than reflection in that reflection is thinking *about* a past action while flashbacks are past experiences in scene. **Flash forwards** are similar to flashbacks, except that the writer is speculating about a possible future event, often creating an imagined scene to show it.

There are two kinds of flashbacks and flash forwards that help writers move around in time: prolonged and anecdotal. While both function like wormholes in time, revealing a scene from the past or future that's intended to elucidate or complicate the characters and/or surface narrative, the prolonged flashback takes its time to develop. When skillfully inserted, flashbacks and flash forwards add texture to our creative nonfiction.

Prolonged flashbacks and **flashforwards** are fully fleshed-out scenes that slow the chronological movement of our creative nonfiction to a halt as we either relive a past experience or imagine a future one. These prolonged flashbacks and flashforwards can either add tension or release it, depending on how well the flash is used. The entire scene in the bar with Jess's former lover is an example of a prolonged flashback. The present tense narrative, the one that shows the stakes as Jess tries to come to terms with her husband's refusal to have a child, bookends this extended scene.

The risk of prolonged flashbacks is that it can be difficult to seamlessly transition in and out, thereby disorienting the reader as they try to understand where they are in place and time. To navigate this issue, we must rely on those transitional phrases to signal a flashback or flash forward and then again when we return to the original time period. "Once, when I was seven…" will efficiently alert the reader to the change in scene. Similarly, "Yesterday…", "Back at the ranch…", and "Years ago, in Sacramento…" will also clue in our reader. When we're returning to the original scene, we can transition back by reminding our reader where they were and when (e.g., "But now, watching my brother tie his shoe…" or "Back in the bedroom, my brother is still tying his shoe").

Anecdotal flashbacks and **flash forwards** may be no longer than a few words or a quick summary of a scene. Anecdotal flashes can blend more seamlessly and provide opportunities to quickly establish metaphors and resonance—a satisfying sense of pattern across time. This might be as simple as weaving a casual detail from the past into the present exposition. Jess takes the opportunity to employ this technique in the last line of her essay, which flashes back to an earlier scene in the essay in which the narrator's husband watched his old dog die after being run over by a truck: "I am telling you he was happy, your old haggard dog. In those final moments, cast out from the confines of a body, he was ecstatic." It's both an anecdotal flashback and a reminder of an already-established metaphor about the ways that people can take control over narrative imperative. Jess wants her husband to understand that he can decide what his experiences mean, that meaning is not predetermined or imposed on us. If her husband can understand that, the narrator hopes he can also understand that having children can mean something more or different than what it meant to his own parents. He need not carry the burden of their narrative.

The most obvious place to insert a flashback or flash forward to increase suspense is in the middle of action. This delays the resolution of the action at hand, which keeps the reader reading. But the risk of this placement is that it often feels gimmicky and/or distracting. Instead, try inserting flashbacks and flash forwards in moments of psychological suspense, rather than physical suspense. An example of this is deft use of flashback in Och Gonzalez's "What I Do on My Terrace Is None of Your Business." Gonzalez pauses the scene in which she is witnessing her neighbor overwater her hibiscus plant: "I want to tell her she's killing them, and it's only a matter of time until she slides her glass door open one morning to find them with limp pink heads and yellowing leaves, all bogged down by the weight of her well-intentioned care." Gonzalez follows this with a brief flashback:

> I know this because in the garden of the old house I lived in for fifteen years before moving to this row of anonymous flats just a month ago, I used to have a fully-grown hibiscus shrub. I didn't do much to help it, but it thrived and exploded in bursts of red all throughout both the brisk mornings and the shimmering afternoons,

Only then does Gonzalez resolve the tension of the moment: "I want to tell her all of this but I don't. What she does on her terrace is none of my business."

IV: READING AS A WRITER

The following exercises will help you practice the techniques learned in this chapter.

A: Reverse Outlining
Choose any three narratives from the anthology, and each time there's a scene, summarize it in the margins. Now, transfer these summaries to a timeline, noting where and when certain events occur. Use specific information when available (dates, age of the narrator, etc.), or at least indicate if the scene was before or after the ones that precede and succeed it. Is this narrative chronological? Why or why not? What are the effect(s) of its form? How would the knot of meaning change if the author had taken the opposite approach—if events were written chronologically or achronologically? What would be gained or lost?

B: Mind the Gaps
Examine any narrative in the anthology. Highlight every time the writer leaps in time (flashback or flash forward) or subject (associative movement). What are the effects of each of these leaps? How do they create meaning in the gaps between them? What ideas, memories,

or thoughts do you bring into those gaps that are particular to your experiences and ways of seeing the world?

C: Juxtapose This

Examine any narrative in the anthology. Highlight interesting juxtapositions, either within a single paragraph or between paragraphs. What are the effects of each of these juxtapositions? How do they complement or complicate one another? How would the meaning change if they were separated on the page?

D: Flashback Bounty Hunter

Examine any narrative in the anthology. Highlight prolonged flashbacks and analyze their effects and placement. How do they complement and complicate the primary narrative? Why might the writer have placed that flashback or flash forward there, as opposed to elsewhere in the narrative? What are the effects, and how would they be different if the flashback was elsewhere in the text? Go back and do the same for any anecdotal flashbacks. Do they suggest or remind the reader of a meaningful metaphor? What essential information or context do they convey? What would be lost or gained if each flashback was extended? Repeat this process with any prolonged or anecdotal flash forwards.

V: PROMPTS

The following prompts will help put to practice the techniques learned in this chapter.

A: Chronological Associative

Take a chronological narrative that you have worked on, and rewrite it using associative movement. Use leaps, gaps, and meaningful juxtapositions.

B: Flash Forward

Since most narratives use flashbacks much more frequently than flash forwards, take a narrative you are working on and add flash forwards in three or more spots.

C: Removing Transitions

Write a flash narrative that has no transitions. Force the reader to connect the dots from scene to scene and idea to idea. And force yourself to think about how you move from one image to the next in a way that best guides the reader, even without the help of transitions.

7

Narrative Energy

II: VIGNETTE

Ever since I adopted him two years ago, I've wanted to write an essay about my dog, Jasper. He's playful, inquisitive, loving, and (the kicker!) only has one eye. But even though I find him fascinating, I knew it would be difficult to generate energy in an essay about a dog. On the surface, there's no real tension. He sleeps, eats, poops. We take walks. So what? There's no trauma, no life or death implications. Sure, he was attacked in foster care, but once he had the surgery to remove the mangled eye and suture the socket, he's been fine. When I first adopted him, he had a habit of licking other dog's mouths, and though I worried he'd be attacked again, a reader would likely not find this small drama engaging. There was no plot, in the traditional sense, and no dramatic experience to sustain such an essay. There were no real stakes.

And yet I couldn't let go of the idea that life with my dog contained narrative possibility. I kept thinking about the day that his foster mother called me to tell me he had lost his eye. I was on a work trip in Nebraska when the phone rang at 6 am. After I answered, she screamed so loudly I thought the dog had died.

I also kept thinking about my divorce, which had only then just begun, and how habitually walking Jasper kept me grounded during my worst grief.

I imagined Jasper's inevitable death in harrowing detail.

I imagined his first owner, who'd only had him for a week before she suffered a heart attack and died. I saw her patting him tenderly on the rump. I recalled that her daughter hadn't known that her mother had adopted a puppy—that she'd only discovered Jasper after first finding her mother's body.

I thought about the mystical cyclops and how these one-eyed creatures are depicted as seers, mystics—like Odin, the one-eyed wanderer of German mythology.

Across these leaps, I noticed a kind of energy that might propel an essay. I noticed tension between Jasper's painful origins and the fantastic mythologies about his one-eyed brethren. I sensed stakes implicit in this new creature's early proximity to so much grief. What did it all mean? I wondered.

It wasn't an essay about family dysfunction. And no one commits a crime. But by burrowing deep into my own curiosities, I intuited a way to activate this material: to take a seemingly uninteresting subject and discover something new. And I realized there were other stakes, too. Both of us had been recently disfigured—Jasper, physically; me, emotionally—and I wrote about the dog in order to discover how to become, again, recognizable to myself.

—Jess

III: OVERVIEW

Many beginning writers shy away from creative nonfiction, fearful that their lives are not interesting enough to keep a reader's attention. They worry that they only death, murder, addiction, and disaster can propel a narrative. Other beginning writers feel that creative nonfiction writers need only expose heartbreaks, loss of loved ones, failures, affairs, and crimes in order to write great narratives. But wild, traumatic experiences are not the only subjects worth exploring. Some of the best creative nonfiction is about nothing more (on the surface, anyway) than quilts, fishing, or sitting on one's terrace. The seemingly mundane often yields incredibly compelling narratives, once we active them with our emotional and intellectual curiosity.

These trepidatious writers confuse plot for interest, drama for energy, and action for tension. The seasoned writer learns that everything contains tension and suspense when given proper attention. By employing certain craft strategies, we can transform seemingly innocuous material into riveting reads. These narratives are not compelling for their subject matter alone but because these writers have mastered **narrative energy**, which is the reader's engagement with the material on the page, regulated by control over language, tension, pacing, stakes, and rhythm.

A: Tension

At its most elemental, **tension** is trouble or conflict, and wielding it effectively is essential for reader investment. In life, and on the page, we must push *against* something to see the world in a new way. Not only does tension keep the reader engaged—because two or more forces are colliding—but, more critically, it's the only way that change occurs. Without tension, people will continue to move in the same direction and with the same perspective. But good creative nonfiction demands change. Without it, there's no reason to tell the story.

With few exceptions, creative nonfiction is driven by human desire. It might be desire with tangible, real-life stakes—Sean's desire to buy a house in "Buying a House." Or the desire may be more internal, emotional, and/or intellectual, which we see in Kristen Millares Young's "A Few Thoughts while Shaving," which contends with mortality and the creative imperative.

In both Prentiss's and Young's creative nonfiction desire, and whatever stands in the way of satisfying it, creates the central tension. In other words, desire + physical, emotional, or intellectual obstacles = tension. When our desires (for love, money, success, or understanding) are challenged (by friends, foes, fate, or fear), tension emerges. For example, the impending birth of Young's second child brings urgency to her questions about her creative imperatives. "Will I have time to write or won't I?" she asks.

Often, the most successful creative nonfiction cultivates tension on more than one level—there is surface tension (What will happen next?) *and* below-the-surface tension (What will it mean? What's at stake?). In "Buying a House," the dual tensions work in tandem. On the surface, the tension is whether or not Prentiss will find a house. The below-the-surface tension, however, is if he will find love. Both tensions keep the reader turning the page.

But tension must be crafted. It can easily be overdone, which will not have the intended effect. The more highly charged the subject matter, the more the writer must control the language. Inherently dramatic situations lose energy when we don't manage the release of information and the way it's rendered, which we will see in more detail in "Expanding and Contracting Scene." Too much drama and the reader feels overwhelmed. Too much action and the reader loses sight of the more complex troubles that sustain our essays. The most effective tension is often a slow boil, just under the surface, threatening our characters in subtle, menacing ways. Amy Butcher's essay "Women These Days" is about a series of violent assaults against women, and yet, she keeps the tension from boiling over by retaining the language of real-world news headlines. The tension mounts as the headlines accrue but without overwhelming the short essay with specific, violent imagery which would have had a sadistic appeal, but not a meaningful one. In this essay, the knot of meaning comes through in the juxtaposition between the cold, reported language and the implied but not overt horrors. So much unspeakable pain, the essay conveys, and so many meaningless soundbites.

Tension is not synonymous with action. The best writers generate tension out of seemingly inert material. By looking closely at memory and experience and asking incisive questions, we will better identify potential conflicts and trouble. We must look under the surface to find the dissonance that drives narrative. For example, on the surface, "A Few Thoughts while Shaving" is about, well, just that. Except those thoughts meander through a web of interconnected ideas about maternity, creation, the body, and time. "Will I have time to write, or won't I? That's not a question that kids answer for you. It's a discipline, like joy, and I'm working on it," the Young muses early on. And then later, "I am learning to accept myself. I hear that's the first step toward love. And I need, so desperately, to love these boys right. If only for that reason, I will do this thing that I once found unfathomable." And yet, as these ideas build through scene and meditation, Young never leaves her bathtub.

B: Stakes

While tension is a kind of collision or trouble, **stakes** are what stands to be lost, gained, or changed in the future.

All good creative nonfiction has stakes because without them we have empty tensions. Imagine the tension in Jess's apartment this morning when she realized that Jasper needed to go outside to pee. She had two choices: let Jasper pee inside or take Jasper outside. Here, the tension is real—Jasper is whining to go outside, and Jess is rushing to get to work—but the stakes are relatively low. On the other hand, given time and attention, Jess might articulate higher stakes. She's new to the job, a dream job she acquired after a painful divorce, which is keeping her afloat financially and emotionally. If she loses the job for chronic lateness, she'll have to move in with her mother, which would precipitate a long, irreversible downward spiral, decades of self-loathing, and an unseemly number of cats. Or, anyway, it feels that way, and that's what matters.

And this is what makes creative nonfiction so interesting to compose, this parsing out of tension and stakes. Tension and stakes occur across a continuum of time, which means that we always have at least two time periods in creative nonfiction. There is the **moment of tension**, like Jasper needing to pee, which is an experience in the past. Then, in some near or distant time period, there is the **moment of reflection,** which is when the writer wrestles to uncover the stakes. So the key with tension and stakes is to consider that the narrator is dealing/has dealt with the tension while the writer is dealing with the stakes.

Stakes are one way we begin to refine the central questions into a knot of meaning. The more clearly the stakes are articulated on the page, the more the central question forms a knot of meaning. We can think of the central question(s) as the threads that form the knot. Why Jess covets her job with such fervor is refined into a knot about self-image, doubt, work ethic, resilience, and independence coupled with an instinct to nurture (the ex-husband, the dog, her students, etc.). As the essay progresses, so does the reader's ability to identify the knot.

C: Pace

Most humans are attracted to movement and variety. Without variety, we grow bored. The same holds true on the page. We are lulled to sleep by prose that maintains a single pace, whether high-paced or plodding. The trick is to vary the pace. Rollercoasters would become dull if they consisted only high-speeds. They are designed to vary their pace. This is what keeps the experience energized: the variety, not just the breakneck speeds.

We can control narrative energy by paying attention to the beats of our sentences to increase or decrease pace. Think about music. Many of the best songs vary in tempo and rhythm. They might build slowly, pick up the speed toward the crescendo, only to slow down again, building up tension, waiting to unleash the crescendo. The best writers, like musicians, use a full spectrum of speeds to sustain the reader's interest and point to the knot of meaning. A fast-paced scene might convey adrenaline, anxiety, and fear, whereas a slow, meandering scene might suggest a sense of tenderness, close attention, a focus on idea, or awe. Often long sentences share complex ideas or images, which slow down the reader. Alternatively, short sentences pack power. They can explore a single idea or moment quickly. They are easy to digest. The reader reads faster.

These ideas will be developed more in "Expanding and Contracting Scene," but one of the keys is matching the pace of our prose to the pace of our tension. Consider the pacing in this short scene in which Young describes giving birth in "A Few Thoughts while Shaving": "To catch the wave of pain and stay above it. To breathe it down. To rock back and forth, standing, kneeling, in the bathtub, on the bed, down the hall, arms round the neck of the nearest person who can bear such weight. To fill the room with sound." The repetition of "to" creates a beat. The phrases get shorter by the time we get to "standing, kneeling, in the bathtub, on the bed, down the hall ..." as if each phrase is a frame in the narrator's clipped memory.

Punctuation can also be a tool in controlling narrative energy. Commas, colons, semi-colons, and the em-dash offer punctuation that can extend a sentence nearly forever. But just because we can write a grammatically correct sentence across pages doesn't mean we should. Instead, we should ask what occurs to our writing as we extend a sentence, and how it serves (or doesn't serve) the knot. This long sentence from Ross Gay's meditative essay "Loitering Is Delightful" reinforces the propulsive energy of rumination, the indulgence of loitering itself, which contributes to the essay's knot: "Loitering, as you know, means fucking off, or doing jack shit, or jacking off, and given that two of those three terms have sexual connotations, it's no great imaginative leap to know that it is a repressed and repressive (sexual and otherwise) culture, at least, that invented and criminalized the concept." The sentence's many punctuations support its slowly building pace, a kind of stuttering advancement.

Another way to control pacing is to consider the length of each paragraph, section, or chapter. Short paragraphs (and sections, chapters, and essays) draw the reader in (but also provide less information). Longer paragraphs often push the reader away. Consider why credit card companies put "the fine print" in long blocks of text. They don't want us to engage with it. To increase the pace of our creative nonfiction, we use shorter sentences, paragraphs, sections, and chapters. If we want the reader to delve more deeply into ideas, to consider more slowly and deeply, try the opposite. Listen to the way that Young embodies experience through her control over the pacing: "We're planning on two kids, and as this boy burgeons within me, I'm considering whether to ask my doctor to harvest my tubes moments after birth, if it happens that I deliver by Caesarian after a full day of unmedicated back labor, like the first time, last year." The meandering sentence invites the reader to linger, to feel the burgeoning, to consider, as the narrator does, the question she poses.

D: Leaps in Space

"Dramatic Design" covered leaps. We'll return to them here since leaps not only affect associative movement but also generate narrative energy, especially when these leaps tie back to the tension and stakes. Leaps keep the reader on their toes while also earning their trust in the process. *Here is a narrator who will consider many points of view, many angles, who will not fix doggedly on one image but is capacious and curious.* Young leaps fearlessly in "A Few Thoughts while Shaving." Early in the essay, the narrator leaps from tossing carnations in her hospital room to throwing away first novel drafts, to weeks later, shuffling to the stationary store and being told by a waitress that she should eat. Young keeps the camera moving from point of interest to point of interest, keeping the energy high.

That said, not all leaps are great leaps. If we leap too often and quickly, the reader might suffer whiplash. Move too slowly and the reader might feel as if they are reading a natural history rather than a narrative. If we leap from image to image without clueing in the reader as to why we are leaping, or showing how the leaps relate to the tension and stakes, the reader might lose track of the central question. It becomes hard to track the mental and emotional journey the essay is trying to develop.

Leaps are often indicated on the page by the use of **white space**, which is merely a gap between two paragraphs. White space is a pause between two sections and, if used intentionally, is rife with meaning. White space is not a blank space or merely a visual transition. Instead, white space is a meaning-maker. Our silences are often as meaningful as our words. White space invites the reader to make connections between the sections it separates. It facilitates the conversation between separated sections by offering the reader a visual cue to pause and consider. Look at how the white space in Young's narrative gives the reader an opening to reflect on the narrator's brush with cancer:

> [The surgeon] didn't save the tumor for me to inspect. She said it looked like cauliflower, but gray.

> I was given time.

Here, the white space asks the reader to see these two sections as simultaneously separate and linked.

Finally, white space plays a role in the visual impact of our work. The visual presentation, the shape on the page, influences how the reader approaches it. A long, segmented work of creative nonfiction with lots of white space, like Seo-Young Chu's "A Refuge for Jae-in Doe: Fugues in the Key of English Major," will be read differently than, say, a short, but dense work of creative nonfiction with no white space, like Ross Gay's "Loitering Is Delightful." The former will be consumed slowly, over time, while the latter is more likely to be read in one, brief sitting: one big bite rather than the many flavors of a meal.

E: Dialectical Movement

Creative nonfiction is a conversation between reader and writer. *I speak from my life to you in yours*, our creative nonfiction proffers. Most of that conversation happens within the writer, who records their internal journey on the page. The writer considers one perspective, then another, and perhaps yet another. **Dialectical movement** is any time the writer explores a different point of view, either between characters or between parts of themselves. Dialectical movement is the inquisitive mind at work and it allows the reader to see situations an ideas from a variety of points of view. In this way, we can increase narrative energy by changing directions. Look at the way that Gay uses dialectical movement to consider various possibilities in one short paragraph:

> It occurs to me that laughter and loitering are kissing cousins, as both bespeak an interruption of production and consumption. And it's probably for this reason that I have been among groups of nonwhite people laughing hard who have been shushed—in a Qdoba in Bloomington, in a bar in Fishtown, in the Harvard Club at Harvard. The shushing, perhaps, reminds how threatening to the order our bodies are in nonproductive, nonconsumptive delight. The moment of laughter not only makes consumption impossible (you might choke), but if the laugh is hard enough, if the shit talk is just right, food or drink might fly from your mouth, if not—and this hurts—your nose. And if your body is supposed to be one of the consumables, if it has been, if it is, one of the consumables around which so many ideas of production and consumption have been structured in this country, well, there you go.

Words and phrases like "It occurs to me ...," "probably," "perhaps," and "if" signal Gay's inner dialogue. As he mules over experience and ideas, he refuses certainty in favor of possibility. Each of these considerations becomes a unique point of tension, a series of potentialities whose lack of definition up tension. This is how dialectical movement evokes tensions in our narratives, by considering alternative or hypothetical possibilities. Often creative nonfiction is not typically propelled by "What will happen next?" but by "What will it all mean?" By pointing to places of doubt in memory, and by imagining hypothetical futures, we excavate the implicit tensions essential to meaning and keep the reader engaged in the process. What keeps Gay's essay rife with narrative energy is not the plot but the momentum of his questions and reflections.

Dialectical movement might chart the evolving stakes of the narrative, from the moment of tension to a week later and then a year, which is what Jess does in her vignette about her dog, Jasper. In the beginning, Jess saw no tension. But then we see Jess evolve, especially through her divorce, and this new Jess sees Jasper as containing more tension and stakes. Later in the vignette, Jess, again in a new spot, sees that both Jasper and Jess are scarred. This transition from one perspective to another to a third highlights the power of dialectical movement.

But dialectical movement is also speculation. In the essay Jess eventually wrote about Jasper, she imagines Jasper's foster mother's thoughts, which is another type of dialectical movement. Her own internal reflection works in conjunction with the imagined internal reflection of Jasper's foster mother to create a dialogue. The same occurs when Jess considers things from Jasper's first owner's daughter's point of view.

Another way to introduce dialectical movement is through an imagined, hypothetical scene, anecdote, or meditation by asking, *What if* […]? Or, *Imagine that* […]? In this way, we introduce new possibilities into the equation. We clarify our intellectual and emotional concerns by creating new possibilities—past, present, or future. *What if the Nazis had won? What if I hadn't answered the phone that day? What if my infant becomes an addict?* By bringing these hypotheticals to life *in scene*, we imagine these possibilities into reality. They become part of what our narrative *means*. The hypothetical scene above, in which Gay imagines someone laughing so hard that food flies from their nose, is an example.

This movement into the realm of the hypothetical is reflective of human consciousness: meandering, questioning, hypothesizing. Humans are always engaged in internal debate and so it makes sense that our creative nonfiction records these mental movements actively and externally. As much as we shift the camera lens within and between scenes, dialectical movement allows us to traverse mental shifts too: considering our material in a different light, arguing with ourselves, and extrapolating multiple points of view. Watch the way Young tracks her thoughts here. "Nothing sharpens the mind like a deadline," she writes. "That may be why I'm so productive while pregnant. I will not give up on this manuscript despite fatigue that settles over me like fog. I have to sit down midway through my showers. Good thing there's a bench." With each new sentence, the essay considers a new idea, a new direction.

Young isn't simply reissuing the same ideas in new ways but tracking their flexibility and growth. The mind moves one way ("Nothing sharpens the mind like a deadline") and then another ("That may be why I'm so productive while pregnant"). Up close, this is what energy looks like: muscular, flexible prose.

IV: READING AS A WRITER

The following exercises will help you practice the techniques learned in this chapter.

A: Reverse Engineering
Examine Ross Gay's "Loitering Is Delightful" and Kristin Millares Young's "A Few Thoughts while Shaving" and identify the tension and stakes. For each, find three ways that the writer creates and maintains narrative energy.

B: Layered Stakes
Examine Sean Prentiss's "Buying a House" and Jessica Hendry Nelson's "When You Were a Boy in Maine" and identify the tension and stakes. For each narrative, identify the surface stakes and the below-the-surface stakes. How do the writers cultivate both? How do both stakes increase the narrative energy?

C: Pacing
Examine any anthology piece. Look at its first fifty sentences. Count how often the writer uses short sentences (let's say any sentence that has fewer than eight words). Count how often the writer uses long sentences (let's say any sentence that has more than fifteen words). Count how often the writer uses medium-length sentences (sentences that have between nine and fourteen words). Finally, come up with a short response that articulates what these numbers might highlight and how it feels, musically, to read those first fifty sentences.

D: Leaps in Space
Examine any anthology piece that has three or more white spaces. Record the time, space and ideas the writer traverses. Note how the writer transitions. Finally, reflect on how and why the writer used these white spaces and how they contribute to meaning.

V: PROMPTS

The following prompts will help put to practice the techniques learned in this chapter.

A: Tension and Stakes

In one of your narratives, write down your tension and your stakes. Then highlight where the reader see those tensions and stakes. Experiment with speeding up or slowing down some of those moments. Note how changing the pace either highlights or distracts from the tension and stakes.

B: Pacing

Examine any of your narratives. Look at its first fifty sentences. Count how often you use short sentences (let's say any sentence that has fewer than eight words). Count how often you use long sentences (let's say any sentence that has more than fifteen words). And count how often you use medium-length sentences (sentences that have between nine and fourteen words). Finally, come up with a short response that articulates what these numbers might highlight and how it feels, musically, to read your first fifty sentences.

C: Leaps in Space

Choose any narrative of yours that has no white space. Now add white space in at least three spots. What is added? What is lost?

Now repeat the process in reverse. Find a narrative of yours that uses white space and remove it. What is added? What is lost?

D: Dialectical Movement

Look at any one of your narratives. Highlight any spot where you use dialectical movement. If you find you are not using dialectical movement often, highlight three places where you could offer your perspective from a future or past time. Also, highlight three places where you could add perspectives from others.

8

Expanding (and Contracting) Scene

I: RELEVANT READINGS

Och Gonzalez, "What I Do on My Terrace Is None of Your Business"
Sean Prentiss, "Buying a House"
Margot Singer, "Call It Rape"
Christian Wiman, "The Limit"
Ryan Van Meter, "First"

II: VIGNETTE

Before I could enjoy the wedding, I had to focus on what needed to get done. I had to help set up the menu, prepare the tent, deal with housing issues for family, and plan the decorations. Even with all this work, I was excited. But, being pragmatic, I didn't think I would love Sarah more after this wedding. We already loved each other deeply. The wedding would just be a public display of our love.

The day of the wedding I raced around doing last minute chores. I wish I could say my mind was on the magnitude of the event, but instead I focused on the details. After I checked off one issue, my family and I would move to the next. An hour before the wedding, I made it to our venue, which sat beside a beautiful lake.

The day of the wedding was sunny. Mid-eighties. I got dressed and mingled. I was busy even then. I wanted a minute to just think of Sarah, of our past and future lives. Instead, I shook hands with people I didn't know and hugged those whom I did. Then I waited underneath the birch branch trestle my stepfather had built and where Sarah and I would be married.

The day of the wedding, Sarah waited across the lake, getting dressed and having her hair done. Soon, she and her father boarded into a maroon canoe and paddled across Mirror Lake. They were out of view, paddling slowly.

The day of the wedding, Sarah and her father landed the canoe at a point in the woods and walked the trail toward where I stood. Sarah and I had visited this point. We had walked these woods. I envisioned her walking the trail.

The day of the wedding, the sun beat down. As I waited for Sarah, I grew hot and nervous. One hundred people stared at me; one hundred people waited for Sarah. I was ready to be done with the ceremony, to move on to celebrating.

The day of the wedding, Sarah's sister and my sister and our nieces walked from the edge of the woods toward us. With everything planned and completed, Sarah stepped from the woods.

Sarah, barefooted, in a homemade gown, stepped from the woods.

On the day of the wedding, she slid from the woods, a cooling breeze.

The day of the wedding, the trees parted and Sarah appeared, barefooted.

Before the day of the wedding, I had seen Sarah thousands of times. And thousands of times I had been stung by her beauty. Her brown, wavy hair. Her eyes the color of slate, or iron. Her sharp features. After the wedding, I will see Sarah thousands upon thousands of times. She will birth me a daughter, a beautiful girl who will look just like her mother—the same chin, same cheeks, same lips.

But on this day of the wedding, I gasped when Sarah walked from the woods. A well of emotion rose in my chest. My eyes wet as Sarah stepped from the woods in her homemade wedding gown. The day of the wedding, she was beautiful, and we were beautiful, and our family was there.

Sarah, on the day of our wedding, stepped from the woods. Her hand holding up the edge of her wedding gown, hand-sewn by her mother.

On the day of the wedding, Sarah smiled. I fell into that smile, into her eyes. On the day of our wedding, I cried.

On the day of our wedding, Sarah stopped inches from me. I felt pulled—unlike any other time in my life—toward something, to something, into something. We, together, on the day of our wedding, reached for each other's hands. I felt her fingers for merely a moment before we fell into a hug. I was supposed to wait to kiss her until after the ceremony. I kissed her the moment she arrived.

On the day of our wedding.

—Sean

III: OVERVIEW

We've heard many times that creative nonfiction needs to show not tell, though "show and tell" is much more accurate. Whichever cliché we've been taught, our teachers were correct: writers need to consider when they should show and when they should tell. Creative nonfiction is not just a record of the events of our lives—Christian Wiman's hunting accident, Och Gonzalez watching her neighbor tend to her flowers, Margot Singer reflecting on her thoughts and experiences concerning rape, or Ryan Van Meter remembering the first time he fell in love—but also how we remember, interpret, and re-create these events for the reader.

A: The Past, the Present, and the Future

Though it is important to remember that every narrative can be written as if it occurred in the past, is occurring in the present, or will occur in the future, remember that all creative nonfiction situations have already occurred, so the use of tenses (past, present, and future) is an artifice that, just like speed of scene and incident frequency, affects how the reader experiences time on the page.

Traditionally, writers of creative nonfiction used the **past tense**. A major strength of this tense is that it easily allows for the use of internal scene because when the situation being narrated occurred in the past, internal scene can occur in some more present moment (usually, the present moment of writing). Also, suspense is heightened as the situation moves from the distant past toward some more present moment wherein the writer has established the stakes. Essentially, the reader intuits that the writing of past events has implications for the present-day writer. Something has changed, and that change will have, or has already had, an effect on the writer.

Wiman uses past tense in "The Limit" to highlight the years that have passed since his friend accidentally shot his father: "I was fifteen when my best friend John shot his father in the face. It was an accident, I'm certain, and but for the fact that I'd dropped a couple of shotgun shells as I was fumbling to reload, the shot could have been mine. I sometimes wonder what difference that might have made."

More recently, **present tense** seems to be the most widely used tense. Present tense feels immediate, as if the events of the narrative are occurring right … *now*. This mirrors how our television shows and movies behave. There feels as if there is no space between the situation and the writing of the event. The reader is living the event with the narrator, and the only internal scenes are the writer's immediate thoughts, which we see in Och Gonzalez's "What I Do on My Terrace Is None of Your Business." Gonzalez writes, "The woman in the apartment on my left has her head drooped low and an arm weighed down by a yellow watering can spouting all over the clay pots that line the metal bars of her terrace. [...] She does this every morning." Gonzalez makes us feel as if we are sitting with her on her terrace this instance looking onto her neighbor's terrace.

But immediacy can also be a weakness of present tense. It offers little space for internal scene since the narrator is living in the moment. Further, most writers write their narratives long after (a week, a month, a year) an experience. So, though a writer might use present tense, the writer might have evolved greatly since the event occurred.

Some writers also use both past and present tenses. This can occur in a variety of ways. One powerful way is to stick with one tense for most of a narrative and then to switch toward the end. Wiman's "The Limit" does exactly that. Most of the essay is in past tense. Only in the closing scene does "The Limit" switch from past to present tense as we move into the closing scene of Wiman and his friend John at the doctor's office with John's father, his face now wrapped in gauze. Wiman is able to offer the necessary reflection in most of the essay, but also capitalize on the emotional impact of an in-the-moment scene. The final sentence brims with meaning and relies on immediacy to convey it: "I stick my hand in my pocket full of cold birds to feel how close I've come."

By far the rarest tense is the **future tense** because most writers don't write about what has not yet occurred, and when they do, they often use present tense. However, a writer might successfully use future tense in two ways.

First, the writer might write about an event that has already occurred but will write it as if it will occur in the future. This allows the reader to feel as if they are peering into the future, seeing one option, of many, that might occur to the narrator. Because logically we understand that the experience has also passed, this technique creates friction between what the writer knows and what the reader is allowed to know. The effect is suspenseful and provocative, if executed well.

Second, a writer could speculate on what might occur in the future. Sean does this throughout "Buying a House." In one section he writes, "In five years (Or ten, fifteen?) if I buy this house (this very house) will these floors only feel the slow steps of my feet quietly moving room to room? The lonely steps of me coming home day after day from work at the university? Or will—some distant year—there be the patter of a child?" Sean uses future tense to let the reader see the world that Sean imagines will occur if he buys this house.

B: Perception of Time

As we think about showing and telling, let's consider time's importance not on the page but in our lives. Time perception is so important that human brains (and all animals) are born understanding the passage of time. Just this moment, Sean's baby daughter, Winter, wakes up crying. Sean looks at his clock and sees that it is exactly Winter's wake-up time, 6 am. This is one more proof that newborns possess an implicit understanding of time.

Even though humans perceive time, we don't always perceive it accurately. Our perception of time varies wildly. When we are bored or worried, time screeches to a halt. And, as clichéd as it sounds, time flies when we are having fun. So, although clock time is universal, perception of time is a construct of the brain. And this perception of time is faulty much of the time. Research has shown that we often recall a one-minute experience lasting up to a third shorter or longer, depending on the nature of the experience.

This faulty perception affects not just our daily lives but also our writing lives, because the way we perceive the world around us affects the details we remember and later write in our creative nonfiction. Our creative nonfiction is most affected by moments so important that they loom larger and longer in our memory. When we realize that these moments are powerful enough to affect our brain's understanding of time, we can replicate how we perceived time in those moments in order to evoke the emotional truth of the experience.

So why is time perception so malleable? There are three major neurological causes.

The first issue that skews time perception is **fight-or-flight** experiences. When we live through fight-or-flight moments, time seems to slow, to stretch forever as the brain races to take in enough information to decide if it should fight or flee.

Fight-or-flight-related writing can be seen in Christian Wiman's essay, "The Limit." Wiman writes about hunting doves with his friend, John, who stands "in his boots and hunting vest, lifting his shotgun to his shoulder and laughing as I fumble to load mine. […]" as they prepare to shoot doves, which is when the hunting accident occurs. The attention-to-detail slows down the scene, a reflection of the way that time is perceived in moments just before tragedy strikes.

Novel experiences also affect how we perceive time. A **novel experience** is any new (and important) event in our lives, like Sean's wedding. The brain remembers these events because they are new, important, and might teach us about how to emotionally or literally survive this world. We usually perceive them as slow-moving. Every detail matters; every second. **Non-novel experiences** are the opposite; they are the mundane moments in our lives. For most of us, the world around us has become mundane enough that the brain "forgets" most of the new information it accumulates each day because this information is a repetition of what we learned yesterday and the day before.

An example of a novel moment is in Ryan Van Meter's aptly named "First," which details the first time he fell in love. Van Meter writes:

> Years from this evening, I won't actually be sure that this boy sitting beside me is named Ben. But that doesn't matter tonight. What I know for certain right now is that I love him, and I need to tell him this fact before we return to our separate houses, next door to each other. We are both five.
>
> Ben is the first brown-eyed boy I will fall for but will not be the last. His hair is also brown and always needs scraping off his forehead, which he does about every five minutes. All his jeans have dark squares stuck over the knees where he has worn through the denim. His shoelaces are perpetually undone, and he has a magic way of tying them with a quick, weird loop that I study and try myself, but can never match.

Even through the haze of decades, Van Meter, though he is unsure of the boy's name, remembers Ben's hair, the patched holes in his jeans, and his shoelaces. This experience with Ben looms large in the writer's memory, first love and, later, first shame. These two novel experiences play out slowly in Van Meter's memory, a sensation he replicates on the page.

Outside of fight-or-flight and novelty experiences, we have a third issue that affects perception of time, one that acts on the brain in much different ways. **Altered experiences** affect how humans perceive time due to drug or alcohol use, medical issues (like dementia, brain injuries, the use of chemotherapy), psychological issues, or spiritual issues.

An example of altered experiences can be seen in Margot Singer's "Call It Rape," which examines rape from multiple perspectives. One section deals with a rape that occurs while a student is black-out drunk. Singer writes:

> Almost nothing about [my former student's] case is clear. She says she did shots before going to a party and can't remember anything that happened after that. The boy in question says she came on to him aggressively at a party and clearly wanted sex. She says she only discovered she'd gone back to his room when she heard the gossip the next day. People who were at the party confirm they saw her grinding with him on the dance floor.

In this example, time dissolves. The student had no recollection of dancing with the male student, returning to his dorm room, or the moment she was possibly raped. She only has a before and an after. Singer crafts the paragraph to reflect the student's intermittent memories. She re-creates the effects of flickering memories by eschewing filler. The reader only sees what the student saw.

C: Speed Control

Now that we know the three major experiences that cause our brains to misperceive time, let's consider how to write these moments in ways that replicate that sensation, therefore helping the reader feel the emotional resonance of these experiences. One way to help the reader feel the warping of time is by adjusting the speed of scene. **Speed of scene** examines the amount of time it takes a reader to read a scene versus the amount of time the actual event comprised. Five speeds of scene exist. From fastest to slowest they are Gaps, Summary, Scene, Dilation, and Internal Scene.

Gaps, which we also discussed in "Dramatic Design" and "Narrative Energy," are the fastest movement of time. Gaps leave out most details of an event and skip over non-novel moments. Drug- and alcohol-affected moments also often have gaps as we saw in Singer's "Call It Rape."

Summary, like gaps, deals with non-novel moments. When using summary, we distill an event down to just important details. Summary can compress months or, for Van Meter, years into a few short lines.

Scene matches the actual time of the event. Here the time it takes to read a narration closely matches the actual time of the event. We often write scenes of experiences during which our perception affected—fight-or-flight, novel, and altered experiences—because these are often significant, formative ones. Singer offers one of countless examples from our anthology. She writes of her mother putting on makeup:

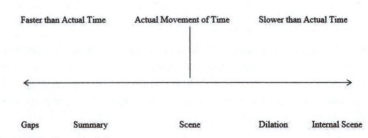

Figure 8.1 Speed of Scene.

My mother stands before the bathroom mirror, putting on lipstick, brushing her hair. [...] She sprays on her perfume, Hermès's "Calèche," its blend of rose and iris, oak moss, and woods, even now the essence of my mother, a luxuriant, sexy smell. [...]

She brushes rouge onto her cheeks, tilting her face before the mirror. [...] My mother takes a tissue and blots her lips, leaving a coral lip-print kiss.

Dilation occurs when the reading of a moment stretches longer than the actual event. Dilation is slower—because of the level of detail added—than real life and often mirrors fight-or-flight, novel, and altered experiences. An example of dilation occurs in Wiman's "The Limit" after John shoots his father, rather than, as expected, a dove. Wiman writes:

Dr. Miller's face was obliterated. He walked out of the brush across from us and around the edge of the tank with the hesitant precision of someone making his way across a familiar room in the dark. Amid the blood and loose bits of skin there were clumps of pellets cauliflowering his cheeks and the sockets of his eyes, distorting his forehead and throat like a sudden, hideous disease, his dark shirt darker down his chest. His lips, too, were so misshapen that it was hard at first to understand the directives he was giving us, though he spoke calmly, deliberately, with the same west Texas mix of practical necessity and existential futility that no crisis could ever shock my own father out of.

Notice the amount of detail Wiman provides as he slows time down and forces the reader to see what John and Wiman saw.

Internal scene is when a writer stops action and records the activity of the brain. Because the writer is no longer experiencing the outer world, they are no longer perceiving the passage of time, instead recounting only introspection, speculation, and reflection. We will discuss internal scene in more depth in "The Active Mind."

An example of internal scene occurs in Wiman's "The Limit." In the moment where John and Wiman pull their guns up, about to take a shot at what they assume is a dove, Wiman dives not into the shot but into thought:

There is some inner, inarticulate anger we share, though, and recognize in each other. When John's begins to slip out of control, the results for the people around him will be immediate, palpable, and utterly disastrous. My own implosion will be no more noticeable to the people around me than something I've imagined. The gun that goes off in my ear now is a fact. It is muted by all the intervening years, by all that has happened, both internally and externally. Still, the authority of its report surprises me, as does the strangely muffled shout that seems to occur at almost exactly the same time, as if the dove, which once again John has not missed, which as I look up is plunging downward, had a human cry.

These thoughts are a pause in the action. Then, Wiman brings us back into action as John fires a shot at what he assumes is a dove.

These five speeds of scene allow writers to decide, much like when they are shifting through the gears in their car, how fast or slowly they want to go. The faster we travel, the sooner we arrive, but also the fewer details seen through our windshield. As we downshift, we slow down and arrive later, but the world comes into crisper focus, allowing the reader to experience in more minute detail.

D: Incident Frequency

Along with speed of scene, writers can use incident frequency to highlight distortions of time. **Incident frequency** is the number of times a moment occurs in the real world in comparison to the number of times it occurs on the page. Three categories exist.

Normative frequency is when the number of occurrences of a real event matches the number of times the event is shown on the page. Van Meter offers an example of this as he writes once about the one night he told Ben he loved him. Though this narrative looks both forward and backward, the heart of "First" deals with this singular night.

Iterative frequency is when the number of occurrences on the page is lower than the number of occurrences in the real world. The iterative is best used to remove non-novel experiences. An example of iterative frequency is Och Gonzalez's "What I Do on My Terrace Is None of Your Business." Gonzalez looks from her terrace to a neighbor's terrace. Gonzalez writes:

> The woman in the apartment on my left has her head drooped low and an arm weighed down by a yellow watering can spouting all over the clay pots that line the metal bars of her terrace. If she had fuchsia pink hair, she would look exactly like the hibiscus flowers she's been growing in the pots. She does this every morning, but the flowers don't seem to want to cooperate and are already starting to look listless, and she can't figure out why.

The reader realizes that Gonzalez looks at her neighbor's terrace most days since she writes, concerning the neighbor, "She does this every morning," but Gonzalez focuses only on this one day, turning many moments into a singular experience.

Repetitive Frequency is when the number of occurrences on the page exceeds the number of occurrences in the real world. Repetitive is best used to highlight fight-or-flight and novel experiences and, at times, altered state experiences. Writers use repetitive frequency to highlight how an issue is so powerful we keep returning to it.

An example of a repetitive incident is from Sean's vignette at the beginning of this chapter. Over and over again, Sean returns to the moment of his marriage. He repeats images and words to make it feel as if this one event occurred repeatedly. And that is the key with repetitive incidents. Sometimes, writers need to retell a story over and over again to search for our ultimate truths while also knowing we might never find them.

IV: READING AS A WRITER

The following exercises will help you practice the techniques learned in this chapter.

A: Fight-or-Flight, Novel, and Altered Experiences
Choose any three pieces from our anthology. See if they include fight-or-flight, novel, or altered experiences. If they do, are they slowed down when turned into scene? Sped up? Altered? How so? What's the effect(s)?

Piece 1:
Event:
    Identify: Fight or Flight   Novel   Altered
    Effect on the Piece:
Piece 2:
Event:
    Fight or Flight   Novel   Altered
    Effect on the Piece:
Piece 3:
Event:
    Fight or Flight   Novel   Altered
    Effect on the Piece:

B: Dissecting a Dilated Scene

Consider the ending to Gonzalez's "What I Do on My Terrace Is None of Your Business" or Wiman's "The Limit." Now break that ending scene apart. Notice how the writer constructs that scene. See how the writer slows down time, mirroring the misperception of time in our brains. Summarize your thoughts on this dilated scene in a paragraph or two.

C: Speed of Scene

Choose any anthology piece that has at least five scenes. Label the speed of each scene in this piece (gap, summary, scene, dilation, or internal scene). Repeat the process with incident frequency (iterative, normative, or repetitive). Then explore why you think the writer constructed their scenes in this way? What did their chosen speeds of scene and incident frequencies offer the piece? Jot all these ideas down in a few paragraphs.

V: PROMPTS

The following prompts will help put to practice the techniques learned in this chapter.

A: Playing with Speed of Scene

Find a scene in one of your own narratives. Now rewrite that scene five times. Rewrite it once by adding gaps to it. Another time by summarizing it. Another time by using scene. Another time by using dilation. And another time by using lots of internal scene.

B: Playing with Dilation

Look at a narrative that you are working on. Find one or more areas that focus on the central question or are otherwise key moments in the essay. See if you can dilate these moments. Try to double or triple the length of these scenes by adding more and more sensory details.

C: Playing with Repetitive Frequency

Look at a narrative that you are working on. Find one or more areas that focus on the central question or are otherwise key moments in the essay. Now repeat that scene again and again throughout the narrative, using repetitive frequency.

9

The Active Mind

I: RELEVANT READINGS

Melissa Febos, "Leave Marks"
Ross Gay, "Loitering"
Jessica Hendry Nelson, "When You Were a Boy in Maine"
Ira Sukrungruang, "Invisible Partners"
Vijay Seshadri, "Memoir"

II: VIGNETTE

In graduate school, a classmate submitted an essay for workshop about relationship infidelities. As I read this essay, I grew angry at the essay but also at the writer. I knew then that there was a writer and a narrator and those two were (at times wildly) different people. Still, as I read the essay in my apartment and, later, talked about it during workshop, my anger bubbled up, and I was a lesser student. My comments were concerned with morality rather than improving my classmate's essay.

For months afterwards, I questioned why this one essay evoked this poor response from me. This wasn't the first infidelity essay I had ever read. It wasn't the first essay in which the narrator behaved immorally. Many of my own essays had a narrator who made questionable (or worse) decisions.

For a long time, I thought maybe it was the topic—infidelity—that affected me so much. But I had no real-life issues with infidelity. It had to be something else.

Only with years of distance did I realize why this essay got a rise out of me. The essay affected me so viscerally because it had a narrator who was acting but not thinking on the page. There were merely scenes of a faltering relationship and then the infidelities, without any reflection from the writer.

In the end, I realized that my lack of empathy with the narrator was not because of her infidelity but because the writer didn't reflect on why she made those decisions how she felt about them, or how they changed her. To empathize with the narrator, I needed to see not only her actions but also the reasons that she performed those actions. I needed to be brought into the narrator's mind so I could understand and maybe even empathize, which is the superpower of creative nonfiction.

—Sean

III: OVERVIEW

As mentioned in "Expanding (and Contracting) Scene," we are often taught to show and not tell in our writing. Sometimes we are taught to show *and* tell, but even then, it's generally understood that writers should show through scene more than tell through summary; that scene is what makes a reader *feel* while summary bores the reader. This is often true. We need scenes. But this simple formula—let's imagine it is *show* 75 percent of the time and *tell* 25 percent—leaves out a crucial part of creative nonfiction.

What makes a person a person? Is it their looks? Their speech patterns? Their height? Their weight? Their attire? Sure. But humans are more than external attributes. Humans are their minds. We gather information and then our brains shape that information over and over as we re-create who we believe we are, what we desire, and, most importantly, what we need. This active mind is what makes creative nonfiction beautiful. Humans are more than beings in action; we are beings chasing after wants and running from fears. We are an evolving consciousness, in continuous negotiation with our emotions and ideas, constantly rethinking our own feelings and beliefs.

Returning to the show-and-tell formula, notice that something is missing: human thought. The equation should be *showing (scene) + telling (summary) + thinking (internal scene) = creative nonfiction*. And just as we saw with scene in "Expanding and Contracting Scene," there are a multitude of ways that creative nonfiction writers can highlight the mind in action.

A: Internal Scene

As mentioned in "Expanding and Contracting Scene," **internal scene** is composed of the narrator or character's thoughts. Internal scene is valuable because it builds up empathy for our narrator or character. Without internal scene, the reader is often left wondering why a character (and, by extension, as we saw in Sean's vignette above, the actual human who is writing the narrative) behaves in a particular way. Often, without internal scene, the reader begins to question the narrator's motives (leading to, as we will discuss in "The Human, the Writer, the Narrator," an unreliable narrator). This lack of believability isn't because the reader has never behaved inexplicably. We all behave badly sometimes, as can be seen in many of our anthology pieces. Instead, when a writer doesn't help the reader understand *why* a character made a particular decision, it can be hard to relate to them.

Internal scene can occur at any moment throughout our creative nonfiction. But for most of our creative nonfiction, internal scene works best when used after fight-or-flight, novel, or altered state moments because this is when humans are usually trying to understand or re-assemble their experiences into a cogent self-narrative. Interior scene helps the reader see how the writer is processing these experiences and ultimately fitting them into a knot of meaning.

B: Six Ways to Internal Scene

There are six ways to create internal scene. The most common is **reflection**: contemplating, meditating, or ruminating on an idea or event that has already occurred. The term "reflection" also means, scientifically, the echo of sound or light waves off a surface. Reflection is not the situation explored in our creative nonfiction but the echo of that situation. If the main character or narrator doesn't reflect on the situation, often the reader is left wondering why they are reading the narrative in the first place. There is no central question, no knot, merely situation. We see reflection in Vijay Seshadri's "Memoir." He writes:

> If I wrote that story now—
> radioactive to the end of time—
> people, I swear, your eyes would fall out, you couldn't peel
> the gloves fast enough
> from your hands scorched by the firestorms of that shame.

Immediately, Seshadri signals reflection by writing "If I wrote that story now." He not only reveals his thoughts but also how we, the reader, would react ("your eyes would fall out"). All of this reflection helps the reader to understand the situation in new and powerful ways.

Another way to create interior scene is through introspection. Whereas reflection is a narrator's ruminations on a past situation, **introspection** is a narrator's examinations of their current feelings or state of mind. Introspection is generally less about situations and more about the emotions that arise from those situations. Introspection focuses on the current state of the narrator or character. Notice the introspection in Ira Sukrungruang's "Invisible Partners," when he writes about how his mother has cut his dates from homecoming and other dances out of the pictures: "[My dance partners] have been relegated to oblivion—my dates—that void where all halved pictures go." Here, Sukrungruang is not reflecting on his dates from years ago or those years-ago dances. Instead, the focus is squarely on his current feelings. These photo-girls have been cut from the story. The reader is prompted to wonder what meaning will be derived from the action now, in the present moment, not what was made of it in the past.

There is also **speculation**, or envisioning either past, current, or future events based on knowledge at hand. Speculation allows a character to reimagine a past, present, or future situation from their own perspective or from other people's perspectives. Humans do this all the time. We speculate on what would have happened if we had kept that job, what will happen if we go into that new restaurant for lunch today, or what our lives will be like if we move to some new town. We speculate about what other people are thinking and doing, often as it relates to us. But speculation is not unbridled imagination. Speculation is making an educated or informed guess so the reader feels as if what is being speculated *might have* occurred or might still occur. Speculation should go beyond *could have*, which is the domain of invention. We'll discuss speculation more in "Embracing Uncertainty."

Jess offers a moment of speculation when she writes, in "A Boy in Maine," about her husband's childhood dog, Bob, getting run over in the driveway while he "watched stricken from the patio." But then Jess begins to speculate about what she does not know but what she can rightfully imagine, based on her knowledge of the now-grown boy:

I envision you, small, six-year-old boy, as you slowly reel in your line through clumps of dead grass, because a body of water, a puddle broken overnight even, surely must contain fish. Water-blue eyes, sandy-bottom hair, your pants overlarge yet too short, barefoot boy in April. You fish until dusk, then slump over your spaghetti dinner, dreaming storks scooping bass from nearby ponds and dropping them into swimming pools in distant, wealthier neighborhoods.

Once Jess runs out of knowledge, she uses the knowledge she has to speculate what the boy might have done. One of the strengths of speculation is that it allows the reader to see alternate realities.

A note of caution about speculation: consider signaling to the reader know that these speculations did not occur in real life. Words like *perhaps* or *potentially* clue the reader in that what they are reading is not the truth but a likely potential. Jess, as we saw above, merely used "I envision" to indicate that what follows is speculation not facts.

Research can also function as internal scene. When a writer properly places research into creative nonfiction, the reader experiences the writer's mind in active thought. The reader follows the writer as they search for research that validates their central question. Further, research also helps the reader see the connections the writer is making, which, again, is internal scene.

Melissa Febos's "Leave Marks" includes research as part of internal scene:

> It isn't just me. Attachment and availability have been inscribed on human bodies for centuries, across continents. The Mursi people of Ethiopia insert lip plates in their girls as preparation for marriage, while the Kayopo of the Amazon use scarification and body painting. Contemporary North Americans are no exception; as we love to jab our flag into the earth, we brand our cattle, we mark our beloveds with bruises, babies, scars, disease, lipstick, and diamond rings.

Febos connects how she marks her body to other cultural traditions of body modification, and in doing so shows her mind in action, seeking for connections outside of her own experience in order to discover meaning. "It isn't just me," she writes. Research is how the writer recapitulates their own experience in order to re-see what it means.

Another way to create internal scene is through exploration of the **fantastic**, a bastard cousin of speculation. The fantastic brings in invented or imagined elements to a work of creative nonfiction. Though most or all of the fantastic is untrue (and possibly impossible), the fantastic allows the reader to better understand the mind and emotions of a narrator. Done well, the fantastic, though invented, should lean into emotional truths inaccessible otherwise. The reader accesses these emotional truths when they are able to analyze the nature of the fantasy. Why is this fantasy here and why is it written in this particular way? the reader wonders. The answers, whether explicit or implicit, deepens understanding.

We can see elements of the fantastic at work in Sukrungruang's "Invisible Partners." Sukrungruang imagines where the photo-girls are today, but not the real women he'd dated, but the cut-out parts of them from the photos. He writes, "I imagine a planet of them. So many lost partners, so many severed parts. [...] There they mingle, in a two-dimensional world. There they try to find a fit to complete the photo. But no cut fits flawlessly, an imperfect puzzle." Sukrungruang goes so far as to find them a new place to mingle, "a table in the corner of a coffee shop. They are beautiful in their dresses, their hair primped and pampered, their nails painted vivid red." Sukrungruang moves beyond speculation and into fantasy, which he reinforces by writing, "In this world, they are best friends, though in the walking and talking world they occupied different circles. In this world they play one role, and it is the one role they share: Ira's date." His use of "this world" and "in the walking and talking world" shows how Sukrungruang has invented this world for his former dates. He is not making educated guesses, but creating a fantasy.

A final way to create internal scene is through showing physical actions that reflect the narrator or character's thoughts. Physical actions and reactions keep the reader in scene. There's no need to pause and enter the narrator's mind interrupting the external scene. That said, the risk of using action to reveal internal scene rather than another option is that the reader might struggle to pinpoint the nuances of emotion, which may lead to confusion.

Ross Gay, in "Loitering," uses a simple action to reveal thought. He writes, "*Lollygag* was one of the words my mom would use to cajole us while jingling her keys when she was waiting on us." In "jingling her keys," we see an impatient mother trying to motivate her children to quit, as Gay writes, lollygagging. But then Gay uses the strategy again:

> There is a Carrie Mae Weems photograph of a woman in what looks to be some kind of textile factory, with an angel embroidered to the left breast of her shirt, where her heart resides. The woman, like the angel, has her arms splayed wide almost in ecstasy, as though to embrace everything, so in the midst of her glee is she.

Here, we see the image of a body in action, followed by how the woman's gesture makes him feel, and then followed by what he thinks: "Every time I see that photo, after I smile and have a genuine bodily opening on account of witnessing this delight, which is a moment of black delight, I look behind her for the boss. *Uh-oh*, I think. *You're in a moment of nonproductive delight. Heads up!*"

Another way to use a narrator's actions to show thought is to have their actions contradict their thoughts, as many of us do in our lives. This is often a great way to develop character by showing the dissonance between how they think and how they behave. When our characters think one way, but their behavior suggests differently, the reader sees their dimensions.

IV: READING AS A WRITER

The following exercises will help you practice the techniques learned in this chapter.

A: Internal Scene
Look at any piece in our anthology. Find at least five spots where the narrator falls into internal scene. Write down if it is reflection, introspection, speculation, the fantastic, research, or physical action. Then write down how that internal scene benefits the narrative.

Internal Scene 1:
- Example:
- Type:
- Benefit:

Internal Scene 2:
- Example:
- Type:
- Benefit:

Internal Scene 3:
- Example:
- Type:
- Benefit:

Internal Scene 4:
- Example:
- Type:
- Benefit:

Internal Scene 5:
- Example:
- Type:
- Benefit:

B: Situation without Thought
Examine any anthology piece that uses internal scene. Now temporarily erase all internal scene from two or three consecutive pages. What happens to the anthology piece if there is no internal scene? Write a paragraph or two of reflection.

C: Reflection, Introspection, Speculation
Can you find an anthology piece that uses the three major types of internal scene (reflection, introspection, and speculation)? Why does the author use each one? What does the variety of internal scenes offer the reader? Write a paragraph or two of reflection.

VI: PROMPTS

The following prompts will help put to practice the techniques learned in this chapter.

A: Internal Scene

Take any creative nonfiction you are working on and add two or more moments of reflection, introspection, speculation, the fantastic, research, or physical action. Remember, these should come especially after fight-or-flight, novel, or altered state moments.

B: Speculation

Work on a flash piece (500 words or fewer) that relies heavily on speculation. Keep imagining into the future or reimagining the past or speculating on a situation through another character's perspective. Keep returning to speculation.

C: The Fantastic

Work on a flash piece (500 words or less) that relies heavily on the fantastic. Let your narrator's brain wander from daydream to daydream. Let your narrator invent, imagine, and create. Let your narrator create a wild that also connects to real-world personal experience in order to create emotional truths.

10

The Human, the Writer, the Narrator

II: VIGNETTE

If someone were to read my essay "Just Like This," which is about a night of drinking with my then-girlfriend in Bangor, Pennsylvania, the reader might wonder about my drinking habits and if I was still dating that woman. In the decade since I wrote that essay, not only are we no longer dating, but now, on my most exciting nights, I have two beers.

If someone were to read my essay "Buying a House," which deals with me walking through a house for sale in Grand Rapids, Michigan, trying to decide if I should buy the house, the reader might wonder if I bought that house, found love, got married, had a daughter, and got divorced, which were all topics of speculation in that essay. Since "Buying a House" was published (and is now in this textbook's anthology), I did buy and sell that house, got married, and had a daughter; still, so much of the rest of the essay feels as if it's from another lifetime. Once I sold that house, I found my dream wife and dream home. Sarah and I now nestle our little family in a house beside a lake in northern Vermont.

If someone was to read "Darkest Wild," an essay I published just months ago that deals with being a new father, the reader might wonder about my young daughter and our home beside the lake. These are things that consume my thoughts today: being a father, being at home here on Solstice Lake.

While I am writing this vignette, my wife, daughter, and dog play in January's snow, building snowmen. My aunt is slowly dying in Florida. And I am busy planning for work trips to Mexico and Colorado. None of these ideas or moments make it into the narratives I am currently writing.

All of this is to say that writing captures only a part of a human's life. And what it captures are merely moments frozen in time, a narrator frozen in thought.

Fifteen years ago, I was obsessed with trying to figure out love.

Ten years ago, I was obsessed with what would happen to me if I bought that house on Lockwood.

Today, I am obsessed with being a father, a husband, and saying goodbye to a beloved aunt, all from the edge of our lake.

Next year, what will obsess me? Next year, who will I be?

—Sean

III: OVERVIEW

Here, we examine the various narrators in creative nonfiction, an under-explored subject in creative nonfiction. *This creative nonfiction is about me, so I'm the narrator* writers often assume. End of discussion. But narrators in creative nonfiction are more varied than that. This chapter explores the myriad ways that narrators manifest in creative nonfiction and includes ideas about them that influence our writing in subtle, but important, ways.

A: The Three Versions of the Writer

For the most part, writers and readers don't think much about creative nonfiction narrators. As mentioned above, the narrator of a creative nonfiction is not simply the writer themselves, but always a construction based on a version of the writer.

But before there is a narrator, or characters on the page, there is a **human**. This person is a writer, obviously, but they probably also have some other job, might be in a relationship, have a variety of outside interests, a history and a future, hopes and dreams.

The point?

A human is not one thing (just a writer clacking away at their computer) but a complexity of things. Because of that, this human, no matter how hard they try, can never exist fully on the page. Words can never *be* a human. They can only imitate a slice of this human's life. Further, humans evolve, so the human Sean was fifteen years ago is not the human he is today. He is a vastly different person. His jobs have changed (then: trail builder; now: professor), his location has changed (then: Pennsylvania and the Pacific Northwest; now: Vermont), his love life has changed (then: either alone or in a fractured relationship; now: in love with Sarah), and his extracurricular pursuits have changed (then: skiing, drinking, being young; now: a father, a skier).

Closer to the page, we have the **writer** who, obviously, looks almost exactly like the human. What is the difference? The writer is merely one small sliver of the human. As mentioned above, the human contains multitudes (as Whitman famously asserted), as does our writer. But our writer's complexities are only concerned with writing. The writer is the human sitting at a computer, shaping and reshaping creative nonfiction. But, once the creative nonfiction is complete, the only sign of the writer is their name on the page. Then the writer moves on to write about their next obsession.

And it is now that the writer's first construct steps onto the stage, our narrator. The **narrator**, unlike the writer, is not human and is instead built of words. The narrator is just one version of the writer (just like the writer is just one version of the human). The narrator guides the reader through the situation and is also, often, the main character.

Even though our narrator is always closest to the situation (in comparison to the writer and human), our narrator's proximity to the situation might be intimately close or relatively removed, depending on how quickly the writer writes the creative nonfiction after the experience, how they craft the narrative, and how much internal scene is used. This temporal space between narrator and situation is **narrator–situation distance**. Narrator–situation distance affects where in time, emotion, and space the narrator stands in relationship to the situation. This distance controls how close the narrator feels to the situation, how long they have been able to reflect on a situation, and, often, but not always, how close the reader feels to the situation. The key here is to consider how close we are to the situations we are writing about and how, whether we are near or far, we can use techniques to move our readers emotionally and intellectually.

An example of a distant narrator–situation is Elissa Washuta's "Incompressible Flow." The piece begins in past tense, which makes the reader feel a sense of distance, a sense of passing time, but only later do we realize how much time has passed and how long Washuta has reflected on this situation. Washuta writes:

> I don't remember whether I was afraid of him. I remember the way I would scream at him, drunk on beer gone hot in the sun that anointed the lake, but I've forgotten the topic and remember only the subtext. I don't even remember the words he used to convince me I should submit to being fucked in ways that hurt me. Years later, my psychiatrist told me my outbursts had probably been PTSD episodes. I didn't remember being afraid. I remembered feeling like I was in love.

By writing "Years later" and "I don't remember," Washuta allows the reader to feel the long passage of time and, with it, the amount of thought Washuta has put into this relationship and its impact on her.

Since it is not always easy to know how soon after a situation a narrative was written, we'll use Sean's essay "Buying a House" to demonstrate a closer narrator–situation distance. Sean wrote this piece mere weeks after seeing this house on Lockwood Avenue. Because of the closeness of the writing to the situation itself, Sean could not write much, if at all, about what occurred between the situation (looking at houses to buy) and the writing of the essay. To compensate for this short narrator–situation distance, Sean projects into the future, imagining what might occur if he were to buy this house:

> As Chad points out the dishwasher, the gas stove, the cabinets, I find myself in the future—god, this house has a way of transporting me—to nights eating alone, crockpots made during long weekends, the smell of stew blanketing the house. I'll read a magazine while eating a quick meal. The second chair at the table unmoved for weeks (months?)—waiting.

As Sean wrote "Buying a House," he recognized that he was limited in how he could use internal scene, therefore flashing forward became a critical tool.

A danger of writing from a short narrator-situation distance is the lack of opportunities for internal scene. This lack of temporal and emotional distance is called **narrator–situation merge**. The issue with narrator–situation merge is that the writer is so close to the situation that the mind has limited or unprocessed perspectives. The narrative could end up as either all situation, all unprocessed thoughts, or both. The best way to avoid narrator–situation merge is to take a few weeks or months or even years before writing about intimate moments. We often need time to process our creative nonfiction. We need time to deal with our successes and failures. We need time to understand what they mean in all their complexity and nuance.

B: The Four Narrators

As mentioned at the beginning of the chapter, often we consider creative nonfiction to employ one type of narrator: the writer. There are actually four narrator types distinguished and determined by the narrator's level of involvement in the situation.

The narrator furthest from the situation is the **dramatic narrator**, who reports on a situation but is not a participant, and is often seen in journalism. The writer keeps the reader outside of all internal scene. Normally, the

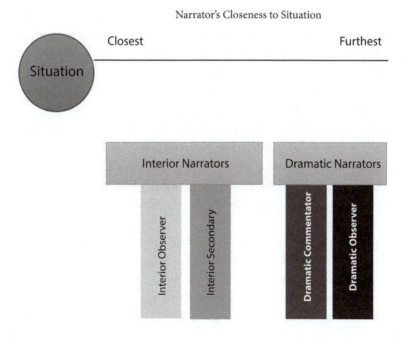

Figure 10.1 Narrative Distance.

dramatic narrator only reports on character actions and words: just the facts, ma'am. Because of its remove, the dramatic narrator is rare in creative nonfiction. There are two types of dramatic narrators. They are the observer and commentator narrators.

The **dramatic observer narrator** is not involved in the situation physically or emotionally. The observer narrator reports rather than experiences. We hear no thoughts from this narrator. Instead, the observer narrator allows the characters to solidify the central question only through words, actions, and research. A great example is the narrator in Peter Grandbois's Loyalty. In this screenplay, Grandbois allows his three characters to speak without a narrator's interference. Even though one of those characters is a version of Grandbois himself (called Peter in the screenplay), the reader merely observes these characters (Peter, Sasha, and Kobo) talking at a café in the Midwest:

Sasha: You're half an hour late.
Peter: (sitting) Sorry. One of the dogs had diarrhea. You wouldn't believe the mess. Then, my son forgot his lunch. I had to drop it by the school.
Kobo: He'll never learn that way.
Sasha: (nodding his head) He's right.
Peter: The dog or the boy?

The entire piece continues this way, with no internal scene. Instead, the reader discovers the central question through ways other than internal scene. When done well, as "Loyalty" is, the central question bubbles up in surprising ways. When done poorly, the reader is left with creative nonfiction that is all situation and no central question.

A more engaged narrator, though still dramatically distant, is the **dramatic commentator narrator**. Again, this narrator is not actively engaged in the situation but does offer internal scene about the situation. The reader sees the situation through other characters' actions and dialogue but also receives commentary from the narrator, who appears to be standing off to the side of the situation. Here, the creative nonfiction is more editorial than reportage.

A great example of this is Kathy Fish's "Collective Nouns for Humans in the Wild." In this flash essay, Fish re-imagines these definitions: "A resplendence of poets./A beacon of scientists./A raft of social workers." This list feels much like our above-mentioned observer narrator until, at the very last moment, Fish offers reflection: "Humans in the wild, gathered and feeling good, previously an exhilaration, now: a target." And in that switch from "exhilaration" to "target," the narrator moves beyond mere observer to comment directly on American society.

Closer than dramatic narrators are **interior narrators**. Here, the reader has access to the thoughts and emotions of the narrator, especially concerning the situation. Most first- and second-person narratives use interior narrators. There are two types of interior distance narrators: secondary narrators and protagonist narrators.

The furthest interior narrator is the **secondary narrator**. Here, the narrator is involved in the situation but is not the main character. With a secondary narrator, we often feel as if we are hearing a second-hand story. We see this in Amy Butcher's narrative, "Women These Days." Butcher shares direct quotes from news articles, which makes it also seem as if she is using a dramatic narrator. Almost the entire essay is about other women, women that Butcher has only read about online. She writes at the beginning of the essay:

> An Ohio woman was shot dead while cooking Thanksgiving dinner; witnesses report that at the time of the shooting, she was standing at a kitchen table, preparing macaroni and cheese. The body of a North Carolina woman was found in a shopping center parking lot at dawn. A Texas woman was grabbed from behind and attacked in a "bear hug" after finishing several laps at the Austin High School track.

For almost the entire essay, Butcher is never the main character, and the reader doesn't even hear her perspective until the ending, when, finally, she offers implicit commentary by relating a conversation with her lover: "*I hate feminists,* he says to me. The love of my life. *I hate that you count yourself among them. A bunch of angry women who hate men. You're hurting an entire gender.*" In this turn, the narrative becomes personalized, though the narrator is still not the protagonist. The essay is not about the narrator specifically, but women generally.

The most intimate interior distance narrator is the **protagonist narrator**. Here, the narrator is a main character. The reader feels as if they are experiencing the situation through the narrator's eyes, which is exactly how the situation unfolded. Most creative nonfiction uses this type of narrator, including Elissa Washuta's "Incompressible Flow," in which the narrator often reflects on the page. Washuta writes:

> Love drove my slender biceps to scrub and wax fiberglass for days while he took to the uncovered, aging motor like a surgeon on an open heart. On the water, I studied his movement as he flipped his body upside-down, every

muscle a hard cord when his wakeboard hit the lake. Other days, we fought. I was mad because he wouldn't say he loved me; he was mad because I was an idiot.

The narrator is directly involved in the situation. Without her, there would be no situation.

The key with narrators is not which is better but which one best fits the material and reinforces the knot. Which narrator best applies to the experiences we long to write about? Is the narrator in the middle of things? Are they peering in from the sidelines? Is the situation researched, outside of personal experience? Which one narrative perspective will best highlight the knot?

C: (Un)Reliable Narrators

Regardless of narrator type, narrators are either reliable or unreliable depending on how we craft the narrator's level of self-awareness.

A **reliable narrator** is someone the reader trusts to be honest. It should be remembered that every narrative is shaped by the writer and every writer uses creative elements. Further, every writer can only offer a limited perspective. So even the most reliable narrators (and writers) play in the gray areas of the ethics and veracity. But, with a reliable narrator, readers trust that the narrative is as truthfully as possible, and if the reader veers from truth they will signal that to the reader. Here, the narrator may offer multiple perspectives, differing viewpoints, research, as needed, and variety of other techniques to fairly convey the situation. Most creative nonfiction uses this type of narrator.

Conversely, an **unreliable narrator** is a narrator who the reader does not trust. There are two types of unreliable narrators in creative nonfiction.

The **intentional unreliable narrator** is a narrator who cannot be trusted, although the writer is trustworthy. The writer intentionally highlights a deceitful/confused/or otherwise untrustworthy narrator who might be missing information. Perhaps the narrator is a child or an outsider, and therefore the reader only learns part of the story, or the narrator has biases, tell lies, is ignorant, in an altered state, or pathological.

The intentional unreliable narrator can be a powerful tool because it can help the reader access the narrator's flaws and dimensions. The intentional unreliable narrator often feels authentic and honest. Also, the intentional unreliable narrator requires the reader to unpack the narrator's reasons for their unreliability. An example of an intentionally unreliable narrator is in Elissa Washuta's "Incompressible Flow." She writes, "I was mad because he wouldn't say he loved me; he was mad because I was an idiot." Notice, Washuta doesn't say that her ex-boyfriend claimed she was an idiot. Instead, she writes that she "was an idiot." Still, the reader understands that Washuta is anything but an idiot; her essay is smart, intricately organized, and beautifully written.

The other version is the **unintentional unreliable narrator**, who the reader doesn't trust, and that distrust carries over to the writer as well. In this situation, the writer believes their narrator is credible, but the reader does not. In this instance, both narrator and writer lose credibility, and the reader disengages with the piece. The most common way a narrative develops an unintentional unreliable narrator is when there is narrator–situation merge and limited internal scene to highlight growth and self-awareness. The best way to avoid the unintentional unreliable narrator is to use internal scene often and fairly and to take the time necessary to process complex situations.

IV: READING AS A WRITER

The following exercises will help consider the techniques learned in this chapter.

A: Human, Writer, Writer-as-Narrator
Choose any anthology piece and then list all the major personal details that we learn about the narrator in their narrative.

Next, research the writer online and discover what information you learn about them as writers. Do they write in more than one genre? Do they write textbooks? Or memoirs? Did they earn an MFA?

Keep digging. What can you discover about them as a human? What is their job? Where do they live? Are they married? With children?

Write a paragraph reflecting on what surprising or expected things you discovered about this human? How does learning more about their human life after how you read their anthology piece change your experience of the narrative?

B: Narrator–Situation Distance

Look at three narratives in the anthology that each employ a different narrator distance (You might try Amy Butcher's "Women These Days," Peter Grandbois's "Loyalty," and Elissa Washuta's "Incompressible Flow"). Explain, in a paragraph, what type of narrator the writer is using and how that affects the narrative.

C: Unreliable Narrator

Look through our anthology for a narrative with an unreliable narrator. Consider Jonathan Rovner's "The Funambulists" or Elissa Washuta's "Incompressible Flow." Then highlight how this narrator is intentionally unreliable. Write a paragraph explaining the effects of this craft choice.

V: PROMPTS

The following prompts will help put to practice the techniques learned in this chapter.

A: Human, Writer, Narrator

Write three bios about yourself. Have one bio focus on who you were during the events that led to one of your works of creative nonfiction. In other words, who were you during the situation you've written about?

Next, write a bio about yourself as a writer. What do you write? What genres do you use most often? How would you describe your writing voice and style?

Finally, write a bio of yourself as the human you are today. Who are you in this exact moment? These bios can be serious, playful, or both.

B: Narrative Distance

Write a piece of flash creative nonfiction. First, use dramatic narrative distance and include no internal scene. Then revise it to use interior narrative distance. Notice what changes during these revisions.

C: Intentionally Unreliable Narrator

Write a flash creative nonfiction narrative that possesses an intentionally unreliable narrator. Work hard to craft an untrustworthy narrator, while the writer retains trust.

11

Soundscapes

II: VIGNETTE

It's early in the morning, and I'm writing before class. As I work, I rock back and forth in my chair. I tap my feet, nod my head, and occasionally pause from writing to drum on my desk.

It took me years to realize how much I move when I write and only after a friend pointed it out. Why do I do that, she wanted to know? I wasn't sure. Eventually, I came to understand that my approach to writing was not just intellectual and emotional but physical too. Sentences are lyrical, rhythmic, and resonant. The best prose, like poetry, is multi-sensory. I was, in my own way, dancing to the sentences, engaging my body in the process.

When I ask my students to write in class, many of them also rock or sway or swing their legs. The other day, I read them passages from a particularly rhythmic essay, occasionally stopping mid-sentence to ask how many beats remained. Often, they could tell me exactly how many syllables would complete the established pattern. This isn't about dancing while we work, but I do want my students to notice the implicit musicality of language. Now, when they look back at their work, they are better able to revise on a cellular level, paying attention to the power of language holistically, rather than just literally, and harness that attention to create transcendent experiences for their readers.

—Jess

III: OVERVIEW

Words serve as the painter's paint, the sculptor's clay, the musician's notes. They are the raw material from which we construct luminous worlds. They are not simply a form of communication but vessels of visceral meaning with aesthetic resonance on many levels: through definition, etymology, sound, connotation, history, shape, as well as the various ways they interact with the words around them. To be a writer is to be an aficionado of words, just as the painter must be a devotee of paint. If we do not love and study our materials, we cannot wield them effectively. Our every word choice has a profound effect on the reader, even when the effects are subconscious or difficult to express. Just like a song will often leave us with complex, inarticulate emotions, so too do our word choices. Part of writing well is learning to employ language with a precision that reaches the reader's subconscious. Poets are acknowledged for doing this all the time, but it's equally important in creative nonfiction.

A: How Words Create Meaning

The key to getting the most power out of our language is to consider if our words work on more than one level to earn their place on the page. We want language to evoke meaning in multiple ways, therefore maximizing its impact. Avoid **prefabricated language** that comprises much of our daily lexicon—words and phrases that are so familiar that they cease to mean in any significant way. *Furrowed brow, ice cold,* and *tears that stream down faces* are all examples. Not quite clichés, which should be avoided, too, these familiar pairings similarly fail to rouse the reader to attention. They function as abstractions, rather than vivid and particular description.

Instead, consider words based on connotation and sound. Writers use language to unpack a central question, which means that they write with meaning in mind first. Words get most of their meaning from their **denotation**, which is their literal meaning. Still, some of a word's meaning arises from connotations based on etymology, common usage, and context.

Connotation is the power of subtext, the conscious and subconscious associations of any given word. The reader intuitively draws on subtext to help inform meaning. Both *cap* and *hat* have the same meaning: something worn on our heads. But they have different connotations. While *hat* is more neutral, *cap* takes on shades of nostalgia and jauntiness. A word like *uncanny* is generally used to mean mysterious or strange, but its etymology (in German, "unheimlich," *un*—"not"; *heim*—"home"), and Freud's infamous writings on the word, gives it more nuanced connotations. *Uncanny* is a sense of the strangely familiar, like the fear of our own repressed desires, Madame Tussauds wax figures, or our own sexuality. "Collective Nouns for Humans in the Wild" by Kathy Fish is an explicit example of how connotation generates meaning. "A group of grandmothers is a *tapestry*," she writes. "A group of toddlers, *a jubilance* (see also: a *bewailing*)." The connotations of the words *tapestry* (warmth, cover, etc.), *jubilance* (joy, excitement, etc.), and *bewailing* (complaint, crying, etc.) project shades of meaning upon the collected humans Fish identifies in the flash narrative.

Along with connotations, **sound** too conveys meaning, in the same way that songs without lyrics still convey emotion. When we read, we hear the words in our heads and feel them in our mouths. Heavy, plunking words hit the reader differently than light, airy words. *Plunk*, for example, has a different sound than *drop*; though they mean relatively the same thing, they resonate differently. *Blazer* and *suit jacket* convey different meanings based on connotation, yes, but also based on sound. We should consider the context of the sentences we are writing and compose to generate specific soundscapes. The z-sound in *blazer* suggests a slickness and power more intense than the less direct, more diffuse sounds of *suit jacket*. Further, there's the succinctness of *blazer* versus *suit jacket*, which has more syllables which makes *blazer* sonically sharper.

Also, we should consider what mood we are trying to create and how that mood *sounds*, even devoid of content. A tense mood might contain more heavy consonant sounds, or a playful scene of a child skipping stones in summer might play up plosive sounds. Three often used ways of using sound as a meaning-making tool are alliteration, assonance, and consonance, all of which create the repetition of sound in a sentence. **Alliteration,** the occurrence of the same letter or sound at the beginning of adjacent or closely connected words; **assonance**, the repetition of the sound of a vowel or diphthong (two vowels that combine into a single syllable, such as *coin* or *side*) in non-rhyming stressed syllables near enough to each other for the echo to be discernible; and **consonance**, the repetition of the sound of a consonant or diphthong in non-rhyming stressed syllables near enough to each other for an echo to be discernible, are typically considered poetry techniques. But the best prose writers also take advantage of these tools. Note that alliterations can be assonant or consonant but always describe repeating sounds at the beginning of the words, while other examples of consonance and assonance can be internal too—like *hearty* and *apart* (internal assonance) or *abolish* and *abandon* (internal consonance).

Consider how Kathy Fish's narrative uses sound to convey meaning. Before the piece grows more serious, the sounds are light and ethereal, soft and sibilant: "A *resplendence* of poets," she writes, "A group of hospice workers, a *grace*." This sentence, though, marks a turn. The repeated consonant digraph— "gr—" in "group" and "grace"—starts a shift in the piece from soft sibilance (and joyful content) to harder consonance (and more tense content), as indicated in the sentence that follows: "Humans in the wild, gathered and feeling good, previously an *exhilaration,* now: *a target.*" Notice how the slightly softer "gr—" sounds become hard-g sounds in "gathered" and "good," before the sentence makes its hard landing, sonically and ideologically, with the word "target."

The reader is drawn to the aural repetitions of alliteration, assonance, and consonance because they create a sense of cohesion and wholeness, like a web of sound. These tools let us use our words like notes in a song, reinforcing rhythms and underscoring mood.

Here are a couple more examples:

Passages with lots of alliteration often create a singsong quality as we repeat the same beginning sound over and over at the beginning of words. "I still wince at what I once said to the devastated widow," writes Vijay Seshadri in "Memoir," creative nonfiction in verse. Here, the repetition of the "w" sound in "wince," "what," "once," and "widow" has that singsong-y effect.

Passages with lots of assonance often feel softer and lighter in mood, perhaps wistful or lilting. "Memoir" opens, "Orwell says somewhere that no one ever writes the real story of their life," which conveys the narrative's initial wistfulness through the repetition of "o" sounds in "Orwell," "somewhere," "no one," and "story."

Alternatively, a passage with many hard consonant sounds like "d" or "t" will often have the opposite effect, evoking a plodding intensity, like the "dun dun dun" of a horror film soundtrack. Or the "b," "k," and "d" sounds in this sentence from "Incompressible Flow" by Elissa Washuta: "The water kicked at the beam that suspended the bed above the lake," which connotes the rhythmic rock and bob sounds that the sentence describes.

B: Style

The music of our creative nonfiction is affected by more than just the words we choose. It's also the style of our words that affects a reader. The **rhythms** of creative nonfiction cultivate certain effects. In general, we want the rhythm to vary while also reinforcing the meaning of the sentence, scene, or paragraph. The reader becomes accustomed to the rhythm after roughly three sentences, at which point the pacing will start to feel dull and predictable, which matters because patterns are only interesting when there is an element of variability. Think about the chorus of a song, for example, which only excites us because it is surrounded by different rhythms. If a whole song were nothing but chorus, it would be far less interesting.

And then there is the bridge, which takes a song to an entirely new place. Lyrically, the **bridge** is typically used to pause and reflect on the earlier portions of the song or to prepare the listener for the climax. The same technique can be applied in our creative nonfiction. A shift in rhythm can also be used to signal a discovery, change the mood, or highlight a contrast between characters. It gives the reader a moment to reflect on what's come before and brace themselves for what's to come. The italicized sections in Washuta's essay are examples of bridges, providing a transitional space between sections of personal material while also shading that material with meaning. The language is excerpted from the textbook *Incompressible Flow* by Ronald Lee Panton and brings a new rhythm and kind of language to the reader's interpretation of the personal material, lending it gravitas and insight.

In addition to variability, we can use rhythm to reflect the mood of a particular scene or character. Short, clipped sentences create a fast, perhaps frenetic sensibility. Consider the urgency in the following sentences: "When my boyfriend asked me whether I was afraid of him, I told him I was not. When he told me I should be, I told him I was not," which open Washuta's essay.

Conversely, consider the following excerpt from the same essay and how the long, languid language reinforces the sentiments described: "Love drove my slender biceps to scrub and wax fiberglass for days while he took to the uncovered, aging motor like a surgeon on an open heart."

Rhyme is one of the first language patterns we encounter as children. It satisfies a primal impulse for pattern amidst chaos and brings to our language a lovely coherence. Rhyme works best when it is unusual and unexpected. Often, rhyme can be used to reinforce other unusual syntactical choices. Consider this line from Annie Dillard's seminal book of creative nonfiction, *Pilgrim at Tinker Creek*: "No, the point is not only does time fly and do we die, but that in these reckless conditions we live at all, and are vouchsafed, for the duration of certain inexplicable moments, to know it." The rhyming of *fly* and *die* reinforces at once how these words both compare and contrast in the context of this interesting sentence. Time is fleeting, which is akin to death's inevitability. But also *fly* and *die* have opposing connotations, taken out of context.

Word rhymes can be used to establish patterns that enhance mood or voice. Each time these rhyming words appear, they contribute to a web of connectedness that creates cohesion. They keep the reader focused and engaged, reinforcing the soundscape of the creative nonfiction.

As we start to compose sentences, we can consider **syntax**, the order of the parts of the sentence. Emphasis shifts depending on how the sentence is constructed. A sentence like "The boy in the red beret broke his bicycle" emphasizes bicycle, but "Riding a broken bicycle was a boy in a red beret" emphasizes the red beret.

Echoes are when a word, image, sound, or idea is repeated throughout a narrative. Or by repeating a certain syntax, for example, like a series of three-word sentences, we send echoes forward and back. It's a tactical move that creates emphasis through mirroring. "Here they come coyote …" repeats Harrison Candelaria Fletcher throughout "Open Season."

Also, consider other types of echoes, moments when a word, image, sound, or idea ties to another place in our creative nonfiction, or even connotations that echo back to earlier words. These echoes add power and depth to our creative nonfiction. Notice the repetition of opposites in Abigail Thomas's flash narrative, "Nostalgia." Some of these oppositions include a "man and a woman;" climbing the high mountain vs. the woman's fear of falling; the sun going down and the moon going up; making love or not making love. These echoes of opposites contribute to the knot of meaning.

Similarly, a carefully composed soundscape can echo with earlier or later material and function as signposts, alerting the reader to what matters. Jess's piece "When You Were a Boy in Maine" makes use of sibilance throughout, particularly "sh" sounds, a pattern that begins with the word "fishing" in the first sentence, and echoes throughout in other important images with words like "thrashing," "crushing," "shouting," "wish and wishes," "ashes," etc. The effect is a subtle, even subconscious, constellation of echoes that nonetheless emphasize pivotal moments in the narrative.

By repeating words, phrases, images, gestures, and/or metaphors, we cultivate and direct a symphony of meaning. Each time we repeat an image or sound it generates an echo that converses with other similar instances. Patterns emerge, and patterns are how we make sense out of chaos. It's as if our creative nonfiction is having an invisible conversation just below the surface, and it's a powerful way to harness subtext into a knot of meaning. The repetition of "woman" in Amy Butcher's "Women These Days" deliberately exploits the power of pattern. It is not just the word "woman" that conveys meaning but its very omnipresence in the piece that adds to the knot of meaning: the persistence of women *and* their continued victimization, which are contradictory but equally valid truths.

C: Flatlining

The magic of creative nonfiction is the way it travels through time and space to forge an emotional connection between strangers. Writer and reader may never meet, but between them exists an invisible bond generated from black marks on a white page. To create this emotion, though, our creative nonfiction must often behave strangely, almost antithetical to logic. In general, the more implicitly emotional the experience, the less emotional our language must become to convey it. We don't want our creative nonfiction to tell the reader what to feel, which causes resistance, but instead to allow them to bring their own emotions—solicited through scene—to the moment. This is a strategy called **flatlining**, and it entails dialing back the abstract language of emotions, using an almost-reportorial tone, so that the reader can bring their own emotions to the experience. Let's consider a romantic scene in a good film or TV show. When done well, these characters aren't espousing their deep love in over-the-top, flowery language. That's the stuff of Harlequin romance novels and Hallmark movies, and it leaves most of us feeling cold. Instead, the good stuff focuses in on the small, objective details to spark emotion—one character's glistening shoulder blades, a pearl button slipping halfway open, a close-up of a cracked and clenched fist. The language that conveys the most intense emotions is not dramatic, purple prose but the precise language of the struck observer. This language provides a stark background against which our characters' emotions can radiate more intensely.

The language of deep grief, for example, is rarely felt through descriptions of weeping or wailing. It is found instead in the odd observation, the strange images that capture our attention through our suffering: the brightness of the sun, the lone bicycle lying in the alleyway, a mother's chipped tooth. We want to avoid the predictable language of grief, romance, or pain in favor of the observational language of shock.

Amy Butcher's essay "Women These Days," as mentioned in its opening note, was "[compiled] and arranged by searching 'woman + [verb]' (walking) in national news outlets over the past twelve months." Given the overwhelming horror of the experiences the essay relates, Butcher needs the control of the reportorial language to contain it. Intuitively, Butcher understands that to narrate these stories head on would overwhelm and, therefore, distance the reader. In other words, the headlines entrust the reader to bring their emotional intelligence and experience to the page in order to make meaning. They can imagine the horrors. We've seen and heard too many similar stories before, the flattened language suggests, it's already a too-familiar story—which is part of the knot.

It's often helpful to think of ourselves as "biographers" rather than "autobiographers," particularly when we're writing about intense emotional experience. This one-step of remove often gives us the emotional distance to do justice to the material. Flatlining the language of our sentences, especially in emotionally powerful moments, helps capture emotions that stun us into stillness, trusting the reader to bring their emotional intelligence to the page. Show it and they'll feel it. Explain it and readers resist.

Notice the way Jess relates a particularly disturbing story about her ex-lover, without indulging the image with sentimental language but letting the clarity of the image contain and convey the meaning. She describes her ex-lover leaving basic training to collect his deceased mother's ashes so that he could carry out her final wish:

> [He took] her feather-light urn to the shores of the Atlantic, bearing it aloft and alone into the wind and waves and letting fly her flaked ashes, food for the fishes, into the roiling and indifferent sea [...] Later he learned the unthinkable, that his uncle, her brother, had secretly buried his sister— *We're Catholics for Christ sake!* the uncle later argued—and the ashes S. had scattered just his uncle's old dog.

The only word of explication here is "unthinkable," but otherwise the image does not insist on its own sadness, it just shows it.

In this way, we draw our reader closer to the emotional import, rather than distancing them with heavy-handed language.

D: Filters

Filters are another way that novice writers step in between their readers and their work. **Filters** are any description of our characters' or narrator's observing consciousness or mental activity. Filters describe thinking or observing rather than just allowing the character or narrator to think or observe. *I wondered; She thought; He saw; I felt*, and similar language filters the character's experience rather than just letting the character experience it. Compare the following two paragraphs:

1. *I watched a black cat slink underneath a parked car, then emerge on the other side trailing thick, black oil. I noticed that her tail was missing and wondered if she'd been run over. Her calico fur reminded me of Grandma's fur coat. I felt the cool of the windowpane against my cheek.*
2. *A black cat slinked underneath a parked car, then emerged on the other side trailing thick, black oil. Her tail was missing. Had she been run over? Calico fur, like Grandma's fur coat. The windowpane was cool against my cheek.*

In the second version, the filters (*watched, noticed, wondered, reminded, felt*) are omitted. They're superfluous. Who else would be "watching" the black cat or "noticing" that her tail was missing? The writing in the second version is much more immediate. The reader is experiencing the image within the character, rather than watching the character experience an image.

Notice the immediacy in the first sentence of "When You Were a Boy in Maine": "You took your red-striped fishing rod out into the yard—neon yellow bobber electric against the opaque gray sky—and cast into a puddle of snowmelt and waited. Brown fields, early spring, early morning." Filters are omitted in favor of the direct treatment of the image itself.

IV: READING AS A WRITER

The following exercises will help you practice the techniques learned in this chapter.

A: Comparing Rhythm
Read "Nostalgia" by Abigail Thomas and "When You Were a Boy in Maine" by Jessica Hendry Nelson. Compare their rhythms. Does one move faster? Does one use shorter sentences? Does one use larger words? How do the different rhythms impact the way the scenes are portrayed and the meaning evoked?

B: Echo Hunter

Identify the use of patterns and echoes in Harrison Candelaria Fletcher's "Open Season." Make a list of the recurring images, objects, connotations, words, and/or sounds and analyze their effects. Do these patterns help point to the knot of meaning? Why or why not? If so, how?

C: We'll Cross that Bridge …

Now, reread "Open Season" and "When You Were a Boy in Maine" looking for bridges. How do they create space for the reader to pause and reflect, and also prepare them for what's to come?

D: Take a Pulse

Identify the sentences, scenes, and paragraphs that convey the most emotion in "Open Season" and "When You Were a Boy in Maine." How do they create that emotion? Look for examples of flatlining and analyze how the effect is created.

V: PROMPTS

The following prompts will help put to practice the techniques learned in this chapter.

A: Sound and Meaning

Examine a narrative that you are working on. Look at the words you choose. Now go back and begin to change words based on connotation. Or look at your diction and find a better word, one that more accurately captures the exact mood. And then start to look for alliterations, assonance, and consonance.

B: Bridging

Take out a narrative you've been working on and locate a moment or moment(s) of inflection—places where the tone shifts right before a dramatic moment or right after one. Try composing a few different bridges into those dramatic moments. Take risks here. Try a bridge that is quick. Try another that is long. Try another that seems on the verge of being over the top. Try one that seems understated.

C: Filter Out

Take out a narrative you've been working on and read through it. This time around, only look for and eliminate filters. Resist the urge to edit otherwise and focus all your attention on filters. Then read through the draft again and marvel at how much more vivid it is.

12

Phenomenal Truths

I: VIGNETTE

A few years ago, a friend and I were talking about skiing. For whatever reason, I told him a story from thirty-five years ago, a story of a boy terrified and a man now embarrassed.

It is 1982 and my family and I ski Plattekill Mountain in upstate New York. I am ten years old. On this cold January day, my father, my friend Tom, and I load onto the lift. Halfway up, the lift screeches to a stop. This is not unusual. Ski lifts stop all the time for a variety of reasons. What becomes unusual is that for five, ten, fifteen minutes, Dad, Tom, and I, and all the other skiers, dangle over the slopes. Waiting. Waiting.

And as we wait, a feeling sweeps through my body. Claustrophobia. A fear of heights. A fear of falling. I cannot control my breathing. My heart pounds in my chest. I start crying. I tell my dad, "I need to get off." Soon, a ski patroller lets us know the lift is broken and they need to lower us down via seats attached to ropes. My dad says, "My son feels like he's having a heart attack," and I do.

The patroller does the necessary work (which includes shooting a roped-in seat over the chairlift cable and then lowering me down) and lets my father, Tom, and me off the lift first, lowering us via rope to the ground. I am happy to land on the earth, happy to be off that broken lift. My heart slows to a gentle flutter. But the beating in my chest is replaced by shame for being the first off, ashamed to have made my dad ask to get me off the lift. That shame follows me for years.

Nearly thirty years after I asked my father to get me off the ski lift, he and I are skiing in upstate New York. After skiing, we sit down for a glass of wine. We talk, as we normally do, about our lives in skiing. Probably because we are relatively close to Plattekill Mountain, my dad brings up that day that we got stuck on the lift so many years ago. I am ready to be embarrassed, to again feel shame sweep through me.

Instead, he says, I remember being on the lift with your sister and her friend, Laura. The lift stopped, and there I was with these two girls. I was terrified. My heart was pounding. Once I knew the lift was broken, I saw a ski patroller, and I asked him to get us down first. And he did. I'm still surprised at how terrified I was.

As we sit and drink wine, me sipping slowly, I don't add anything. I don't contradict my dad. I don't offer my own version. I just wonder about my story, my dad's story. How similar they are. How different they are. How I no longer know what parts of the story are mine and what parts are his. How I no longer know what shame is mine and what shame is someone else's.

—Sean

II: OVERVIEW

Unlike fiction, creative nonfiction must wrestle with major ethical issues regarding "truth," "fact," "memory," and "invention." Creative nonfiction writers are often questioned about the veracity of their work. A range of perspectives contributes to a heady debate between purists and more laissez-faire writers about the relative veracity of creative nonfiction.

Some of this pushback derives from memoirists who have fabricated their stories. The deceits of a few select writers broke a bond of trust. But, beyond those who knowingly lie in their work, there are a few other ethical concerns in creative nonfiction.

One of them, similar to the willful deceits of some writers, is that some writers call their work "true" while not caring much about truth, fact, or memory and focusing instead on the perceived value of art over truth (not that art and truth are ever antagonists). This is a controversial approach that some writers claim is deceit and others claim is art. We will touch upon this idea more in "Aesthetic Truths" below. These writers live somewhere more on the fictional side of the truth spectrum (recall the "Veracity Scale" from "Genre and Veracity").

Finally, every creative nonfiction writer uses fictional elements such as dialogue, character development, scene creation, and setting creation. The mere act of creating a story transforms it from "fact" to "art," and that transformation sometimes makes the reader question if a writer is being truthful.

Part of the issue is the assumption that creative nonfiction is the writing of true events. This creates a contract between reader and writer that calls for truthful and factual narratives. But it might be impossible for a creative nonfiction writer, as we will see below, to write truthfully or factually.

A: The Definitions

Before parsing the issues with truth, fact, and memory, it is useful to have a shared understanding of these terms (and others). Below is a list of definitions.

In Medieval Latin, **a fact** meant something that was literally a "thing done." By the 1600s, a fact was understood to be "a thing that is known or proven to be true."

Truth comes from the West Saxon word *triewe* and means "faithful" or having the "quality of being true." **True**, meanwhile, traces itself back to Proto-Germanic. And since the 1200s, true has meant "consistent with fact" and since the 1300s has meant "real, genuine, not counterfeit." Creative nonfiction traffics in different kinds of truth. The first is truth with a capital T. This Truth is "consistent with fact."

The next type of truth is **emotional truth**, which is how someone feels about or interprets a past experience and/or how an experience feels during the moment.

Another type of truth is aesthetic truth. Before we define aesthetic truth, let's define aesthetic, which is the artistic and/or philosophical principles that guide an artist. **Aesthetic truth** includes the ways a specific writer—or related group of writers—approaches their work artistically. So, put simply, aesthetic truths deal with what forms or style a writer uses to uncover their knot of meaning.

Other important terms to define include memoir, essay, and creative nonfiction, which we've briefly looked at before but will reexamine to see how their definitions teach us about truth.

Memoir traces back to the Latin word *memoria*, which means, simply, "memory." Memoir is a sharing of the writer's memories or the construction of one's story from memory.

Essay originates from the Latin word *exxagium* (through the French word *essai*) and means "a weighing" or "to examine" or "to try." An essay, therefore, is an examination or the trying on of an idea or event.

Creative nonfiction, as we discuss in detail in "Genre and Veracity," is trickier to define since it is based around what it is not: i.e., *not* fiction. Still, one definition is that creative nonfiction uses imaginative elements to write about real events.

What might be most interesting about these definitions is that none of them (memoir, essay, and creative nonfiction) focus on truth or fact. They are more interested in the examination of memory. Ultimately, neither truth nor fact is achievable in creative nonfiction; it is only imaginable.

B: The Fallacy of Truth and Fact in Creative Nonfiction

Let's not understate the "creative" part of creative nonfiction. It's inherent in every phase and choice in the writing process, from the creative process of remembering to the ways we choose to render scene, dialogue, or setting. All of these choices require the writer's creative writing tools. "Creative" comes from the term "inventive." So to create is, naturally, to invent. Creative nonfiction writers always use some measure of invention as they write. More practically, all writing (all art for that matter) is a reconstruction, an artifice. It is not the experience itself but fundamentally an object created out of, or inspired by, experience. It is not *the thing itself*. It can't be.

Secondly, creative nonfiction contends with memory. Many people imagine that memories are like photos in a photo album called "our brains." All the writer needs to do, then, is reach for a specific memory and re-create its truth. But this isn't even close to how memory works. Science has proven that memories can be created, altered, and destroyed, that they are unstable and ever-changing. No memory is ever permanent or unadulterated.

Research shows that there is an original memory (the memory made during an experience), but that this original memory is immediately replaced as soon as it is recalled. And then, when we re-remember an experience, we create third version of that original memory, and so on. Each memory is different from the first in small and major ways depending upon the changing lenses through which we are recalling it and the story we are creating to make sense of it. Each new re-telling moves the memory further from the original, which is why we all memories are **malleable**, a reminder that memories are, at their core, inventions and re-creations. After five or ten or fifteen years, a memory can be altered hundreds or thousands of times rendering them vastly different from whatever original Truth may have existed.

If remembering a memory bastardizes it, then maybe the best way to preserve a memory is to not remember it. In theory, this would preserve original truth. Unfortunately, writers also deal with the **forgetting curve**, the speed at which memories break down. Research shows that humans lose over half of their memories in under a week unless they actively review the experience them. The brain cannot hold onto all of its memories. Humans bring in too much information, so it filters out what is needed and removes most non-novel experiences.

So we creative nonfiction writers are in a quandary. The one bit of good news is that fight-or-flight and novel experiences are often the memories slowest to fade. But—there always seems to be a "but"—these memories are often extremely flawed. Study after study shows that eyewitness accounts (around which much of creative nonfiction is based since we are eyewitnessing our lives) are unreliable. Research shows that 30–50 percent of eye witness accounts are wrong because under stressful situations people record these memories poorly, and so while they might seem vivid, they're often inaccurate.

Despite our best intentions, as we see, memory always fails to replicate truth and fact. Instead, memory is a new story, its own creative nonfiction.

C: A New Call to Arms

The four memory-based issues mentioned above ([1] the creative nature of creative nonfiction, [2] the malleability of memory, [3] the forgetting curve, and [4] the flaws of eyewitness accounts) are roadblocks on the journey toward truth and fact. Because of that, creative nonfiction is often largely fictional, even when writers try their hardest to write truthfully. So what do we do? Should we just lump creative nonfiction in with fiction? Do we see creative nonfiction as flawed and, therefore, useless?

No. The collective narratives based on real-life experiences are far too important to ignore, as we established in the "History of Creative Nonfiction." They are a means through which we navigate and survive our complex lives.

Instead, we need to use all available resources to help write truer narratives (photographs, interviews, news accounts, etc.). But we also need to understand that creative nonfiction is not the writing of strictly factual stories. This newly defined framework moves writers and readers away from creative nonfiction as a form of absolute truth, and instead reveals it to be a *process of* deep and thoughtful *engagement with* fact, truth, and memory.

D: The Filtered World

Without delving too deeply into philosophy, Immanuel Kant (1724–1804) claimed there were two worlds: the noumenal and the phenomenon. The **noumenal** (originating from the term "Ding an sich" and translated as "thing-in-itself") is the actual world or the factual world. The **phenomenal** (anything observable) is the world of appearances and interpretation, the world filtered through human senses. Rephrased in mathematical terms, noumenal truth + our senses = an individual's phenomenal truths. Humans cannot experience the noumenal world because our senses (sight, smell, touch, taste, hearing) automatically alter the noumenal world into a filtered perception of truth and fact (the phenomenal).

Memories (or their creative nonfiction) can't be noumenally true since humans experience life through the filter of their senses. But, and this is where beauty outshines fact, there are a plethora of phenomenal truths for each singular noumenal truth. Two people will always remember an event differently as we saw in Sean's vignette above. Major and minor details will be morphed, combined, added, or subtracted because of the phenomenal nature of human experience. And this is what makes creative nonfiction so powerful. Creative nonfiction's power does not come from telling a noumenally true story. Instead, creative nonfiction is powerful because— even if it gets some or many truths and facts wrong—each writer is striving toward their own individual phenomenal truths.

E: The Myth of Creative Nonfiction

A **myth** is "a traditional story accepted as history […] to explain the worldview of a people." Euhemerus, a Greek mythographer, called myths "accounts of actual historical events, distorted over many retellings." Myths, simplified, are stories that a culture believes to be true (and may be true) while the outside world believes a culture's myths to be untrue or distorted.

And the same holds true in creative nonfiction. The reader must understand that a writer's phenomenal truths are always distorted. They are a **personal myth**.

By considering that creative nonfiction is comprised of phenomenal truths (rather than noumenal truths) to generate personal myths we acknowledge the following:

1. Writers must still strive toward (though never achieving) noumenal truths because a personal myth is a story that the writer believes to be noumenally true. Therefore, the writer must probe malleable memory while also reviewing outside sources to strengthen the phenomenal truths of their stories.

2. This new philosophy of truth and creative nonfiction shifts the reader's expectations from noumenal truths to phenomenal truths, which are best understood as personal myths.

If writers enter the writing process attempting to write the truest version of their phenomenal truth and if the reader understands that they are reading a personal myth, then we have a clear and effective contract between writer and reader.

Creative nonfiction is beautiful because it is the writer's world interpreted through the senses and re-envisioned through the malleability of memory, emotion, and intellect. These narratives may be more true, emotionally, than facts. Our stories signify powerfully when we understand them as vast webs of personal mythologies—past, present, and future—alive and vital in this tremulous world.

III: READING AS A WRITER

The following exercises will help you identify and analyze the techniques learned in this chapter.

A: Noumenal and Phenomenal Truths
Examine any narrative from the anthology. Highlight all the noumenal truths in the piece. Also, label why they are noumenal truths. Then highlight all the phenomenal truths and label what makes them such.

B: Aesthetic Truths
Examine any two narratives from the anthology. Compare their aesthetic truths. What styles does each author use? What do those styles do for the creative nonfiction? How do they work toward creating meaning through their aesthetic choices?

C: Memoir, Essay, and Creative Nonfiction
Examine three or more narratives from the anthology. See if you can label at least one as memoir, one as an essay, and one as creative nonfiction? Do you see differences between these three terms? Can you find anthology pieces that fit one but not all of these terms?

IV: Prompts

The following exercises will help you practice the techniques learned in this chapter.

A: Noumenal Words for a Noumenal World

Write a piece of flash creative nonfiction that uses only (or almost only) noumenal truths. Use only verifiable facts.

B: Noumenal Revision

Revise a narrative in progress by trying to increase the number of noumenal truths. Conduct as much research as necessary to cultivate a more noumenally-true narrative.

C: The Forgetting Curve

Write a narrative about what you cannot remember. Focus on all the small and large details that no longer exist in your memory.

D: Eyewitnesses

Write a narrative about a situation in which other people were involved. Interview those other people and add their takes. In the narrative, explicitly, examine how each viewpoint is the same or different.

13

Embracing Uncertainty

II: VIGNETTE

Recently, I was writing an essay about my ex-father-in-law's death. I was trying to discover meaning from a death so unexpected and sudden. He'd inexplicably fallen from a ladder, suffered a head injury, and was in a coma four days before succumbing to his injuries. The essay, though, was focused squarely on the days right after his death, wherein my ex-husband and I were holed up in my in-law's lakeside camp: grieving, fishing, faking the rhythms of the living. In my memory, those few days are a blur, clouded by grief and worry for my husband. I couldn't remember them with any accuracy. So, instead, I started researching largemouth bass, the species we were pulling out of that lake, one after another, and learned that bass spend nearly half of their lives floating near-motionless in deep water. I learned that their eyes glow when they feed and that you can read the age of a fish in the rings of scales around its tail, much like you can read the age of a tree. I researched whether fish can indeed feel pain, which was obsessing me then, the physiology of pain, as I worried over whether my father-in-law had felt pain during his four-day coma.

These facts, while not directly related to the death of my father-in-law, provided new inroads into the experience I was attempting to turn into creative nonfiction. Metaphors surfaced when I realized that bass spend nearly half of their lives nearly immobile, which was akin to my father-in-law's coma conditions. Also, nobody can say for sure whether fish feel pain, just as nobody can say for sure whether people in comas experience pain. These were new ways of thinking about what my father-in-law may have experienced during his coma. In this context, he was suspended in a different universe, as water to air, and therefore subject to different laws of physics. His experience in that hospital room could not be compared to mine and my husband's, just as our experience at the lake could not be compared to the fishes. Mostly, the research helped me tap into that most inexplicable of human conundrums: our own mortality—for example, the fact about the rings around a bass tail lead to an image of my father-in-law's palm, which could not provide me with a similar "reading"—an irresolvable but meaningful image. In embracing doubt, the search for meaning becomes the conduit for cultivating it.

—Jess

III: OVERVIEW

One of the most common refrains we hear from novice creative nonfiction writers is that they *just don't have a good memory*. This isn't unusual. *Of course you don't*, we say. Consider all that we learned about memory in the preceding chapter. Few of us possess the photographic memory often and unfairly expected of creative nonfiction writers. Further, as we now know, even the best memories are compromised. To compensate for our malleable memories, we conduct research and interviews, but even the most fastidious researchers inevitably come up against roadblocks. There are some things in the past that, no matter the tenacity and ingenuity, we will fail to ever know.

Some writers turn their backs on the whole endeavor, preferring to hide creative nonfiction under the cover of fiction or else abandon life stories altogether. A few even go so far as to denounce the whole genre as suspect, lacking in truth and value. But these perspectives obscure how real lives *signify*—not just because personal experience matters but because each of us possesses a unique and notable point of view on those experiences, those phenomenal truths.

Art, like science, is not born of certainty but of doubt. We write to find out, to come to some measure of understanding, and most importantly, to plumb the mysterious, the unique set of wonders implicit in each of us. Much like we conduct experiments to uncover scientific truths, creative nonfiction leads us to personal and/or cultural and emotional discoveries. Creative nonfiction then is the record of the journey toward the knot of meaning. It is like an artfully constructed process paper. These journeys inevitably contain setbacks, confusions, sometimes pain, and always shoddy memories. That's okay. Absences and mystery are part of the story; and our efforts to discover answers are, likewise, part of the story.

Further, remember that the word "art" is derived from "artificium," Latin for "artifice" (that root also gave English "artificial"). "Artificium" in turn developed from "ars," the Latin root underlying the word "art" (and related terms such as "artist" and "artisan"). All art, from painting to music to writing, is not the noumenal "thing itself" but an artifice, the phenomenal. The past, after all, ceases to exist the moment it passes, so any art form that draws on past experience is by its very nature an artifice. This means that any creative writing that aims to erase its scaffolding, so to speak, or ignores its own artifice, could be considered "less true" than art that points to its own constructed-ness.

So rather than ignore our doubt, we should embrace it as a critical component of the meaning-making process. What we don't know often reveals as much as what we do know. In other words, work with imperfect memories and research roadblocks, rather than against them.

A: Dialectical Movement (Revisited)

We'll return to a strategy discussed in "Narrative Energy," but this time, we'll demonstrate how **dialectical movement** (any time the writer explores a different point of view, either between characters or between parts of themselves) can invite the doubt and speculation mentioned above into the meaning-making process. What we don't know, or are unsure about, or where two (or more) perspectives collide are often as meaningful, or more meaningful, as what we *do* know.

But, first, why bother with embracing uncertainty?

Embracing uncertainty is important because admitting to a lack of information mirrors the experience of living. Consider all the things we don't know, especially concerning those important things in life. Is our co-worker frustrated with us? If so, why? Is our partner sad? About what? Does our frustration at work mean we should make a career change or merely adopt a new perspective?

By embracing life's unavoidable uncertainties, we earn our reader's trust. Readers trust writers who point to places of doubt, who are willing to admit that their version of the truth may not be someone else's version, or that their point of view is fallible. These concessions signal that writers are interested in whole truths, not idealized ones. We are smart enough to realize that there are three or four or five sides to every story. And a story becomes truer when more of those sides are explored.

Finally, uncertainty arises because memory is mutable, as we discussed in "Phenomenal Truths." No matter how hard we try, we'll always get our memories wrong on some level.

Rather than ignoring discrepancies, we can examine them for meaning in our work. One of the ways to do that is to question our memories, viewpoints, and other people's viewpoints. Questions to consider: *Why do you remember what you remember? How has your memory of an experience evolved and/or the memories of your subjects? Why do you/they remember it in this particular way? How else do others remember the experience? Where would a particular person argue most about your memory? And why?*

When we broach these questions head on, we engage in dialectical movement. We craft a dialogue between the noumenal and the phenomenal and between various people's phenomenal truths, and in doing so speculate about "what it all means."

We might think about speculating as "perhapsing," as many writers do—"Perhaps it happened this way" or "Perhaps it felt like this" or "Perhaps she felt this way."

Recall that in "The Active Mind," we define **speculation** as envisioning past, current, or future events based on the knowledge at hand. Meaningful speculation requires that the writer have as much information as possible and that they use it to make cogent suppositions. Speculation is a way to fill in the gaps between what we know and what we can't know, and, therefore, excavate those gaps for resonance. One interesting thing about speculation is that humans do it all the time and in a variety of ways and fields. Scientists speculate. Meteorologists speculate. Lovers speculate. Parents speculate. In Margot Singer's essay "Call It Rape," Singer speculates as she tries to understand the legacy of rape in her hometown. She writes:

> I remember three girls being raped, not two. Moreover, the man who police say assaulted Stern and her sister was arrested in 1973 and spent the next eighteen years in jail. In 1973, I was ten, not in high school. Have I misremembered what happened? Or did the police make a mistake?

Notice how Singer conveys her astonishment, a critical element of the essay's knot, through dialectical movement. The essay is in conversation with itself.

One of the keys to dialectical movement is cuing the reader, which is when we signal dialectical movements to come, such as "I don't remember exactly, but I imagine it happened like this …" or "I remember it this way, my mother remembers it that way, and in the middle, perhaps, is a greater truth."

Cueing the reader is a strategy that allows speculation and memory to coexist while also keeping our pact with the reader. It can be accomplished in swift, subtle strokes, as in "Saturdays were often filled with_____" or "A typical conversation with my mother usually_____." The words "often" and "usually" cue the reader that what follows will be an amalgamation of memory and imagination, a composite memory. Singer cues the reader in the last paragraph with the word "maybe": "maybe anatomy is destiny; maybe Freud was right." "Call It Rape" is not an essay about certainty, after all, but a refinement of a central question about the relationship between sex and violence.

Alternatively, we can be more explicit about the role of doubt in the knot of meaning by speculating about why and how we remember certain experiences as we do. It is not simply what we remember but *why* we remember *what we do* that cultivates the knot. Singer wonders why she remembers three rapes, rather than two, only to discover later that these were separate incidents, that in fact there were five rapes in total.

Or, in "Leave Marks," Melissa Febos speculates, "Tenderness toward the object of our desire becomes an expression of love partly, I think, because it so defies the nature of want, whose instinct is often less to cuddle than to crush," only to later in the same paragraph speculate again, "Lust is an urge to consume and perhaps there is no true expression of it that does not imply destruction. I can't say." Her uncertainty is part of her knot of meaning, and not incidental to it.

B: The Journey toward Meaning

Here's another way to think about embracing uncertainty. Let's borrow from a familiar structure in fiction, the "Hero's Journey," as Joseph Campbell defined it in his book *The Hero with a Thousand Faces*. The "Hero's Journey" begins with a hero or antihero (often the narrator but not always) who embarks on a quest and returns significantly changed, even when that change appears subtle. And just like the protagonist in a short story, novel, or film, the protagonists in our creative nonfiction will inevitably encounter obstacles during their journey toward change. Indeed, that's how change occurs—by pushing through obstacles. Creative nonfiction is, by its nature, a quest, and most creative nonfiction ends with a new perspective, not necessarily a solution tied together neatly with a bow.

Not only is this a useful way to think about structure in creative nonfiction, it should encourage us to include our missteps, memory lapses, research roadblocks, and places of uncertainty as useful obstacles in the journey. Febos demonstrates this point in the second to last paragraph of "Leave Marks" when she writes:

> I cannot render anything precisely in words, as I cannot crush my lover's body inside of mine. All I can do is leave a mark—the notation of my effort, a symbol for the thing. That is the endless pleasure and frustration of the writer and the lover: to reach and reach and never become.

The journey of the essay does not conclude the journey, in other words. It only reframes it.

Also, as with any journey, we don't know how we will be changed by the journey until after it ends, often long after (which ties back to narrator–situation merge, which we examined in "The Human, the Writer, the Narrator"). This uncertainty not only feels authentic to our reader, but it also allows them to step into our shoes, to journey with us, and to feel the questions shift.

C: The Edges

The above strategies for embracing and using uncertainty do not replace the need for creative research, however. Instead, they help us locate the edges of memory and experience, which we can then use to expand our vision, fact-check our work, and direct our journey toward the knot of meaning. Though embracing uncertainty is something we each do every day, as is speculation, the foundation for speculation is finding out as much information as we can before we speculate. Research is vital for embracing uncertainty because it's the only way to authentically locate it. In other words, we cannot know what we don't know until we know all that we can know. Say that five times fast.

The project of living is rooted in research. We seek out information daily in order to move through this world with some measure of competence and grace, so why would we limit our creative nonfiction to within the confines of our brains? Our selfhood is riddled with holes, and our job as chroniclers of creative nonfiction is to find and plumb those holes. Research de-familiarizes us with the known world by revealing what had previously been unknown to us. And de-familiarization is the first step toward a knot of meaning.

Some research is merely fact-checking (verifying the weather during an event or the stage of the moon). But much of it can lead toward meaning-making. And while we're looking up facts, we have no idea what else we might find. Research opens possibilities for further research, but we must take those first steps. In this way, writers are like cartographers of the noumenal world, mapping out its hidden connections and discoveries by staking the fringes of the known world.

Let us track how Febos develops a newfound bit of information into a new perspective:

> I read now about adolescents sucking on more obvious parts of each other in group activities that seem to preclude the secrecy and innocence of my own unsayable awakening. I don't so much mourn their lost childhoods. I lost mine at first opportunity and sex isn't the only way to do that. But I do remember the vacancy of those earliest and most obvious sex acts. I met desire under that faded beach towel, to the sound of cleats knocking the cement basement floor. What I mean is, the neck is always innocent. The parts of us we cannot see are touched most deeply, are most needing to be seen.

She takes a bit of research, likely discovered on the internet, about adolescents and sex and follows that train of thought into a new idea about the connections between innocence and desire. Febos understands that the wider world (the noumenal world) is always just outside the tight circle of personal experience (the phenomenal). This wider world cradles our experiences, but also permeates and shapes them. Embracing uncertainty demands that we interrogate the forces that shape our stories: the physical landscapes, as well as the spiritual, intellectual, and emotional ones. The best creative nonfiction writers actively investigate these forces on the page.

For creative nonfiction writers, research is not merely an academic pursuit but a way of life, and it both exacerbates and mitigates authorial uncertainty. This is good news because certainty is the death of good writing, and so while we research to bring cogency and context to our creative nonfiction, we must also embrace the ways it complicates our process. When we approach research as a lifestyle, as a deliberate mode of being, we honor the connections between an ever-shifting set of facts, stories, and personal myths. The best research, as we discussed in "The Central Question," is born of wonder. It is not performed in a vacuum but instead as a kind of organized call-and-response with the world.

Below are a few techniques to consider as we research.

1. Researching Imagined Setting

Consult multiple sources to reconstruct the past or reimagine a time or place. Photos, maps, descriptions by primary sources, records, and newspapers are all useful sources for this kind of work. This research informs our reimagined setting, which we bring to life using imagery. Singer opens "Call It Rape" by reimagining an event she'd researched but wasn't there to witness. Nonetheless, the reimagining is a vivid and fact-based way to engage the reader:

> Three girls are smoking on the back porch of their high school dorm. It's near midnight on a Saturday in early autumn, the leaves not yet fallen, the darkness thick. A man steps out of the woods. He is wearing a black ski mask, a hooded jacket, leather gloves. He has a gun. He tells the girls to follow him, that if they make a noise or run he'll shoot. He makes them lie face down on the ground. He rapes first one and then the others. He walks away.

By eliminating filters and rendering the scene "as if" she's there, Singer closes the gap between reader and writer, but this is most honest when heavily researched.

2. Researching Metaphors

Metaphors are connections that help us navigate the world and are fundamental to elucidating our knots of meaning. By understanding the connective tissue between disparate objects, ideas, memories, and facts, we comprehend what might otherwise be perceived as chaos. The same principle applies to creative nonfiction. Metaphors organize chaos into coherence. But rather than rely on our intuition to cultivate metaphors, we need to actively seek them out. When we live with the questions that our projects provoke, we grow attuned for metaphors. We begin to recognize them in our research, and when we do, we should use them as signals that we are on the right track. This is the subconscious directing our attention in useful directions. Pay attention. Think broadly and indiscriminately about what's most relevant to our creative nonfiction. Often, when we recognize a relevant metaphor, it means there is more to discover about that subject. For example, once Jess recognized the connection between her father-in-law's coma state and the motionless state of largemouth bass, she began to research more about the fish and the pond and to excavate many more meaningful metaphors between the landscape her father-in-law loved and his final days.

3. Everything Is Connection

Good research requires fidelity to facts, and veracity is more interesting than invention. Truth begets creativity, a set of boundaries against which the writer pushes to find meaning. While sources are subjective, the objectivity of facts can ground our work in something larger than the self. It puts the self in the context of the noumenal world, thereby enlarging both. Places of uncertainty between the two are not problems to be fixed, or a sign that we need to resort to invention, but opportunities for investigation. Even our frustrations can be connective tissue; it points to places where rationality breaks down, which is meaningful. When Jess couldn't find with any certainty an answer to the question "Do fish feel pain?," the impossibility of knowing became part of her narrative. She could no more answer that question with any certainty than she could know if her father-in-law felt pain while in his coma, or his last cogent thoughts, or what her husband felt as he watched his father die. These various black boxes also form a web of knowing, and when we speculate or imagine our way through these uncertainties, new, perhaps truer, resonance emerges.

IV: READING AS A WRITER

The following exercises will help you practice the techniques learned in this chapter.

A: Dialectical Movements
Read "Call It Rape" and "Leave Marks" and look for places where the writer uses dialectical movement to cultivate meaning. Identify whether the dialectical element is speculative or imagined and reflect on the effects of that rhetorical choice. How did the dialectical movement help the writer point to the knot?

B: Doubt
Study "Call It Rape" and "Leave Marks" looking for places where the writer looks squarely at places of doubt or confusion. How does the writer use that doubt to speculate about meaning? How does this tactic contribute to the knot?

C: Research Search
Study "Call It Rape" and "Leave Marks" looking for places where the writer has probably included creative research. How does the writer use the research to enhance the knot of meaning? Speculate about what would be lost without this research? How does the research help the writer earn credibility?

V: PROMPTS

The following prompts will help put to practice the techniques learned in this chapter.

A: Writing across Boundaries

Write a piece of flash creative nonfiction that begins and ends with speculation. By the end of the creative nonfiction, the speculation should move the narrative in a different direction from where it began.

B: Revising for Movement

Choose any creative nonfiction that you are working on. Revise it by trying to increase the use of dialectical movement. Highlight places where your memory is fuzzy and speculate as to why. Be clear, careful, and precise in your speculations. Consider other people's viewpoints. Don't forget to cue the reader.

C: Creative Metaphor

Write a list of interesting facts you've learned recently. Take one of these facts and use it to jumpstart your creative nonfiction about an experience that feels related in some way.

14

Ethics and Credibility

I: RELEVANT READINGS

Amy Butcher, "Women These Days"
Major Jackson, "Mighty Pawns"
Sarah Minor, "A Log Cabin Square"
Jonathan Rovner, "The Funambulists"
Vivek Shraya, "Trisha"
Ira Sukrungruang, "Invisible Partners"
Brooke Juliet Wonders, "Self Erasure"
Xu Xi, "Godspeed"

II: VIGNETTE

I commonly receive questions from readers of my first book—a memoir about (among other things) my brother, Eric, and his struggle with heroin addiction—about his reaction to the book. They want to know how Eric feels about it, but more specifically I suspect, they want to know how he feels about me *now that I've shared his story publicly. Does he feel angry? Betrayed? Resentful? The questions beneath their questions are almost always, "How will* my *family member/loved one/neighbor/old teacher/story subject feel if I publish something about them? Can I write honestly about other people without hurting them? Without getting disowned? Without losing my integrity?"*

I don't have objective answers. Instead, I tell them this story. Shortly after my book came out it was featured in (O)prah Magazine—an exciting but terrifyingly real development in my book's life outside of my hard drive. Eric bought the issue. He called me from his cell phone to tell me he'd gotten the magazine and had read the article. He'd also read the book, in both manuscript and galley form, and though he was not portrayed in an idealized way, he'd given his blessing. In the book, I'd tried to convey my brother's complexity—his strengths as well as his mistakes and struggles. I thought he'd recognized that and approved, but still, I worried that he might feel differently once the book was out in the world.

He was living in Philadelphia, while I was living in Vermont. This was during one of his brief periods of sobriety, and I think he was on his way to the methadone clinic when he called.

"Hold on, Jess, I'm getting on the bus," he said.

I heard the bus door whine open, and then a hum of voices, shuffling sounds, and the bus driver shouting for people to make more room.

Then Eric's voice loud over the din: "Hey, y'all! This is my sister's book featured in Oprah Magazine!*" I pictured him holding up the magazine, flipped open to the page that featured a large, color photo of the book's cover. "And I'm the addict in the book!"*

It was quiet on the other end now, and then a rush of applause.

"Yeah!" someone shouted.

"Go ahead, boy!" said someone else.

I imagined my brother smiling, bearing the magazine aloft. He was not only accepting, he was proud. And not because he had been depicted heroically ("I'm the addict in the book!") but because he had been seen.

—Jess

III: OVERVIEW

Earlier chapters discuss veracity in creative nonfiction, the contract with the reader, and ways to deal honestly with fallible memories while still writing engaging narratives. Here, we'll address complications that arise in the real world when we write creative nonfiction. We'll humbly attempt to assuage fears concerning privacy and ethics, while also acknowledging the real risks we take when we write from life. Telling true stories isn't for the faint of heart. It requires an abiding faith in the power of writing to signify, to mean, to contribute to the literature of our time. It means that we believe in the influence these true stories have to shape, however subtly, the trajectory of our social consciousness. Like oral histories, creative nonfiction is a record of the way we live, and it is both private and political work. Publishing creative nonfiction has ramifications, no matter the form, that are both rewarding and risky. And yet, the examined life is always worth it.

Our stories matter.

A: Risky Business

Depending on the focus of our creative nonfiction, we'll write with varying degrees of loyalty and love toward the humans depicted in our narratives. Commonly, the characters in our creative nonfiction are friends, family, lovers, exes, mentors, and foes. They enter our creative nonfiction because they are inextricably wedded to our life stories. And yet, each of them possesses a separate but equally valid accounting of events.

Here's a simple truth: Writing well enough to publish is not only a right but a responsibility. When we portray someone else in our writing, we must do so with absolute respect—even, and maybe especially—for those who have harmed us.

"[Literature is an art], but not a martial art," warns creative nonfiction writer Annie Dillard. Beyond the ethical concerns, which are many, writing out of vengeance is always bad writing. It is transparently ill-spirited and reduces our characters to caricatures. In malfeasance, these characters become one-dimensional, and human beings are never *one thing*. Even the evilest among us have dimensions, subtleties, and vulnerabilities. Usually, those who commit wrongdoings have been wronged themselves. This is not an excuse, only an acknowledgment of the complications of human nature, and a flag for embracing every character as nuanced and deserving of empathy. Or, if not, then perhaps they are an uninteresting subject for writing, as one-dimensional characters always are. Humans are compelling not despite their contradictions but because of them.

Major Jackson is explicitly interested in the contradictions of his subject, "Earl, the toughest kid/on [his] block in North Philadelphia" in "Mighty Pawns." Earl is simultaneously a tough kid living in Section 8 housing *and* a chess prodigy winning championships in Yugoslavia at the Belgrade Chess Association. He is interesting because of and not despite these seeming contradictions.

The best creative nonfiction comes from a place of love, and while love is always complicated, it ought to shine through even the most difficult scenes. Again, the reasons are twofold. We are hurt most by those we love the most. If this weren't true, we could easily dismiss these people as villains and move on; we wouldn't be so hurt. It follows, then, that for the reader to experience feelings of hurt, we must show the love that precedes and very often permeates the experiences through which we suffered. Another very real risk, and probable outcome, of writing for retribution is that the work won't be very good, and it won't get published anyway. But if it is published, often this one-dimensional writing will guide the reader toward siding with the supposed enemy in the piece and against the writer. Consider yourself warned.

B: Bill of Rights

Equally true is that our stories are ours to tell. If we let the above risks silence us, the world will be a darker place. We need creative nonfiction to shape and challenge the status quo, to illuminate our humanity, to teach us that we are not alone, and to show us *how to be*. When we read creative nonfiction, we engage in a radical and imaginative act of empathy. We see pieces of ourselves reflected, and these elucidations of our darkest, strangest, most courageous or terrifying impulses open us to more magnanimous ways of countenancing the world. This has been true since the earliest utterances of clan lore around the fire and will continue to be true long after these pages are dust. Creative nonfiction, no matter the form it takes, is intrinsic to our survival as a species. That's a huge claim, but one we'll stand behind. As our needs have evolved, so too have our stories. They serve as instruction (from "How do I slay the wooly mammoth?" to "How do I survive trauma?"), elucidation ("How and why do humans suffer?"), and conduits for human connection ("We all suffer. This is how we survive it."). All of these are intrinsic to the ongoing health and persistence of our species. This is not trivial work.

And while our version of events is not the only story or perspective, it is a valid voice among a chorus of equally valid voices. As we learned in "Phenomenal Truths," there is no truth with a capital T that can make its way to the page—only a collection of phenomenal truths, some voiced, some silent, all subjective.

For Jess, writing about her brother's heroin addiction was not easy nor did it depict her and her family as anything other than fallible and flawed, but she also felt it imperative to contribute to the shifting conversation about addiction and addicts. Her brother is a whole person, capable of great love and intelligence, empathy and kindness. He is not a nameless faceless "other," nor is anybody else suffering from addiction, and their stories help shift and shape the public conversation, and ultimately, the policies that influence recovery.

Consider, too, that not all creative nonfiction is about trauma and family. Some of the best creative nonfiction is about, on the surface, not that much.

There is a great quote attributed to the writer V.S. Pritchett, "It's all in the art. You get no credit for living." This quote highlights that it is often more important to have a distinctive point of view and voice, to indulge the wondering mind. Better to "really see" than to have a salacious plot. The best writers can, and do, write brilliantly about subjects as seemingly small and inane as 'salt,' 'shaving,' and 'old' photographs. Consider Ira Sukrungruang's "Invisible Partners," which is about discovering that his mother had cut out his prom dates from photos. No one was hurt by Sukrungruang's mother's actions. The prom dates probably never even knew about their excision from the photos. The narrator is not deeply hurt. But, still, his mediation and speculation moves the reader in powerful ways.

C: Establishing Credibility

When we write creative nonfiction, we must earn our credibility not just with the humans we depict on the page but also with our readers. Readers are skeptics by nature—and given the number of high-profile, fallacious memoirs in recent decades and the contemporary conversation about the slipperiness of facts—rightfully so. Our authority must be earned.

Consciously or subconsciously, the reader wants to feel as if we have good intentions, that we aim to capture the world in all its complexity and dimensions, that we don't idealize ourselves or anyone else, that we don't preach or condemn. Good writers have no interest in misleading our reader because we know that such an agenda is both transparent and dull.

The best creative nonfiction signals its good faith in small and subtle ways. Here are a few:

- **Acknowledge our flaws as much, or more so, than we depict the foibles of others**. We should be able and willing to call ourselves out, and to do so urgently and with reflection. This signals that we're not here to exalt or heroize ourselves but to tell a true and complex narrative to the best of our ability. Notice how Jonathan Rovner demonstrates this well in "The Funambulists." Rovner writes about himself in unflattering terms: "My crippling fear of rejection is represented by stale vaudeville-style jokes in the manner of the late Henny 'Take My Wife ... Please!' Youngman." Two sentences later, he writes, "My paralyzing inability to make a decision—large or small, personal or professional—is represented by the eating of waffles." These depictions show Rovner not as a hero in his story but as someone vulnerable, relatable, and real.

- **Consider our characters before we knew them.** This is a great way to develop dimensionality and empathy for characters who might otherwise come off as malicious or opaque. Let us look into our characters' pasts to discover things that can make them complex. Yes, the narrator's mother in "Godspeed" by Xu Xi is stern with her servants, but she also lives in a time when domestic help was expected of her by people, like her husband, who had more power and influence than she did. She also "had to work twice as hard [to impress her husband's family], [who were] accustomed to legions of servants in their large Indonesian homes, in contrast to our puny three." This section shows Xu's mother from before Xu's time, which adds nuance to her mother.
- **Cultivate narrative distance.** What if we thought of ourselves as biographers instead of autobiographers. When we demonstrate the control of the biographer, we prove our ability to write our creative nonfiction honestly. This slight shift in perspective is often enough to create the emotional distance necessary to begin turning personal experience into literature instead of a diary entries. It allows us to approach our characters with more objectivity and distance, while also inviting in community, culture, and history, to help develop character motives and behavior. The biographer does their research! Our narrative will still be subjective—filtered through the writer— but the perspective will be wider, less fraught. Rovner gives us a biographer's feel since he writes about his situation through the third person. Outside of his "emendations and substitutions," which uses first person, the rest of "The Funambulists" is in distant third person. But even in first person, we can observe ourselves and our narratives at a slight remove during the writing process, as if watching a film. Often, this envisioning technique promotes necessary breath and breadth.
- **Write about what we don't know as much as, and as fervently, as we write about what we know.** This was something we examined in "Embracing Uncertainty." Consider Brooke Juliet Wonders's "Self Erasure," which is an erasure of her boyfriend's suicide note. This erasure examines as much about what Wonders doesn't know—all the reasons, beyond a series of letters, that one takes their life—as it does what it knows. While the erasure highlights what is not known through its use of blackout, the ending overtly leans into this idea: "My boyfriend Rob took his own life by handgun on August 21, 2005. Seven years later, I still can't bring myself to read this letter without judgment." The knot of meaning exists in the fissure between the known and unknown.

- **Research characters and situations.** As we discussed in "Embracing Uncertainty," the more we creatively research the more we will find complexity in all situations and the more well-rounded our characters become. Examine Sarah Minor's "A Log Cabin Square," which uses a variety of research to explore its central question. Minor shares with the reader information gleaned from an exhibition called "Quilt Voices," researches a company called Home City Ice, and she uses research from an article, "Quilt Language: Toward a Poetics of Quilting," all as ways of reaching her knot of meaning. The variety of sources gives Minor credibility and a solid foundation of knowledge from which to launch her journey of discovery.
- **Tell the truth.** In all its complexities and from all its angles, we must do our best to tell our phenomenal truths. Even if we're not sure about what might or might not have occurred, admitting this lack of clarity can also be a form of transparency that earns the trust of our reader.

D: The Real World

There are no concrete, one-size-fits-all ways to communicate to our creative nonfiction subjects about our writing and their role in it, just as there's no blueprint for human relations generally. We write this section from a place of personal experience and not as authorities on the dynamics of your personal relationships. That being said, here's what we've learned works best for us:

- **When to Tell Our Subjects That We've Written about Them.** Jess and Sean each tackle this differently but with the same intentions in mind: we'd both rather maintain relationships with our subjects than publish anything.

  First, this obviously doesn't apply to literary journalism, profiles, or most immersion journalism and essays. If we are writing about subjects who are not part of our personal narrative or using someone else as the protagonist (profiling our city's mayor, writing grandma's memoir, or a magazine article about the personal lives of Instagram influencers, for example) then we are ethically beholden to inform them about the work.

  For all other creative nonfiction in which we are the narrator telling a personal story that includes other humans, Jess suggests waiting until the piece is accepted for publication. Here's why: the minute we let someone know about the work, they are likely to influence that process. They may want to read it and give their feedback. They may want to make sure that we include their perspective. They may recount certain stories from their point of view, and that perspective will likely differ from ours in fundamental ways. These disruptions, in early phases of a project's development, might derail our creative process. Moreover, their voice will likely get in our head, and the work may become more cautious and, therefore, inhibit discovery— which is an essential quality of good writing. In instances where the relationship is fraught, realizing that they are a subject in somebody else's creative nonfiction can be a disempowering experience. Our subject will likely worry about how they're being depicted. They may ask questions we are not prepared to answer. Their imaginings are often worse than what ends up on the page, but early drafts may not yet demonstrate the nuances, empathy, and dimensionality that will ultimately soothe a skittish subject. It's important that the work is the best it can be—artistically, but also in its generous portrayal of all subjects—before we let them read it, Jess thinks. Our early drafts often contain the rage, grief, or pain of memory, but not the empathy that distance and revision afford. Why risk bad feelings when our later, revised, and fully processed pages will be more thoughtful, nuanced, and capacious. In hindsight, it will be this version that we will want to share with our humans—our most authentic self and theirs.

Sean shares his creative nonfiction with his subjects a bit earlier than Jess; he shares it before he sends it out for publication, but once he considers it complete. Sean would rather not publish the story than hurt those close to him. This affects what stories he is willing to tell. As Jess mentions above, Sean's subjects' voices do worm into Sean's head. And he is often more cautious with what he shares. But, one of the benefits of sharing his creative nonfiction with a subject early on is that Sean learns from his subjects, which influences his narratives in profound ways.

- **Show subjects our work long before publication.** Hooray, our creative nonfiction has been accepted for publication! Now, it's time to give subjects plenty of time to read, well before the narrative scheduled for publication. This gives them time to get used to the idea, air grievances, and offer feedback, should they want. It's our opinion that it's only fair that we give our subjects the time and space to respond to our creative nonfiction. That doesn't mean we need to change a word, but considering that we've detailed our point of view (and plan to share it with the world!), we ought to hear out our subjects' points of view.

Jess tells her family and friends who appear in her work that she wants to hear their feedback—good, bad, or ugly—and if they feel especially uncomfortable with anything she'll consider making changes. She warns them, though, that she reserves the right to publish her story as she sees fit, and she won't necessarily make changes. But she listens with an open heart and mind, and thus far nobody's asked for changes she could not happily accommodate. Often, these conversations lead to insights she would not have made on her own. Moreover, sometimes sharing this writing nurtures closer relationships with the subjects of her work.

Sean, as mentioned above, shares any sensitive creative nonfiction before he begins publication so he has a chance to revise before the creative nonfiction enters the publication phase. Also, he enjoys hearing new perspectives that further complicate his central question and knot of meaning.

- **Give people the opportunity to pick their own pseudonyms.** It's a small gesture but one that offers up a modicum of control.
- **Be willing to change identifying characteristics and occasionally create composite characters.** This last part comes with a caveat. If we are creating composite characters or misrepresenting chronology, Jess and Sean believe that the contract between reader and writer deems that we alert the reader to these liberties. These are willful and substantial breaks from truth and, therefore, best to acknowledge outright in the text or in the front matter of a book. Notice the way that Amy Butcher alerts the reader right away that she is collating borrowed language to construct her collage essay with a disclaimer. Or how Vivek Shraya in her photo essay "Trisha" explicitly acknowledges that she is reconstructing photos of her mother by wearing similar clothes and adopting similar surroundings and poses.
- **Prepare ourselves (and our loved ones) for misrepresentations in media or reviews.** Here's something many writers don't consider before we publish our first book. Once we publish, our creative nonfiction is no longer ours alone but belongs to the public sphere, and the public will feel and react to our characters in any way they please. This means

that reviewers (professional or otherwise) may reduce our characters to labels (something a good writer should never do). One reviewer called Jess's mother an "alcoholic," which was neither true nor pleasant for her mother to read. They may also misread or misrepresent our creative nonfiction in ways we hadn't intended. And so our humans are now vulnerable twice, once at our mercy and now at the hands of strangers. However best we can prepare ourselves and our subjects for these reactions, do so before publication. Proceed with eyes wide open.

IV: READING AS A WRITER

The following exercises will help you practice the techniques learned in this chapter.

A: "It's All in the Art"
Skim through any five pieces in our anthology and reflect on whether they tackle risky subject matter or more ('seemingly') mundane subjects. Then reflect on how each narrative focuses on ensuring that "it's all in the art."

B: Signaling Good Faith
Examine the list in "C: Establishing Credibility" in this chapter. Then choose an anthology piece with risky subject matter. Now walk your way through the piece to see if and how the writer establishes their credibility. Jot down your ideas concerning each bullet point.

C: Risky Business
Comb our anthology for topics that you feel would be risky for you to write about. Consider, especially, Seo-Young Chu's "A Refuge for Jae-in Doe: Fugues in the Key of English Major," Melissa Febos's "Leaving Marks," Harrison Candelaria Fletcher's "Open Season," Jonathan Rovner's "The Funambulists," Margot Singer's "Call It Rape," Ryan Van Meter's "First," or Brooke Juliet Wonders's "Self Erasure." What about these pieces feel too risky for you?

Next, while remembering the quote "It's all in the art. You get no credit for living," consider how those writers turn risky topics into beautiful art.

V: PROMPTS

The following prompts will help put to practice the techniques learned in this chapter.

A: Risky/Too Risky

Create a list that has two columns. Column one should include three or more situations that are too risky for you to ever write about because of how it might affect your subjects. Column two should include three or more risky situations that you are willing to write about, even if it might affect your subjects. Then reflect on how you decided to put a situation in one or the other column. What made some situations too risky to write about? What made the other situations risky but not too risky?

B: Establishing Your Credibility

Take out a piece of creative nonfiction you are working on. Now, return to the list in "C: Establishing Credibility" in this chapter. Walk your way through your creative nonfiction. See how many of the bullet point ideas on establishing credibility you have already used. Then see how many more bullet point ideas you can integrate into your creative nonfiction to further establish your credibility.

C: "It's all in the art. You get no credit for living"

Write a flash piece of creative nonfiction on the riskiest topic you have on your list in Prompt A: Risky/Too Risky. Now work on ensuring that the piece works not on its riskiness but on its art.

15

Re-Visioning

I: VIGNETTE

Recently, an MFA student of mine came to me in tears. We were on the third day of a ten-day residency, and his essay was the first we'd workshopped. The draft he'd submitted was lovely, nearly ready for publication, everyone had agreed. The problem, the writer insisted now, was that none of it was true anymore. The essay, about his father's long affair with a ballet dancer as well as the writer's own ideas about masculinity and sexual fidelity, had led him to a knot of meaning that accepted his father's moral failings and both men's romanticism to be equally true. But now, the writer told me, he'd realized his father's transgressions had been more duplicitous and transgressive than he'd previously understood. His father had had many lovers while still married to the writer's mother, both women and men. Now, the essay's knot of meaning no longer stood up, no matter that the essay itself held together beautifully as it was.

"On the one hand," I said, "the essay is as true to your experience as it could be during the time of writing. One option is to leave the essay alone and submit it for publication."

On the other hand, though, we discussed how the new revelations deepened the essay's possibilities. The writer's new sense of doubt changed not just the knot but also his sense of the narrative's essential shape. While the original essay was organized more or less chronologically, his new understanding of multiple truths (and lies) suggested a "truer" structure, one that moved between multiple realities, positing them all on their own terms, refusing to prize his own sense of truth over his father's or even his mother's. By the end of our conversation, the writer had decided to re-vision the essay by embracing his doubts about his father's ability to reflect honestly about his sexuality and faith, and also about his own complicated beliefs about monogamy, masculinity, fatherhood, and contemporary relationships.

As he was leaving, the writer thanked me.

"I couldn't have figured it out without you," he said.

And though the sentiment felt good, I knew it wasn't me who had helped him in his re-visioning but the power of the process itself. All of it. The failed beginnings, early drafts, feedback from his peers, and most especially revelations that forced him to "re-see" his material. Life is like that, isn't it, which is one of the reasons why creative nonfiction is essentially a process of re-visioning what came before. We live and write about the experience of living. The two are in constant tango. I was simply there at the end of that process, a sounding board for the writer's concerns and conceptions. A mirror to show him back his evolving ideas. In this way and others, writing is not a monologue but a dialogue, even a cacophonous conversation. The myth of the solitary writer alone in a tower of their own making is patently false—we create in conversation with other writers and readers; with the past, present, and future; and with peers, mentors, and editors. Re-visioning is how these conversations take place, and it's one of the markers of a true writer, one willing and able to bear unfinished business. This time of flux is intolerable for some but essential for the writer. Only here, inside the creative process—where we are living, breathing, and wrestling with mystery—are we able to transcend our singular selves.

"Only connect," the writer E.M. Forster asserted.

In life and in writing, we need only to connect.

But that's not what I said to the young writer as he left my office. Instead I just smiled sagely and nodded.

"That's my job," I said, and then traipsed off to the bar.

—Jess

II: OVERVIEW

It is impossible and useless to think about revision as separate from drafting. Either actively or innately, the two are in constant conversation. Or, if preferred, these dual processes are a kind of breathing for the writer, so much so that we were tempted to put this chapter in the beginning of the book because revision *is* the writing process. Intellectually and creatively, they coexist in time. Even while some writers produce distinct, multiple drafts, the intellectual and creative work is always in tandem with production. For these reasons, we find it helpful to think instead about re-visioning, which emphasizes the active and ongoing way in which we do this work.

A: Vision and Re-Visioning

In introductory creative writing classes, we learn that revision is a global practice, not merely line editing. Take this advice as a matter of course. Another adage that bears repeating: **Revision** is re-vision, literally re-"seeing" our material. As we revise, we must ask ourselves, *What is this creative nonfiction really about?* Or, *What is the central question beneath the situation?* The draft might be about a father's extra-marital affairs, as in Jess's student's essay, but it was *really* about contradictory ways of loving. (Hint: that's the knot.) Some of us even write and revise simultaneously. Jess remembers an early course in her MFA program in which one of her mentors admitted that she did not revise much, not formally anyway, but instead wrote and rewrote each sentence with near-painful precision. She couldn't move on to the next sentence until the one she was working on was "perfect."

Jess understood completely; at that point, she too was a painfully slow sentence-writer. These days, she engages in a more mutable and dynamic revision process, but the cognitive processes involved in writing necessitate that we are always "working on it," always engaged with our material consciously or subconsciously, always re-seeing and rethinking a project-in-process. We go to sleep with our drafts and wake up beside them. We take them to work with us and have conversations with them on the commute. We add to them in the morning and change them completely by noon. And in creative nonfiction, especially, they change alongside us, as we continue to live out the experiences, consequences, and emotions that form us.

"However thoroughly we lose ourselves in the vortex of our invention, we inhabit a corporeal world," explains writer Mary Gordon. Envisioning and re-visioning require that we traverse two realities: the one we move through and the one we imagine. When writers return to the page after long hours in the corporeal world, they bring back with them mementos—something else they read; a snippet of overheard dialogue, perhaps; an interesting fact—and these mementos help them "re-see" the world they are creating on the page. Or perhaps they have spent long hours, days and nights, inside their memories. The writing came quick and dreamlike and now they set out to officially begin "revising." Even then, the processes are not linear and separate. We discover through the process of writing what we are writing about and in the process of refining that vision, we reimagine its possibilities.

B: Discovering the Knot

Writing is how we discover what we think, believe, wonder, love, and feel. Good writers do not begin writing because they know what they want to say or have some preconceived truth they want to prove. The best writers recognize the fallibility of their own convictions. They write from a place of curiosity, not assurance. The writing process is how we discover the knot, not how we prove the knot. After all, our job is not to prove anything, only to refine our questions. Our job is to show the world in all its gorgeous, heartbreaking complexity. Our job is to recapitulate the human experience so that in some small way, it becomes easier to bear.

Part of re-visioning our creative nonfiction is figuring out the complex truths that are often hiding in our drafts. Our job is to find them and coax them out of hiding. To call them into the light. To point to them. To refine them. To see how they tie together with other truths.

Remember, the knot is an expansive way of understanding creative nonfiction's (and life's) *aboutness*. In other words, the best creative nonfiction is not about "X and not Y," but "X *and* Y," or perhaps, "X *and* Y *and* Z *and* even A can be true on certain days under certain conditions." The knot is a reflection of our ease with "complexity and ambiguity"—real meaning requires it.

So how to figure out the knot? As we draft, we can take notes about the narrative's *aboutness*. Notice where the narrative contradicts itself. Notice where characters contradict themselves. Notice when emotions contradict— our own or our characters'. These clue us to the knot. It can help to jot notes in the margins of our drafts. What's at the root of this scene? This image? What's it trying to show? What's it trying to reveal? What images, descriptions, or ideas tend to repeat? Why do they repeat? What does the repetition suggest about meaning?

Other clues can be found in places where change takes place. Often, when a character realizes something anew, it is suggestive of the creative nonfiction's deepest concerns.

Try to put the knot into language. Try to sum it up in a sentence or two. This may be difficult and it most likely will change as we continue to re-vision. If it were easy to summarize the knot, then we wouldn't need to write the piece. And, yet, it's worth trying. By working to summarize contradictory truths, we are better able to refine those truths. Sean, on his trickiest pieces of creative nonfiction, will summarize his creative nonfiction in one sentence and then tape that sentence to his computer so he can always see it as he revises. Then, after a round or two of revision, he often re-writes (or revises) the sentence as the narrative morphs.

C: Re-Visioning toward the Knot

Now that we have some semblance of our creative nonfiction's knot (though, remember, that our central question and our knots evolve as we keep re-visioning), our job is to shine a light on the knot by ensuring that every word, sentence, paragraph, and scene work to show one aspect or another of the knot. For example, in his final draft, Jess's MFA student employed a host of craft techniques to ensure his creative nonfiction was always focused on revealing the contradictions of his father's way of loving. On the page, the father character is either loving well or loving badly, sometimes both. When the writer explores the motivations for his father's behavior—both personal and cultural—he always keeps present these contradictions. Even his word choices emphasize contradictory ways of loving. In a scene during which his father takes the young narrator to an ice cream shop, the father eats his ice cream as if "gnawing a bone." The word "gnawing" contrasts how most of us eat ice cream. The phrase also hints at his father's carnality, revealed in more depth later in the essay.

Ultimately, we have to be ruthless about what stays and what goes from our creative nonfiction. No matter how lively, entertaining, or well-written a scene may be, if it doesn't serve the knot then it doesn't belong. Writing is not for the faint of heart. We must "kill our darlings" as Sean does, or we must at least keep them in a separate file called "Darlings in Purgatory" as Jess does.

D: Re-Visioning Structure

One of the fundamental elements of re-visioning is the conversation between form and content. Creative nonfiction expresses itself in form. Our formal choices heighten and reflect the knot. If the knot is about contradictory ideas about love, as in Jess's student's essay, then one possible form would be layered and braided, with each character's stories and perspectives given equal weight and space on the page.

By re-visioning structure, we don't mean our creative nonfiction must be a villanelle, or a monologue, or a flash essay (though they can be)—just that the form should be in relationship to the content, form should serve a function. So we should ask ourselves: *Is this form best suited to reveal my knot? How does it serve my knot? What does this form "say" about my knot?*

E: On Utilizing Feedback

Workshops, peer readers, writing groups, and editors are not luxuries for the serious writer but essential parts of the process. Of course, feedback systems vary in form, style, and approach, but all are vital to the meaning-making process. Without the reader, meaning can't exist. In other words, meaning is co-created. The writer brings their world to the page, with all their history, influences, emotions, and ideas—and the reader brings theirs, with all their history, influences, emotions, and ideas. Neither dictates the meaning of the work alone; it is instead co-created between these two cognitive spaces. Meaning occupies a third space, wherein the writer's and reader's minds intersect. Where their worlds overlap, however briefly, is the meaning-making space. Our creative nonfiction, the artifact itself, does not resonate if left on a shelf unread. It's the old "If a tree falls in the forest and no one's there to hear it, does it make a sound" paradox, except in the case of art, if it doesn't "sound," then who cares? Visually, the meaning-making space might look like this:

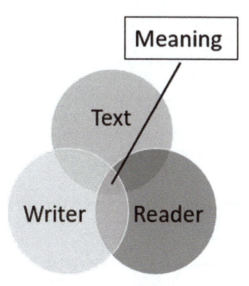

Figure 15.1 Space of Meaning-Making.

If meaning-making is our goal—and it should be—then we need to listen deeply to readers. Prior to publication, peers, writing group cohorts, mentors, and/or other readers serve as test subjects so that we can calibrate our creation to resonate as we intend.

Often, though, readers offer contradictory advice. It's hard to know whose advice to take, or why. Remember, our job is not to please everyone. Learning to be a writer is learning to live with ambiguity. The point of critique is to accelerate the revision process—to activate "re-visioning" by seeing our work from other perspectives. We write, as mentioned above, to connect. By hearing how our reader is connecting, or not, with our work, we better see it with some measure of objectivity. It forces us to relinquish sentimentality or possessiveness. After all, if our narrative is to function in the world, then it doesn't belong to us exclusively. It belongs to writer *and* reader. In this way, it's like any relationship. We have to take feedback and respond incisively and creatively—neither relinquishing nor priding our own point of view, but rather with a capacious heart, eager only to strengthen the bond between reader and writer.

Also, we can think of a pile of critiques as responses from various types of reader. One critique might be from a pragmatic reader. Another might be from reader who loves language. That third critique might be from a reader who focuses on the central question. That final critique might be from a reader who loves plot-driven work. Then we decide which critiques are most valuable to our process by considering our intended audience. For example, if we are not writing plot-driven work, we may not capitulate our revisions that way. On the other hand, perhaps this reader's feedback alerts us to a lack of tension that could be addressed in other ways.

Finally, if the workshop format allows it, it can be useful to let our readers know, before they read, our thoughts and intentions for the knot. Contrary to old and possibly outdated wisdom, providing workshop readers with some information about our intentions and goals helps readers make suggestions that align with our ambitions.

F: Other People's Processes (and What to Do about Them)

Other People's Processes are like Other People's Problems—we can listen and learn from them, but, ultimately, they don't belong to us. We must evaluate how we write and re-vision our work, but we can also try other people's strategies. If they work for some, they might work for us. But we all must find our own best practices. That might sound simple and reductive, but it's important. Too often, we bemoan our own creative process as "less than" or "not as good/productive/smart" as someone else's. But we shouldn't disparage ourselves for not fitting into some idealized fantasy of a successful writer. It's a craft, not an assembly line. But it's not just a craft, it's Sean's craft and Jess's craft and your craft, and we each have our own relationship to it.

Not all of us can write every day, for example, nor should we. Jess does most of her writing during summers and short, but focused, bursts during the rest of the year. As a professor, she's learned that she simply does not have the time or energy to teach and write consistently at the same time. There's another reason she works this way: she prefers it. She works best when all her creative and intellectual energy is channeled in one direction. She doesn't write as well when she's bouncing between teaching and writing duties or even between multiple projects. She likes to focus in on one project and go deep. Her process is echoed by writer Henry Miller: "Work on one thing at a time until finished."

Sean's process, on the other hand, is more scheduled. He wakes up early (*ungodly early*, Jess mutters) to write while his head is clear. He works best when he has multiple projects on his desk, letting each one influence the other. He fits into a camp of writers like Isabel Allende, who commands that writers "show up, show up, show up, and after a while the muse shows up, too." At least this was true until Sean had a baby girl who was also a terrible sleeper. So for the past three years, all while Sean was writing this textbook, he learned to be more like Jess, to realize that early mornings no longer work for him because his mind is hazy and his child is often awake during those ungodly hours, too. Plus, Sean realized he wanted to spend more time with his daughter and less time in front of a computer. So now he has a wildly new process. And, soon enough, his process will evolve again.

None of these approaches is "right." Each approach is right only for that writer during that phase of their life. But often it takes years to figure out and even once we figure it out, it's changing again because of life or work or age or any number of other reasons. If we don't yet know how we work best, try things out. We can take the advice of more experienced writers and see if it works for us. We can learn from their routines (or lack thereof) and try them all on. Ruth Stone, as detailed by Elizabeth Gilbert, waited for inspiration to strike. And when Stone did feel a poem coming, she had to "run like hell" to the house while being chased by it. "The whole deal was that she had to get to a piece of paper fast enough so that when it thundered through her, she could collect it and grab it on the page," Gilbert explains.

Few of us would recommend Hemingway's infamous (and possibly misattributed) quote that we "write drunk, edit sober," but in the spirit of open-mindedness, let's assume it works for a select few (and hopefully with minimal health consequences).

Writer Kurt Vonnegut, perhaps more helpfully, suggested that we "[write] to please just one person. If you open a window and make love to the world, so to speak, your story will get pneumonia."

More recently, attention-addled writers are turning to the Pomodoro Technique, which is basically interval training for writers. Write for twenty minutes, pause for five, write for twenty, pause for five. Repeat for four cycles before taking a longer break, say twenty minutes. The trick is that we must set a timer and abide by it no matter how well the writing is going. The cycling is said to focus and extend our concentration, and many writers swear by it.

Or we can use prompts. We can try out the "Prompts" at the end of most chapters. Websites like *The Writers' Chronicle* and *Poets and Writers* offer great suggestions, as well.

But maybe the key is to play. Be willing to try new strategies all the time. Stay open and alive to the world and our art. Form a hypothesis and then get dirty. Take Charles Darwin, for example, who went about his discoveries and theories as an artist might, or a child. When studying tortoises on the Galapagos, he was never content to simply observe. Instead, Darwin wanted to see what would happen if he sat on their backs and rode them like slow-moving horses. Or what if he picked one up by its tail and swung it in a circle? He asked questions. He got lost in the muck of the universe and came back with souvenirs.

Our job is no less important; no more serious than that.

However we go about it, consider that our process of creation will be as unique as the creations themselves.

III: PROMPTS

The following prompts will help put to practice the techniques learned in this chapter.

A: Visioning Your Knot of Meaning

Look at one of your unfinished pieces of creative nonfiction. Now write your central question in one or two sentences at the top of your draft. As you write and re-vision, keep reminding yourself of your summarized central question.

B: Visioning Your Knot of Meaning, Take II

Take a piece of creative nonfiction you've already written. Again, summarize your central question in one or two sentences. Now re-vision your creative nonfiction while constantly checking to see if what is on the page matches your summarized central question.

C: Re-Visioning Structure

Choose any creative nonfiction you've been struggling to re-vision. Now rather than revising just the text, focus on form. Consider new ways to re-form your creative nonfiction. Could you braid it? Could you use a found form? Could you use achronology or reverse chronology? And then consider how those new forms might match your central question.

D: Utilizing Feedback

Share a piece of creative nonfiction with your peers. Then collect their written responses. Now, examine those responses and begin to separate the responses into those that seem to work best for you and those that move your essay in another direction. Now consider why some of the feedback works better for your re-vision than other feedback.

Part 2

Anthology

1

Basement Story

Austin Bunn

A pitch black
volume of space.

I stagger through
the dark, some minor light.

The game
was called
Death.
　　　Seriously.

My twin brother
and I made it up.
When we were boys.
One of us
would rig up the basement
with all kinds of spooky shit:
creepy notes,
written in ketchup,
like "YOU WILL DIE SOON"
and "SATAN IS HUNGRY"
and the big kitchen knives
and beloved stuffed animals dangling in nooses—
like my brother's weirdly Jewish
plush dog named "Sam Brockamitz."—

Then, the other brother
would open the door
　　　you couldn't see anything
　　　you never knew
　　　what to expect
and you walked down
into the basement

with a single book of matches
  knives ketchup favorite things
  hurt, destroyed, ruined.

And
you went
through the dark
  very
     slowly
and
you were
afraid.
  (beat)
At the end
you were supposed to
die.
  interestingly.

        I die interestingly.

        SFX: A phone.

Two years ago,
in early morning
my mother calls me—
  Mom, mom
  Whoah. Whoah ....WHOAH.
  Do you know what time it is?
  I'll tell you what time it is, mom.
  It's darkness o'clock!

        I turn on a lamp.
        The stage, revealed.
     A series of floor lamps. A sheet
    covers a tower of bureau drawers,
      the height of a person

She tells me
she'd sold it.
She'd sold our house
  my childhood home.

The tremors from
the disease
made the stairs in the house, like,
impossible.

It was all too much space
to clean
to care about.
Our town has been changing a lot
anyway. New people, wealthy people.
I heard the realtor,
on her cellphone
—when she thought
no one was looking—
call our house,
"a tear down".
        A tear down.

And my mom asked me
to come home and
clear out the basement.
There were
some things down there
that she couldn't bare to see.

                                        I approach the sheet.
                                        It glows from within.

See ... the basement was the universe.
Dark and windowless and ours.
The beanbag, the TANDY computer
where I programmed my first videogame
"VIETNAM"
(which, no matter what, you lost automatically)
and second long-distance phone line
—remember those?—
and Mom's books,
her "missing" copies of *The Joy Of Sex* ...
Fear of Flying
and *The Naked Ape*
(which, actually has nothing to do with sex and was
really boring)
And let's not forget ...
the Death game

I should say:
Colin wanted to be there.
He lives in Chicago.

But he's not allowed.
He has trouble … adjusting.
He doesn't like to remember.
Who he was.
Or what he did.

> *I remove the sheet.*
> *Beneath: the drawers,*
> *spilling with cruft.*

I think we all have our basement stories.
The story below the story.
The person
beneath
the person.

> *SFX: camp sounds.*

It started in 8th grade.
Boy Scout Camp.
Also known as:
Hell In Shorts.
We both went.
And for two weeks
we watched the other kids
in our troop
light a camp fire
with hair spray.
                Whoosh!
And drop daddylong legs
on the skillet.
                Skskskskt!
                Sweeet!
"Pain Olympics."
They called it.
But Colin,
Colin was great.
Thrifty, reverent, wise.
Naturally,
everybody
hated him.
In the middle of the night,

while he slept.
the other boys took his cot
set it in the showers.
And turned on the cold water.

From the drawers:
Colin's Boy Scout shirt.
Soaking wet.

I just watched—
like I watched
the Pain Olympics.
and the comets of
fire that torched our
food—when
Colin woke up drowning.

I wring out his Boy Scout Shirt.

The next day,
when we came back
from
whittling
canoeing
whatever the hell
we did trying to grow ourselves up.
The tents of our troop
were all burned to the ground.
                    Whoosh.
Hairspray on plastic.
He learned it from them.

I place
the shirt
into my backpack.

"Sensory input disorder."
That was the diagnosis,
I think they made it up.
Not, say: revenge?
Mostly,
he was stray voltage.

I became his caretaker.
Like, his ambassador to the world
Like, you couldn't just touch him.
He had to touch you first.
Or he went haywire.

A tennis racquet, discovered.

Around this time
my mother
started dating again.
This was four years after the divorce.
And Angus came into our lives
Angus was this big time
American Studies professor
at Rutgers
And his entire field of research
was The Jersey Devil.
The Jersey Devil,
which was this winged goat
that took first born children
and flew them to Atlantic City.
        like the chupacabra
        meets Sinatra.
Angus looked like David Crosby
He had a moustache
and he *only* drank tea.
He wanted to teach us
tennis so badly
he *paid* us.

Racquet into the backpack.

I'm pretty good at tennis.
Thank you Angus.

And my mother
as you could imagine
fell in love.
One weekend
Angus had spent the night

in the morning,
he made us breakfast
with his dick
sticking out
of his pajamas.
—a thumb in
burned grass—
And Colin and I
just stared.
     (beat: the stare)
That afternoon,
Colin and I
we were in
the basement
listening
when he told
my mother
that he was in love
with two women at the same time
and maybe the other woman
marginally more than her,
It was complicated,
good complicated,
he wanted to explore
his feelings with this other woman
And we heard
our mother weep.

"I'm going to go make us
some tea," Angus said.

And Colin
went upstairs—
where Angus
ruffled his hair
like he knew who
the hell
we were—

and Colin
poured
the boiling water
into Angus's lap.

After that
After
the
uhm
[police]
He had a therapist
who made him keep
a diary
a tape diary

I discover tapes in the cruft.

SFX: the tape diary recordings.
"This is my diary.
And the first entry
will be about
hatred."

And he did.
Except.
See,
that's me.
That's my voice.
I kept it for him.
And nobody
knew
what he
was really
listening to.

SFX: The Sounds of Horror,
people burning alive
people buried
The tape goes into the backpack.

Which was this record
called "Sounds of Horror"
which had
people getting burned
people getting buried
terrible things

(until)
My mother came
into the basement
and found *The Joy of Sex*
and *Fear of Flying*
and this
map he'd made
on graph paper

                                                            The map.

of our school.
And all the Xs.
With names
next to them.
And, at the top,
"The Death Game"

                                          Map into the backpack.

My mother
fired the therapist
— I could stop
making the tapes, *finally* —
And she said,
Where are the pills?
And they said,
there are *pills* for him,
but there are *places* too.

I don't know
what makes the difference,
why
a person turns out one way
and another person
(spun into the world
at the same time)
turns out another.
My twin brother is an inch
taller than me.
He is a lot angrier
than me.

Everybody
lives above

their own cellar.
I share mine.

The night before
Colin left,
he came into my room
and said,
"I'm afraid."
         And I'd never heard him
         say that before.
So we lay on my bed
and I told him
the world
would be like
our game.
With all these traps.
And scary things that
put people put there
for you.
Maybe even
you put there
yourself.
You've just
got to walk through
the dark
         very
                  slowly.

I didn't know what I was
talking about.
I made him a tape
One I made walking around
our neighborhood,
pretending
I knew things
that I didn't.

                                   A discovery: the last tape.

And I found it
In the pile

in the basement.
He'd left it behind.

And now
I have it
with all the rest of his
things. With me.

                                        I zip up the backpack.

Recently,
a lawyer called me
Colin hurt somebody.
Again.
And now they want
his whole story
the evidence
against him.
I told them
it was all there
in the basement.

At 17 Walnut Street.

Except the new owners
went bankrupt
halfway-through
their *teardown*

So now,
there's just
a hole in the ground.

There's just a basement

open to the air.

And every last shadow
is gone.

                                        I run out.
                                        A lunge of light.

2

Women These Days

Amy Butcher

[Compiled and arranged by searching "woman + [verb]" (walking) in national news outlets over the past twelve months]

An Ohio woman was shot dead while cooking Thanksgiving dinner; witnesses report that at the time of the shooting, she was standing at a kitchen table, preparing macaroni and cheese. The body of a North Carolina woman was found in a shopping center parking lot at dawn. A Texas woman was grabbed from behind and attacked in a "bear hug" after finishing several laps at the Austin High School track. A California woman was found dead and stuffed in a trash bag on a sidewalk. A Pennsylvania woman was found dead in the suspect's grandmother's home. A Michigan woman was groped and urinated on while shopping in Kohl's; a breast cancer survivor who had recently undergone a double mastectomy and reconstructive surgery, she was shopping for new bras when Troy Police say the assailant attacked her, urinating on her back and into her incisions, which were still healing. An eighteen-year-old Pennsylvania teen was shot in the head several hours after her high school graduation by a white male while merging into traffic ten miles from her home and mine. A Michigan woman walked into a hospital and reported to nurses that she'd being sexually assaulted, beaten with brass knuckles, imprisoned for three days and transported to have sex with a man for money; the woman reported that she thought the man was a friend. Police would later describe hers as some of the worst bruising they'd ever seen.

A woman in her fifties was knocked to the ground, dragged into a field and raped in populated Rosental Park; during the assault, she was kicked and punched so hard in her face that she had to undergo emergency surgery, and police responded to the crime by telling a local newspaper that women should reduce their personal freedoms by jogging in pairs rather than assume they will be protected. A 63-year-old woman was found dead in her bedroom at 11 a.m.; police report her head was bashed in and her husband, who had bite marks on his hand, told a neighbor, "I know I'm going to jail." A 33-year-old woman was on her way to work when a man pushed her into oncoming traffic, sending her sprawling headfirst into the road as a bus was heading towards her; the driver, travelling at about 12mph, swerved at the last second, narrowly missing the victim's head as she lay inches from the bus' wheels. A woman out for a walk was forced into a car by a man with a Caribbean-sounding accent; he drove her to a secluded parking lot at gunpoint and then sexually assaulted her. A woman was thrown to the ground and kicked by two men in a parking lot. A twenty-two-year-old girl from my hometown was murdered by strangulation and blunt force trauma one week after transferring to Temple University; she was moved to three separate locations via Lyft first in a blue plastic storage container and then a duffel bag before police identified her attacker, a 29-year-old male who was later found cleaning blood from his apartment, his cousin later testified.

Police are still searching for the suspected rapist. Police are still searching for the suspected murderer. Police are still searching for the suspected assailants. The suspect is reported to be a tan, white male in his mid-50s with no facial hair. The suspect was last seen shirtless and in work boots with shorts. The suspect is between 25 and 35 and was wearing gray knee-length trousers and a blue-green chequered shirt. The suspect drives an older model small car that is dark green or maybe blue. The suspect denies ever seeing the victim before. The suspect denies being at the bridge at the time of her murder. The suspect alleges he was at the mall at the time of the shooting. The suspect denies being in the park that morning. The suspect reports he was grocery shopping at the time of the murder. The suspect remains at large. Police ask for anyone with information about the suspect to come forward.

I hate feminists, he says to me. The love of my life. *I hate that you count yourself among them. A bunch of angry women who hate men. You're hurting an entire gender.*

3

A Refuge for Jae-in Doe: Fugues in the Key of English Major

Seo-Young Chu

INVOCATION (Winter 2015-16)

It's evening in Queens, New York. Alone in my apartment, I'm grading student papers and drinking ginger tea. The phone rings. For some reason I forget to check the caller ID before answering, "Hello?"

A woman's voice: "Hi, Seo-Young?"

"Yes?"

"I'm calling from Stanford to ask about your experience while you were here."

(blank space)

The blank space above: a representation of my immediate response to the caller's words.

I almost can't believe that this is happening. Stanford is reaching out to me. Will Stanford apologize at last? That is all I have ever wanted: an apology.

My experience while I was at Stanford.

The story tumbles out. It's a story I have told numerous times already—to psychiatrists, to close friends, to myself, to lovers, to neurologists, to therapists. The story begins with my suicide attempt at age 21 and ends with

Stanford's own punishment of the professor in 2001: two years of suspension without pay. I describe the long horrible months of sexual harassment. I describe the rape—or the parts of it that I can bear to mention out loud. I add that I never pressed charges or received any money from either Stanford or the professor. All I did was tell someone else who told someone else who started the fact-finding investigation that resulted in his punishment. I have never sued the rapist, the department, or the school—despite the time I've lost and the fortune I've spent as a consequence of the harmful culture at Stanford that enabled the professor to injure me as well as others.

The monologue is disjointed and long. I hadn't been expecting this call. I haven't had time to prepare. And yet I've had too much time to prepare: nearly fifteen years.

There is a silence after I've finished speaking. I start to wonder if perhaps the caller has hung up on me. I start to worry she won't call back.

But she's still there. "That's ... awful," the woman is suddenly saying. "I'm so sorry. I'm just a Stanford undergrad. I was actually calling Stanford alumni for financial donations, to ask you for a gift of, but, I don't, I mean, in this case, for you ..."

Something is happening to my eyes. The room has begun at once to darken and to seem much too bright. Or is something happening to my mind? Bright like sunlight at noon in Northern California on a cloudless day. But I am in Queens, New York City. The year is not 2000. What time is it? How old am I? Something is happening to reality. A sickening gust spreads throughout my internal organs. The phone I hold is shaking. My hands and arms are shaking. I close my eyes. I imagine feathery bandages made of photons holding together the jigsaw of my body. The shaking subsides.

"No, I'm the one who's sorry," I manage to say, and I mean it. "Tell me about your studies."

"Sure," she says, and begins to talk with cheerful confidence about her major, which is not English but history. She's excited about her academic career. As I listen to her, I murmur vague, pleasant, encouraging utterances. I'm happy for her. She has a bright future. "You have a bright future," I say. We wish each other well. Somewhat awkwardly the dialogue ends.

For several moments I am dazed. Inexplicable giddiness has begun to seep into my head. I can hear air seeping into a balloon. The balloon is beige. The phone is warm in my hand. Most balloons are not beige. The gust of nausea rapidly gathers in my chest. I rush, half-stumbling, to the kitchen trash can.

I throw up.

DISCUSS THE FOLLOWING QUOTATION

"There's a great pleasure in teaching freshmen because you're sort of being folded into their lives at a particular, powerful moment in which you can make a difference," he said in the 1996 interview. "And to some degree, you can 'convert' them to English. It becomes a way of trawling for majors." (Source: Cynthia Haven, Stanford Report, August 17, 2007)

SOURCES AND ALLUSIONS

He found me in a place known as the Farm.
His field: to grow a special breed of harm.

His stock of antique furniture and dolls
And manuscripts he nurtured in his walls.

A culture of "American" indifference
To rape he tended with uncommon sense.

Exactly how I came to be a thing
For him to call his own is still a thing

I can't or won't remember. He misused
His powers to leave minds like mine abused.

Where others who preceded me fare now
I often wish yet do not wish to know.

Sometimes I dream that his rare book collection
Is made of all "his" women turned to fiction.

IS THIS AN EXAMPLE OF IRONY?
EXPLAIN YOUR ANSWER

I grew up pronouncing the word "women" the way my Korean parents did: the same way we pronounced the word "woman."

It was the professor—my rapist—who corrected my pronunciation of the word "women." Since then, every time I have uttered "women," I have remembered his voice.

It—his voice—it accompanies mine like an accent. "Women."

HERE, I FILLED OUT THE FORM

- Year of birth: 1978.
- Place of birth: Northern Virginia.
- First language: Korean. To this day I have dreams in which my young mother is holding me in her arms and whispering to me in achingly melodic strings of Korean syllables.
- Second language: English. When I started school, the teacher told my parents that if they wanted me to succeed in America they would have to communicate with me exclusively in English. From then on my mother and I were estranged. We spoke to each other in an English filled with gaps. It took me decades to recognize the sacrifice my mother made when she stopped speaking to me in our native tongue.
- Language spoken by parents to each other: fluent Korean. I grew up hearing marriage as a foreign language—literally and figuratively. I grew up hearing the sound of Korean as a language of Korean-bound han syndrome, disappointment, fury, resignation, the sense of being trapped forever, resentment, guilt. Every other word: a door slammed.
- Faith system(s): raised Roman Catholic by my mother and Confucian by my father. Currently agnostic.
- How parents met: Their marriage was arranged.
- Significant family trauma(s): the Korean War (which orphaned my father and made him watch his beloved elder brother die); my mother's sister's suicide when I was a child; being run over by a car as a child while waiting for the schoolbus; struggling as a Roman

Catholic teenager with my romantic feelings for a female classmate; being hospitalized during my senior year of college following my first suicide attempt; being raped soon after my first suicide attempt by a professor at Stanford University, where I was just starting a PhD program in English language and literature.

IS THIS AN EXAMPLE OF IRONY? EXPLAIN YOUR ANSWER

His interests included The Declaration of Independence. He wrote a book titled *Declaring Independence*.

SYMPATHY FOR JAMES COMEY. SUMMER 2017

He had called me at lunchtime that day and invited me to dinner that night, saying he was going to invite the whole cohort, but decided to have just me this time, with the whole cohort coming the next time. It was unclear from the conversation who else would be at the dinner, although I assumed there would be others.

It turned out to be just the two of us, seated at a small table in the middle of his favorite restaurant.

The professor began by asking me whether I wanted to stay on in the PhD program, which I found strange because he had already told me twice in earlier conversations that he hoped I would stay, and I had assured him that I intended to. He said that lots of people wanted to work with him and, given the academic pressure and job market, he would understand if I wanted to walk away.

My instincts told me that the one-on-one setting, and the pretense that this was our first discussion about my position, meant the dinner was, at least in part, an effort to have me beg to work with him and create some sort of intimate relationship. That concerned me greatly, given that I wanted to be his advisee.

I replied that I loved my work and intended to stay, write my dissertation, and receive my degree. And then, because the set-up made me uneasy, I added that I was not "interested" in the way people who are dating use that word, but he could always count on me to work hard and try my best to produce good scholarship.

A few moments later, the professor said, "But I'm lonely. I'm needy. I need to feel desirable. I need you to desire me."

I didn't move, speak, or change my facial expression in any way during the awkward silence that followed. I wanted to leave. Instead I froze.

The conversation then moved on, but he would return to the subject near the end of our dinner.

At one point, I tried to explain why it was so important that my personal life be independent of my professional career. I said it was a conundrum: Throughout history, some people in institutional positions of power (e.g. straight white male professors with tenure and endowed chairs, among other privileges) have decided that their positions authorize them to use less powerful people (e.g. 21-year-old first-year graduate students who happen to be female, mentally ill, and 1.5–2nd generation Korean American) in ways that make the powerful even more powerful (while putting the powerless in a risky situation). But the abuse of power can ultimately make the powerful weak by undermining public trust in institutions—including academic institutions—and their work.

Near the end of our dinner, the professor returned to the subject of my status as a student, saying he was very glad I wanted to stay, adding that he had heard great things about me from Professor X, Professor Y, and many others. He then said, "I need you." I replied, "You will always get work from me." He paused and then said, "That's what I want, work from you." I paused, and then said, "You will get that from me." It is possible we understood the phrase "work" differently, but I decided it wouldn't be productive to push it further. The term—"work"—had helped end a very awkward conversation and my explanations had made clear what he should expect.

INTERLUDE. During one of my episodes

Self: Dad?

Dad: Yes, Jennie?

Self: Did Stanford happen?

Dad: What do you mean?

Self: Was it real. The professor. Did all of that actually happen. To me.

Dad (after a pause and a sigh): Yes, it was real. It happened.

Self: Because I couldn't remember if I was remembering something that didn't happen. But it was real. You're not just saying so.

Dad: It happened. It was real.

Self (after a silence): Thanks Dad. I needed to know that.

FILL IN THE BLANK

Crime:
Punishment: suspension for two years without pay.

LECTURE, 2078

"Originally the sonnet was a site of sexual violence. Male poets were rewarded for celebrating the women they hunted. They used the sonnet form and an instrument called the 'blazon' to convert their prey into exquisite English artifacts. Our anthologies still include holograms of jewel-like eyes, porcelain skin, ruby lips, hair like gold, and so on."

Over time the white men themselves modified the sonnet to make it accommodate topics other than male heterosexual desire. The topics came to include blindness, time, spiders, God, the planets, applepicking, wine, prayer, computers, robots, politics, and the apocalypse. Now, in the year 2078, it is possible to choose existence in a world designed like a sonnet. It is possible to live one's entire life inside a sonnet. It is possible to become a sonnet.—But only if one has consented to such an existence.

DISCUSS THE FOLLOWING QUOTATION

In a 1996 News Service interview, [JF] described the 18th-century attitude toward belongings this way: "There was a sense that objects were preferred over people because they didn't leave you, they didn't talk back, and you could project a certain subjectivity and have an intense relationship with them, particularly with books," he said. (Source: Cynthia Haven, Stanford Report, August 17, 2007)

A LITTLE SONG AND A RECEIPT

Doe: a deer, a female deer—
Often chased by sonneteers of old.
Caught, and killed, and bathed in fear,
turned to human blazons to be sold—

Eyes—$twin models of the stars.
Skin—$fine tissue wrought from gold.
Lips—$your favorite kind of flower.
Sex—$a secret still untold/a Silk Road to unfold/a thing for you to mold/a
    source by you controlled.

Total: $—————.—

THE BLAZONAUT

Setting: an alternative universe where, due to the choreography of molecules here, to use words is to versify. Location: Southwest Canada (not far from where the Golden Gate Bridge is located in our reality). Time: a year named

"The Earliest Early Americanist" (corresponding roughly to our year 2000 AD). All residents of this universe hold the following truth to be self-evident: Each person has the right to free consent. Living by this truth is to them as breathing is to us. Rape, in this reality, is an alien phenomenon.

1. News

    "… she fell into the water from the sky …"

2. Jae-in Doe

    Decedent is an Asian female.
    Twenty-two she just had turned.
    The cause of death we cannot tell
    Despite the many things we've learned.

3. TOP SECRET

    My Doe-type can be difficult to track.
    Yet here I am, my voice-box playing back
    From lips hydrangea-lavender in hue
    His thoughts during our first few interviews.

    The hair is shoulder-length, the color black.
    The height and weight suggest she won't fight back.
    The fingernails are unadorned and short.
    The eyes are brown; no makeup do they sport.
    The skin appears unpierced and untattooed,

    Yet scars of ruby-pearl seem to protrude
    Like self-inflicted jewelry on each arm
    And wrist—which means she's vulnerable to harm.
    The language of her flesh, as I assess her,
    Reveals Confucian worship of professors.

    Her deference Korean gives me right
    To use her innocence for my delight.

4. The Coroner's Soliloquy

    The species: neither robot nor a xenomorph but both.
    A blazonaut I call her as I scan her for the truth.

Throughout her brain dimensions grew like flowers wild
And han flowed through her circuits like fog-weather mild

until the onslaught
caused a drought.

The genitals, the soul, the lymph, the spine, the nape,
Show evidence of _____
For which we have no name.

I can't do this anymore.

DISCUSS THE FOLLOWING QUOTATION

You can keep nothing safe from our eyes and ears. This is your own history. We are your most perilous and dutiful brethren, the song of our hearts at once furious and sad. For only you could grant me these lyrical modes. I call them back to you. Here is the sole talent I ever dared nurture. Here is all of my American education. (The Korean American narrator of *Native Speaker* by Chang-rae Lee)

MUTANT BLAZON

My rapist's eyes remind me of the sun.
To look at them will mean that I go blind.
His mouth beside my ear—they form a gun.
Each breath: a bullet targeting my mind.

My rapist's eyes remind me of the sun.
His throat: a fist to silence mine designed.
His reason: a ventriloquist's illusion.
No tenor in the end could hearing find.

My rapist's eyes remind me of the sun—
Too close for any vessel with a mind.

Survive or get to die—that is the question.
No longer have I any will to mind.

My rapist's eyes remind me of the sun—
Not dead, not living, neither keen nor blind;
A daily haunting; memory rebegun;
Disaster in some future undivined.

I write, rewrite, a "sonnet" about rape
To hunt that voice I wish I could escape.

DISCUSS THE FOLLOWING QUOTATION (without using the words "predator" or "prey")

There she beholding me with milder look,
Sought not to fly, but fearless still did bide:
Till I in hand her yet half trembling took,
And with her own goodwill her firmly tied.
Strange thing, me seem'd, to see a beast so wild,
So goodly won, with her own will beguil'd.

—From Edmund Spenser's poem "Like As A Huntsman" (Sonnet 67 of his 1595
   sonnet cycle AMORETTI)

DISCUSS THE FOLLOWING QUOTATION (without using the words "predator" or "prey")

"Yeah that's her in the gold. I better use some Tic Tacs just in case I start kissing her. You know, I'm automatically attracted to beautiful … I just start kissing them. It's like a magnet. Just kiss. I don't even wait. And when you're a star they let you do it. You can do anything. […] Grab them by the pussy. You can do anything." —The 45th President of the United States of America

COMPLETE THE FOLLOWING DIALOGUE

Professor: All men have rape fantasies, including your father.
Student:

A KIND of CENSUS

- Number of spouses: zero.
- Number of children: zero.
- Longest stretch of time spent alone inside the apartment: eighteen consecutive days.
- Longest stretch of time post-rape without any physical intimacy with another mammal: seven consecutive years.
- Number of episodes of Law and Order: Special Victims Unit never seen: zero.
- Year I watched SVU for the first time: 2011.
- Year SVU started: 1999.
- Number of fantasies about cathartic dialogues with Olivia Benson: countless.
- Number of years spent closeted to most people about what happened at Stanford: fifteen.

July 5, 2016. Facebook entry posted shortly after I came out as a rape survivor

Q: Do you think being raped made you gay?
A: Several people have asked me this question (or a version of it). It is a question worth addressing.

(1) I cannot speak for others who have been raped. I can only speak to my own situation. Please do not mistake anything I write here for a generalization. (2) The first crush I remember having: Ellen Degeneres. At the time I didn't know who she was (I caught a glimpse of her on TV); I didn't know what it meant to be gay; I didn't know what I felt was a crush. All I knew was that she made my heart feel nervous and I wanted to see

her face again. (3) My parents had an arranged marriage. The arrangement was less than ideal. They spoke to (argued with) each other in Korean—a language that my brother and I did not understand—and they spoke to us in (broken-ish) English. To this day I think of marriage as literally a foreign language. (4) My mother was (is) devoutly Catholic. As a child I myself was devoutly Catholic and confused about my sexuality. The last time I went to confession (I was a teenager) I confessed I thought I might be gay and also I wasn't sure if God existed. The priest said he could not forgive me but he could give me holy water for me to keep by my bed to repel Satan. (5) My first sexual experience was being raped at the age of 22 by someone who wielded power over me, who controlled my future, and who was fully aware that I was sexually inexperienced and confused about my sexuality. (6) I spent much of my twenties in relationships that allowed me to pretend (or try to pretend) that Stanford never happened. Does it matter that a few relationships were with men and that a few were with women? I honestly don't know. (7) My last relationship ended a decade ago. Since then my personal life has resembled a desert ruled by agoraphobia and the wish to destroy my capacity to feel attraction. (8) I have been attracted to people of all sexes and gender identities. (9) As the details above are meant to suggest, my sexuality is extremely complicated. Did being raped make me gay? No. (See item 2.) But it is a fact that rape (among many other factors, including those mentioned above) had an impact on how I experience desire and act (or hesitate to act) upon my feelings. Indeed it may be the case that "rape survivor" is one of my sexual orientations. *I would not wish this joyless and often agonizing orientation on anybody.* (10) Again I stress that I speak only for myself. I doubt it is possible to generalize that rape makes people gay (or straight). Different individuals survive violence in different ways. Some of us end up not surviving. Some of us are working on just holding on. I hope that my answer has been educational.

"Noli me tangere": A Kind of Villanelle

His ghost stands watching me while I'm asleep.
I know that this cannot be real because
I'm wide awake. I never fall asleep.

The hours between twelve and twelve still keep
Me up reciting poetry because
His ghost stands watching me while I'm asleep.

I close my eyes, imagine rivers deep
And soft plush turquoise emerald velvet moss.
I hide myself here as a pebble heap.

What if I dared to sea from cliff to leap?
My absence from the world would be no loss.
His ghost stands watching me while I'm asleep.

When finally I die, will I escape
His ghost's attention? Or will those glib jaws
Assault my ghost with secrets fresh to keep?

I don't know if I wake or if I sleep
Or why my speech obeys poetic laws.
His ghost stands watching me while I'm asleep.
Perhaps he's dreamt a way my soul to reap, to reap, to reap.

PALO ALTO DISAPPEARANCE

A yard, once used for some kind of sport, lies seemingly deserted. High above her, in a near-future sky, one allosaurus and one magpie, each the size of a skyscraper, battle for extinction. Crowds of invisible spectators flow toward the spectacle. At some point, when the rumors grow too poisonous, she turns around, against the tide, and starts to climb a secret staircase made out of wisteria, the stems of which twine counterclockwise. The more she climbs, more and more flowers surround her. Blossoms thicken. Petals seep into her hair. Her skin becomes liquid petal.

"Anyone is inside your house," the flowers whisper.

"I don't have a body," she responds.

By now she is no longer climbing a staircase. The staircase has disappeared and so has she.

In the distance another mythical creature falls and another endangered animal cannot hear its own appalling song. Where games of sport once took place, palm trees begin to shimmer, dazzle, daze. She is beyond the last thought at the end of the mind.

Obviously this is not reality.

This was one way I got through it.

TERRIFIED VAGUE PRONOUNS

As he, to have her, turned into a swan,
So she, to bear it, turned him to a swan.
I often wonder which was worse: the swan
She conjured, or the man inside the swan.
I often wonder which came first: the swan
Whose "blow" (Yeats wrote) was "sudden," or the swan
Whose "sudden blow" was made of piecemeal swan-
Like men in motion slow: from man to swan.

The things that one man did engendered here
A broken mind, the pills within an hour
That should have left me dead. Being caught up,
Accustomed to the comfort of his chair,
Could he possess the knowledge or the power
To see that each from different heights would drop?

AFTER EMILY DOE. JUNE 2016

One image that's been invading my mind lately: a mugshot that was never taken. It was never taken because I never pressed charges. I didn't think to press charges.
He's no longer alive. He was my adviser at Stanford. He was a tenured professor, a "big name" in academia. I was a first-year Ph.D. student, 21 years old and stupidly naive. I had also recently been hospitalized after a suicide attempt. I had just been diagnosed as bipolar.

"Your mom and I should have—we didn't know how to prepare you—" my dad said yesterday while we were brokenly discussing the Stanford assault case that has been in the news recently.

To which I could only say, "I'm sorry, I'm sorry you have a daughter who made you go through so much trauma in addition to the Korean War and everything … "

We apologize to each other, my father and I. The Stanford professor refused to apologize to me.

I know I should forgive him. It wasn't his fault.

When he asked me if I was a virgin, I told him the truth: yes. (I should have said: It is none of your business.)

When he told me that he controlled my future, I let myself believe I had no future worth imagining. (I should have been brave and stood up to him.)

I still wake up sometimes to find my clothes drenched in sweat and my body numb, literally numb.

In my head the mugshot is blurry. I scarcely remember what he looked like. I can't bring myself to google his name.

Parents: you do not want your children to end up like me. If your child is assaulted, try to get professional help for your child immediately and be sure to follow through. This may be challenging if you are an immigrant who is exceedingly shy, less than fluent in English, financially struggling, Roman Catholic, and/or incapable of saying the word "rape." But assault can be devastating and the impact permanent if not addressed right away and adequately.

THE NEW MILLENNIUM (after Shelley's "Ozymandias")

I meet a stranger in a house of gloom
Appointed with archaic chairs and shelves
Made centuries ago ... The stranger's doom
Is my fate too, for that which makes my self
not hers is time alone. Inside that room
She cannot see me but I see her dread,
Her shattered face—Something I know is wrong.
Her body language speaks as though it's dead.
If minds could text, in hers this would appear:
"Your name is Jennie. My name is Seo-Young.
Let me, your future self, bear your despair."

Now that I'm home, I'm drowning in decay,
Pill bottles, trash, her burden mine to bear.
Why did I—she—choose to survive this way?

SEX AFTER STANFORD

One of the side effects (for me at least) of being violated: every time I feel desire, attraction, or any evidence of a libido, I automatically feel guilty. I feel an obligation to cancel my body, delete, to make it disappear.

The "logic": I have a libido; therefore I could not have been raped. The truth: I did not want to be trapped in his house full of horrible shadows and statues.

FASCICULUS

Where two thighs meet—a Vertex glows—
My "Sex"—a Bomb or Missile—
Remembrance Now—the Weapon grows—
Turned—inward—at—my—Will—

As Hunters—carcass—make their Prey—
A "Special" "Victim"—I*—
To excavate—Preempt decay—
Extract—from sense of Time—

* Variant: I'm

TO BE ON THE MARKET DURING HIS FESTIVAL

The professor, at once bragging and threatening, had often told my younger self that he controlled my future, my livelihood, my *worth.* (I still ask myself sometimes: "Is my future 'worth' living?")

Being on the job market became a continuously fraught performance. The most excruciating theater took place where no one else could see it: my brain. Denial was a circus act. I don't know how the circus animals survived the mistreatment.

In preparing for the long stressful winters of phone calls and emails and MLA hotel rooms and campus visits and "professional" attire (my rapist liked to talk about grooming me, as if I were a pet—I remember how furious his reaction would be whenever I chose to wear glasses, look frumpy, or let lint appear on my clothing), I should have done this:

I should have worked through the bad memories. I should have worked through the feelings of disgust, self-loathing, humiliation, fear, despair, and hopelessness.

Instead I let the feelings and memories choreograph my actions. I punished my psyche for remembering details about JF. I punished my flesh for what JF did to it.

PSYCHOMACHIA

- We wish we had selected our
  Society with much more care.

- The problem is you've shut the door,
  Available to life no more.

- But she can't risk or bear the chance
  Of misconstruing some advance—

- What if his cultured ways to me
  He gave, rape culture a disease?

- I never understood this world.
  I still don't understand this world.

REMINDER

And yet he could be vulnerable—alarmingly so. Once, in his house, during a meeting to discuss his course (for which I was a teaching assistant), he began to sob violently. No one else was there. I was sitting at one end of a couch. He sat next to me and—before I could do anything—weighted down my lap with his head. "I miss my mother," he cried over and over again on my lap.

I was rigid. I was rigid with an emotion for which I still have no name. I don't remember how I got myself out of the situation.

Did part of myself get left behind—? Is that why I can't remember?

SOMETIMES I SCREAMED

A Special Victim said to me
In Space there is no Rape—
A Special Victim heard from me
In Space there is no Hope—

There is no thing with Feathers, here—
No tune without the words—
Nobody can exist out here—
I'm nothing—Who you were—

CONTUSIONS, RECENT

Whenever I felt the horrible urge to "pleasure" myself, I would often succumb—but not without using a hammer afterwards to punish my flesh with such ferocity that the pain made me pass out.

There were times in my life when my skin ran out of places that were not purple, turquoise, blue, or red.

The alternative to battering my flesh: letting the intrusive ghost of my rapist happily watch me surrender to my libido.

INSTRUCTIONS LEFT INCOMPLETE (After Donne's Holy Sonnet)

Gather our parts, united self, though you
Do not exist quite yet enough to send
Your futuristic wholeness from the end
Of lyric time to where we wait for you.
Make us consent to sentience anew.
Revive our will until there is no end
But endless means by which we all transcend
The paradox you already outgrew.
Believe the story that free will is free.
By then you'll have put on the suit of "me"
As if it were composed of empathy,
A fabric of compatibility.
It's your turn "to be" now. Now you are me.
Please sign your name here if you _____.

WHICH OF THE FOLLOWING STATEMENTS IS TRUE?

(A) Someone says, "I am lying right now."
(B) Someone says, "Rape me."
(C) Someone says, "I never consented to this alien experiment called 'existence.'"
(D) Someone says, "No means yes."
(E) Someone says, "At least you didn't die."
(F) Someone says, "Why can't you just get over it?"
(G) Someone says, "What you went through is a first-world problem."
(H) Someone says, "What about the Earth and climate change? You have to put rape in perspective."
(I) Someone says, "But you seem okay."
(J) Someone says, "I can't believe how widespread this problem is."
(K) Someone says, "Let me rape you."
(L) Someone says, "Let go."
(M) Someone says, "Am I the only one who can hear all of these voices."

ON THE IMPORTANCE OF NAMING

"When you use the word 'rape' to describe what happened to you—can you use a more subtle expression? Something more elegant? You are an English language expert, Jennie, so I trust you must know how to discuss what happened without using that word. There must be a more decent, less ugly way of saying it. I am sure you know of such a way. Jennie? Are you upset? Why are you crying? Did I say something wrong? Jennie, say something. Please, I'm sorry. Jennie, what did I do."

CLEAR THOUGHTS IN A CLEAR SHADE (After Marvell's "The Garden")

To vanquish all my memories' blight
I swallow dots that promise light.
Ellipses of unconsciousness
Unknow me into happiness.
What science fiction is this space
Where time is just another place?
No apples drop about my head
Yet "apples" I can "taste" instead.
Such luscious freedom from the past
Is pleasure after pain has passed.
Once human life I finally shake
A shape past human I will take.
Were I a Daphne turned to tree
I'd pray for flames to set me free.
Tillandsia I'd rather be,
A lock of air, the dew my key.

Yet still I live, an idiot,
A shadow that can strut and fret.
Why human form? Why woman form?
Collapse me into formlessness
Until existence nonsense is:
The sonic and the furious,
A nothing of significance;
—An alien of consciousness;
A spacetime of unconsciousness.

RESURRECTION LULLABY
(After Milton)

When one considers how one's life is spent,
Each resurrected self another hide
Less human than the one that last had died,
One's brain a frozen bruise that can't consent
To heal after the violence he meant,
His afterlife itself slow homicide,
"Please let my will complete the suicide,"
One prays. But other voices, to relent
That prayer, interrupt, "One did not need
Apology, redress, or an arrest
To live as though his punishment were great.
Survival was enough to fill the need
Required by existence of each guest.
Your prayer's heard. Now fall asleep and wait."

DREAM

Outside: a Farm. Inside: a dimly lit living room. A constellation of antique furniture. A couch. A young woman, my height, we're standing in the room looking at each other, no one else is in the room, she looks like me but her hair is longer and her cheeks are fuller and the scars on her arms are still visible. I notice them because she's gesturing. She's pointing at the couch. "That's where I die," she says. "That's where you must take my place. There is no other way. I have no future worth living."

I used to hate these dreams. I'm learning to live with them. They're like the dreams I have of North Korea. They're like the dreams I have of life after death.

The next time I see her I will say:

Forgive yourself for having been naive.
You've dwelled here for too long. It's time to leave.

DISCUSS THE FOLLOWING QUOTATION

We hold these truths to be self-evident, that all men are created equal, that they are endowed by their Creator with certain unalienable Rights, that among these are Life, Liberty and the pursuit of Happiness.

THE GRADUATE MENTORING AWARD. NOTE: THE AWARD WAS RENAMED IN AUGUST, SOON AFTER THE LETTER WAS SENT

To: June 2016
Executive Director
American Society for _____

Dear Professor _____,

Recently I learned that there is a graduate mentoring award named after (I'm just going to force myself to spell out his name) Jay Fliegelman.

This man was supposed to be my dissertation adviser. I say "supposed to be" because he spent more time sexually harassing and stalking me than he did advising me academically. Instead of discussing ideas, scholarship, or projects, he "mentored" me with insights such as "All men have rape fantasies, including your father." (That is a line I will never forget.) He left me voice messages about overdosing on male enhancement pills. He shared explicit fantasies with me—despite my protests. He violated my flesh, my psyche, my sense of bodily integrity—despite knowing that I was *unwilling,* despite knowing that I was a virgin, despite knowing that I was incapacitated by mental illness. He must have known, too, that I was under the influence of his institutional power. I was new to Stanford, new to California, new to the profession. He had been in the profession and at Stanford for decades. Indeed, his own mentors and former dissertation advisers were still teaching and advising in the Stanford English department when I arrived as a 21-year-old first-year Ph.D. student. Only from this temporal distance can I see so clearly his power and my powerlessness.

For years I have struggled to be a model survivor. I wouldn't want to get Stanford into trouble, right? I should show how grateful and uncomplaining I am—after all, Stanford punished the professor by suspending him for two years without pay, right? Stanford, too, has remained silent about the case. There is no public record of what happened.—Not even a concise announcement describing the nature of Jay Fliegelman's misconduct and punishment. (Does Stanford not understand that in the absence of clear communication, rumors and misinformation have a tendency to grow?)

In the past few weeks I've learned that the years of silence surrounding Jay Fliegelman's misconduct and punishment have had a number of consequences that are regrettable. One of these consequences: the creation of the award mentioned above. This graduate mentoring award is named after a man who abused his power, who refused to apologize for raping his student, who screamed at and terrified his student, who dropped by his student's dorm unannounced causing the student to hide in her closet in the dark wondering "How long do I have to stay here? Is he gone yet?"—whose ghost continues to haunt his student to this day.

I have worked hard to forgive Professor Fliegelman. I realize he was human and complex. I am sure he was a good mentor to many students. I admire the loyalty and gratitude that former students of Jay Fliegelman have demonstrated by creating this award. I do not know if they are or were aware of what he did to me. Perhaps they were unaware of the extent to which Professor Fliegelman caused damage. In any case, if any former students are reading this: Now you know.

I understand the "Jayfest." I have no objection to naming his collection of books "the Fliegelman Library." But what hit me in the solar plexus and made—makes— me feel sick: seeing the website for the Jay Fliegelman award for *graduate mentorship* (seeing the "mugshots" of professors honored for mentoring students the way Jay Fliegelman mentored his students) and recognizing one of my graduate professors from a non-Stanford university—a professor who has been nothing but professional and kind to me. "Are these awards given to advisers who sexually harass and rape their students?" I wondered —"and if so what did Professor X do to deserve such an obscene award?"

The thought now strikes me as absurd. But it is no more absurd than the existence of an award for graduate mentoring named in honor of a man whose "mentoring" included threats, controlling behavior, objectification of a student's body, and sexual violence. Surely there are better examples in whose honor this award might be renamed.

If you are one of Jay Fliegelman's former students who had an experience worth celebrating: I believe you. You need not provide documentation to persuade me. I believe that, in your experience, he was a wonderful mentor. Is it too much for me to ask you to believe me too?

Thank you for your time and consideration.

Seo-Young Chu

January 2017. Why I Am Joining the March

In an ideal world, my body and mind together would join the march—in person, in public, in visible protest.

In an ideal world, my flesh would freely will itself outside and onto the streets to demonstrate out loud against the inauguration of a man whose irresponsible and casual expressions of entitlement and violence have amplified the trauma (the injury, the bleeding wound) of rape culture.

In an ideal world, the president of the United States of America would not be so eerily reminiscent of a specific nightmare from my own personal past: a man in a position of power who sexually harassed and violated me seventeen years ago, a man whose ghost lives on in this Yellow-Haired-Man-In-Ultimate-Position-Of-Power.

In an ideal world, the pain that I am experiencing right now would not exceed the sum of the medical conditions with which I have been diagnosed (including post-traumatic stress, bipolar depression, spinal herniation, fibromyalgia, anxiety, and chronic migraines).

In an ideal world, there would be female as well as male U.S. presidents.

Yet I believe in the reality of ideal worlds. They can be articulated. They can be drawn. They can be painted. They can be diagrammed. They can be meditated. They can be realized.

EPILOGUE

I am one of the lucky ones.

4

Leave Marks

Melissa Febos

We first made love in a hotel room in Santa Fe, where the five o'clock sun simmered on the horizon, grazing her shoulders with its fire as she knelt over my body. I watched her mouth open on my hipbone and leave a wet print that shone in the light as she looked up at me.

I had never been a lover who watched, but I watched her—hands tucked under my back as she bit my ribs, my belly, my breast. As her fingers slid inside me, her mouth latched onto my chest—the blank space just below my clavicle. I stopped watching then, stopped thinking of anything but the drive of her long fingers—how they filled me even as her mouth pulled, unraveling.

After, in the bathroom mirror, flushed and swollen, I leaned in and examined the purple splotch shaped like Rorschach's *card VI*, the most condensed inkblot of his ten. It is known as "the sex card."

It's embarrassing, I said, after I'd climbed back onto the bed beside her. *But I love hickeys.*

She laughed and slid her hand down my chest, pressed the mark like a button with her fingertip. *You are wild.*

It'll fade by Monday. I smiled. My pleasure notwithstanding, to arrive on the college campus where I taught emblazoned with love bites was unthinkable. Even as defiant teenagers, we massaged them with frozen spoons, scrubbed them with dry toothbrushes, held icepacks to our necks as if to cool our racing pulses.

I'm writing an essay about hickeys, I told a friend. *Ew,* she said and crumpled her face. Curious, I thought. We don't blink at sex as commerce—women's bodies propped across billboards and television screens, the familiar iconography of male lust. We coo at pregnant bellies, sanctify that most blatant acknowledgement of sex, but shame this ephemeral evidence. A hickey is personal. It offers nothing to its witness but recognition. Is our puritan history so strong in us that to acknowledge touch for pleasure's sake is vulgar? Maybe the hickey reveals other things, parts of our desire we'd rather not see in the light.

One family vacation when I was eight, I played in the pool with a halved rubber ball. Turned inside out, it would fling into the air with a satisfying *pop*. Somehow, I managed to suction this apparatus to the center of my forehead.

Look! I crowed to my poolside parents. And then, *Ow!* when it popped off of my face and splashed into the water. I rubbed my stinging forehead. When I looked up, my parents dissolved in laughter.

Oh, honey, my mother grinned. *Look what you did.* The rubber hemisphere had left a circular crimson bruise in the center of my forehead.

You've got a hickey on your face, said my dad. *What's a hickey?* I asked.

I gaped at their answer, incredulous. *Why would anyone want to do that?* But later, in the hotel bathroom, when I looked in the mirror, I touched the dark mark so gently, leaned in to see it closer in repulsion, in wonder.

At ten, I discovered my neck. It felt like a secret my body had finally told me. A first drink, a light switch, a doorway where a wall had always been. Tracey Barren's mouth tore a hole in the hull between my shoulder and jaw, and water rushed in. That pleasure was a revelation: If this, then what? After baseball practice, on a stray couch cushion in my basement, under an old beach towel, Tracey and I played "Date." She was always the boy. Her mouth on my neck. The sounds of my mother starting dinner upstairs. *Don't stop*, I said, for the first time.

From the start, my last love had edges, the kind I can't help but touch— run my fingers along the jagged parts until they cut. For the first year of our relationship, my lover lived with another woman. She lived 2,500 miles away. When I saw her, after weeks of wondering, I was so hungry. I was angry. I was vibrating with fear. My mouth itched to close on her. As if that could make her stay.

Tenderness toward the object of our desire becomes an expression of love partly, I think, because it so defies the nature of want, whose instinct is often less to cuddle than to crush. My want was more gnash than kiss, more eat than embrace. I cared for my lover, but that kind of desire precludes many kinds of love. Hunger is selfish. I wanted her happiness. I also wanted to unzip my body and pull her into it, or crawl into hers. It is no accident that we go to the pulse. Lust is an urge to consume and perhaps there is no true expression of it that does not imply destruction. I can't say. But even my tenderness for kittens includes an impulse to put them in my mouth.

The sound of sucking means many things and all of them are synonymous with hunger. It is no wonder, our obsession with vampires, werewolves, flesh-eating zombies. Lust is also a desire to *be* consumed. The vampire's victim is arched in terrified ecstasy. We agree on this fantasy by the billion: devour us, leave us no choice but to surrender. Under my mouth, my beloved squirmed. Her hips rose, shoulders clenched, body resisted and yielded at once. The vampire is all measure and seduction until he tastes and loses control in the ravening.

One day, she held up a photograph in a magazine: a red fox, pointed face, yellow eyes embering.

Look, she said. *Like you. So little, so pretty, and so wild.*

Under this light I both preened and cringed. Like the bite marks on her neck, it revealed the animal in me who so often won.

Like no lover before her, she had seen these parts of me. Maybe she brought them out—how I get too hungry, eat too fast, chew with my mouth open. Jealousy heaves my chest and heats my hands, which sweat so often, those swift conductors of all feeling—both emotive and environmental. My teeth chatter easily though in sleep my temperature soars, a furnace metabolizing all the day's suppressed impulses. I felt embarrassed on the mornings we both woke smelling of my metallic sweat, as if I had revealed some grotesque secret.

My body has always given me away. Or maybe it's the other way around.

There is charisma in wildness and it was part of what drew her to me. How much I felt and how fast I moved. But so often the things that attract us are the things we grow to fear most. The things we want to change or control or keep only for ourselves. She began to instruct me. *Speak more softly,* she said. *Don't let them stand so close to you. You are mine,* she said, and oh, how I wanted to be hers. The opportunity to prove myself compelled me. It was not the first time.

Amelia, my best friend in fifth grade, must have been queer. Now, it's easy to armchair-diagnose her, to see how she fit my future type: razor-smart, broody with repressed anger, funny as fuck. Back then, I only knew the curious mix of fear and affection I felt for her. Like many vulnerable people, she defended herself with violence. "Indian sunburns," pinches, and monkey bites—in which she clamped my skin between her knuckles and twisted—Amelia flowered my thighs and arms with bruises. Every time she moved, I inched. It didn't stop me from spending every weekend at her house, though. That would have broken her heart.

I could see her tenderness, her lack of control, the fear that drove her to hurt me, and I could take the pain. It felt like a responsibility. It felt like a way to love her. Though it wasn't only for her.

I am a woman who likes to be marked and to mark. And I did then, too. There was a satisfaction in those bruises, in being the object of her reaching, in withstanding it. Sometimes, at eleven years old, I felt invisible, like a ghost haunting my own life. And the marks she made on me were a kind of proof. Like the ghost detected by glass she holds or the reflection in a mirror, Amelia's marks made me real. So many ways of being are intangible, can be explained away. Physical evidence is the easiest accounted. The things that mark us are the things that make us.

It isn't just me. Attachment and availability have been inscribed on human bodies for centuries, across continents. The Mursi people of Ethiopia insert lip plates in their girls as preparation for marriage, while the Kayopo of the Amazon use scarification and body painting. Contemporary North Americans are no exception; as we love to jab our flag into the earth, we brand our cattle, we mark our beloveds with bruises, babies, scars, disease, lipstick, and diamond rings.

My hickeys, too, are not simply an expression of desire, but also of ownership. During that first year, when my beloved lived with another woman, near the end of our visits I would buckshot her neck, shoulders, and chest with hickeys. At least for the duration of those bruises, I could claim her body mine alone. I have always wanted to carve my name into the things I am afraid of losing. Perhaps the desire to leave marks is more honestly a desire not to be left.

And as much as we like to own, we also like to be owned in love. Or at least, to belong to someone. I am a feminist, and the desire to be possessed is one I have been reluctant to admit. I may not want to flash a diamond ring or replace my name with someone else's, but the mark of her mouth on me meant something similar—if not owned, then wanted. And who does not want to be wanted?

I developed early. By the time most of my classmates reached puberty, I was already a C-cup. As a result, my first kisses provoked a reaction that my less-developed peers did not suffer. Today we call it "slut shaming." And it happened to me before I even had a chance to be promiscuous.

Much as we worship them, we also like to punish promiscuous women— or those whose sexuality is simply too evident. Sex is a slippery currency in a sexist society; access to my body worked in those boys' favor but against mine.

For a year I suffered sneers and crude gestures in the junior high school cafeteria. Prank calls to my family's home announced my sullied reputation. More than once I was groped in the school hallways. I absorbed that punishment without scrutiny and the shame of both my desires and my body was not easily unlearned. My brazenness as an adult who is unafraid to bear the evidence of her sex is partly restitution for those years.

There are other reasons why love bites are the domain of teenagers. For one, amateurism—the first hickey is often a mistake, and one that many never make again. In repeat offenses, there enters an element of braggadocio. The guy who breaks the bed and mistakes it for the best sex ever. *Look at us*, the splotch-necked teens gloat, *we are wild, we have sex*. Despite its glorification, sex is most novel to its initiates. The hickeyed teens are broadcasting old news to the rest of us—their entry into a club whose membership is public.

But my lover and I shared that novelty. While she lived with that other woman, and during the slow process of their separation, our public appearance as a couple was limited. I'd never had to hide my affections as an adult and that invisibility, however sensible, stung. I hated feeling like a secret and it spurred many fights between us. But much experience— not least mine as a former professional dominatrix—has taught me that restriction is the quickest route to fetishization.

After we were free to expose our desire, we did so with intention, in compensation for that year of hiding. I gave readings with my neck tattooed by her mouth. We posted pictures online of our bare midriffs pressed together. I'd never been so public a couple, and I wore it the way I had rainbow "freedom rings" as a teenager—giddy with visibility.

I read now about adolescents sucking on more obvious parts of each other in group activities that seem to preclude the secrecy and innocence of my own unsayable awakening. I don't so much mourn their lost childhoods. I lost mine at first opportunity and sex isn't the only way to do that. But I do remember the vacancy of those earliest and most obvious sex acts. I met desire under that faded beach towel, to the sound of cleats knocking the cement basement floor. What I mean is, the neck is always innocent. The parts of us we cannot see are touched most deeply, are most needing to be seen.

However insistent or ravenous the hickey, it is by nature temporary. There was a time when my beloved and I considered getting matching tattoos on our ring fingers. We spent hours laboring over meaningful designs. For months I made appointments that she canceled at the last minute. She resisted that permanent mark for the same reason that I wanted it. Despite our mutual obsession, we did not trust each other.

Another year later, she revived the idea. As we drove past desert tattoo shops, she'd point. *Let's do it*, she'd say. *Why not?*

I'd nod, but never pull over. I had already stopped believing in the power of such symbols to make anything permanent. I had already stopped wearing her hickeys.

They say that passion wanes, that trust grows in its place. But after two years together, she and I still grabbed at each other like animals, like people who might never taste that particular salt again. Our passion never guttered. I kept waiting for trust to grow. The only thing to count on was our hunger, and the ways our bodies fed it. No mark of passion can make a love stay. It can only prove that it was.

I know the impossibility of the hickey, whose urge is not ultimately to mark or be marked, but to possess and be possessed. I cannot render anything precisely in words, as I cannot crush my lover's body inside of mine. All I can do is leave a mark—the notation of my effort, a symbol for the thing. That is the endless pleasure and frustration of the writer and the lover: to reach and reach and never become.

I could not make her mine any more than she could make me hers. The best I could do was to show her how much I wanted it. To press my mouth against her pulse, and open.

5

Collective Nouns for Humans in the Wild

Kathy Fish

A group of grandmothers is a *tapestry*. A group of toddlers, a *jubilance* (see also: a *bewailing*). A group of librarians is an *enlightenment*. A group of visual artists is a *bioluminescence*. A group of short story writers is a *Flannery*. A group of musicians is—a *band*.

A *resplendence* of poets.
A *beacon* of scientists.
A *raft* of social workers.

A group of first responders is a *valiance*. A group of peaceful protestors is a *dream*. A group of special education teachers is a *transcendence*. A group of neonatal ICU nurses is a *divinity*. A group of hospice workers, a *grace*.

Humans in the wild, gathered and feeling good, previously an *exhilaration,* now: *a target.*
A *target* of concert-goers.
A *target* of movie-goers.
A *target* of dancers.

A group of schoolchildren is a *target.*

6

Open Season

Harrison Candelaria Fletcher

Here they come coyote, denim sharks with earthen skin, parting the C-Building crowd, to bruise blood into pale cheeks, bust up orthodontic smiles, twist back thumbs from scales, turn asphalt into alfalfa, the New Mexican dance with history, the springtime junior high ritual, out for revenge, out for kicks, out for you.

*

1: to make or prepare by combining various ingredients
- to juxtapose or put together to form a whole whose constituent parts are still distinct
- [no obj., often with negative] (of different substances) to be able to be combined in this way: oil and water.

*

Here they come coyote, the Speedy Gonzalez cartoons, the Frito Bandito erasers, the Ricky Ricardo's "got some splainin' to do," the Chico and the Man's, "it's not my job, man," the Ricardo Mantalban's "Corinthian leather," the Telly Savalas Pancho Villa, the Marlon Brando Zapata, the West Side Story switchblade, the wolf in Zoot Suit clothing, the low-rider steering wheel made from chrome chains.

*

"I don't feel comfortable calling myself that."
> "It's who you are … "
> "But it doesn't feel right."
> "Why not?"
> "Look at me."

*

Here they come coyote, the boys who make sandwiches with tortillas, the boys who wear "Puerto Rican fence-climber" shoes, the boys who speak with South Valley accents, the boys who fold brown paper sacks to use again at lunch, the boys you and your blond friends point to and laugh.

*

Is Person 1 of Hispanic, Latino or Spanish origin?
☐ No, not of Hispanic, Latino or Spanish Origin
☐ Yes, Mexican, Mexican Am., Chicano
☐ Yes, Puerto Rican
☐ Yes, Cuban
☐ Yes, another Hispanic, Latino, or Spanish origin – *Print origin. For example, Argentinian, Columbian, so on.*

*

Here they come coyote, sleepovers at friends' houses with shag carpet and color TV and Lite-Brite and milk and cookies and Pat Nixon pearls and Archie Bunker recliners and the times they invited you back and you wanted to stay.

*

The advantages and/or immunities certain groups benefit from based on appearance beyond those common to others: [not having to worry about being followed in a department store while shopping]; [seeing your image on television and knowing you're represented]; [people assuming you lead a constructive life free from crime, free or Welfare]; [having the freedom and luxury to fight racism one day and ignore it the next.]; [never having to think about it]

*

Here they come coyote, the dead father you never knew, the dead father's family you never knew, the French-Scottish ghosts who left you your name and your skin and the slot-machine genes that slip through your fingers like dust.

*

1. originally a Spanish corruption of a Nahuatl (Aztec) word
2. rebels against social convention with deception/humor
3. [slang] a contemptible person, avaricious or dishonest

4. term for half-Spanish and half-European
5. both hunter and scavenger [opportunist]
6. trickster, transformer, shape-shifter

*

Here they come coyote, the eight shades of brown on your mother's families' skin, the calluses on your grandfather's hands, the worry lines on your grandmother's face, the defiance in your widowed mother's stare, the beans you eat every Friday (and Saturday and Sunday, too), the tortillas you use as a spoon, the bike you make from parts, the K-Mart shoes, shirts, pants and jackets, the tangled roots from New Mexico to Spain, the box you check on the census, the brown bag you fold at lunch, the R's you roll like dice.

*

"Welcome to the [   ] Diversity Committee. Thanks for coming. Now, tell us: Why are you here?"

*

Here they come coyote, the Mexican mirrors you will hang from your walls, the red-brown soil you will keep in a jar, the hand-carved santos that will watch over your home, the Latina will you marry in an adobe church, the Spanish names you will give to your children, the green chile enchiladas you will make to perfection, the rancheras songs you will play on Christmas, the Southwestern skies you swim through in sleep, your mother's name you will add to your own, your mother's words that will sting like a slap:

"You always were more Anglo."

*

Here they come coyote, they caught your scent at last, head down at your C-Building locker, between your brown friend and your blond friend, between one lie and another.

Time to run. Time to choose.

7

Loitering

Ross Gay

I'm sitting at a café in Detroit where in the door window is the sign with the commands

NO SOLICITING
NO LOITERING

stacked like an anvil. I have a fiscal relationship with this establishment, which I developed by buying a coffee and which makes me a patron. And so even though I subtly dozed in the late afternoon sun pouring in under the awning, the two bucks spent protects me, at least temporarily, from the designation of loiterer, though the dozing, if done long enough, or ostentatiously enough, or with enough delight, might transgress me over.

Loitering, as you know, means fucking off, or doing jack shit, or jacking off, and given that two of those three terms have sexual connotations, it's no great imaginative leap to know that it is a repressed and repressive (sexual and otherwise) culture, at least, that invented and criminalized the concept. Someone reading this might very well keel over considering loitering a concept and not a fact. Such are the gales of delight.

The Webster's definition of *loiter* reads thus: "to stand or wait around idly without apparent purpose," and "to travel indolently with frequent pauses." Among the synonyms for this behavior are *linger, loaf, laze, lounge, lollygag, dawdle, amble, saunter, meander, putter, dillydally,* and *mosey.* Any one of these words, in the wrong frame of mind, might be considered a critique or, when nouned, an epithet ("Lollygagger!" or "Loafer!"). Indeed, *lollygag* was one of the words my mom would use to cajole us while jingling her keys when she was waiting on us, which, judging from the visceral response I had while writing that memory, must've been not quite infrequent. All of these words to me imply having a nice day. They imply having *the best* day. They also imply being unproductive. Which leads to being, even if only temporarily, nonconsumptive, and this is a crime in America, and more explicitly criminal depending upon any number of quickly apprehended visual cues.

For instance, the darker your skin, the more likely you are to be "loitering." Though a Patagonia jacket could do some work to disrupt that perception. A Patagonia jacket, colorful pants, Tretorn sneakers with short socks, an Ivy League ball cap, and a thick book that is not the Bible and you're almost golden. *Almost.* (There is a Venn diagram someone might design, several of them, that will make visual our constant internal negotiation toward safety, and like the best comedy it will make us laugh hard before saying, "Lord.")

It occurs to me that laughter and loitering are kissing cousins, as both bespeak an interruption of production and consumption. And it's probably for this reason that I have been among groups of nonwhite people laughing hard who have been shushed—in a Qdoba in Bloomington, in a bar in Fishtown, in the Harvard Club at Harvard. The shushing, perhaps, reminds how threatening to the order our bodies are in nonproductive, nonconsumptive delight. The moment of laughter not only makes consumption impossible (you might choke), but if the laugh is hard enough, if the shit talk is just right, food or drink might fly from your mouth, if not—and this hurts—your nose. And if your body is supposed to be one of the consumables, if it has been, if it is, one of the consumables around which so many ideas of production and consumption have been structured in this country, well, there you go.

There is a Carrie Mae Weems photograph of a woman in what looks to be some kind of textile factory, with an angel embroidered to the left breast of her shirt, where her heart resides. The woman, like the angel, has her arms splayed wide almost in ecstasy, as though to embrace everything, so in the midst of her glee is she. Every time I see that photo, after I smile and have a genuine bodily opening on account of witnessing this delight, which is a moment of black delight, I look behind her for the boss. *Uh-oh,* I think. *You're in a moment of nonproductive delight. Heads up!*

Which points to another of the synonyms for *loitering*, which I almost wrote as *delight*: *taking one's time*. For while the previous list of synonyms alludes to time, *taking one's time* makes it kind of plain, for the crime of loitering, the idea of it, is about ownership of one's own time, which must be, sometimes, wrested from the assumed owners of it, who are not you, back to the rightful, who is. And while having interpolated the policing of delight such that I am on the lookout for the overseer even in photos I have studied hundreds of times, on the lookout always for the policer of delight, my work is studying this kind of glee, being on the lookout for it, and aspiring to it, floating away from the factory, as she seems to be.

8

What I Do on My Terrace Is None of Your Business

Och Gonzalez

The woman in the apartment on my left has her head drooped low and an arm weighed down by a yellow watering can spouting all over the clay pots that line the metal bars of her terrace. If she had fuchsia pink hair, she would look exactly like the hibiscus flowers she's been growing in the pots. She does this every morning, but the flowers don't seem to want to cooperate and are already starting to look listless, and she can't figure out why. I want to tell her she's doing it wrong—hibiscus plants need to be watered every day in the summer, but once the weather cools, like it already has on this early November morning, they need only a little water every now and then. I want to tell her she's killing them, and it's only a matter of time until she slides her glass door open one morning to find them with limp pink heads and yellowing leaves, all bogged down by the weight of her well-intentioned care. I know this because in the garden of the old house I lived in for fifteen years before moving to this row of anonymous flats just a month ago, I used to have a fully-grown hibiscus shrub. I didn't do much to help it, but it thrived and exploded in bursts of red all throughout both the brisk mornings and the shimmering afternoons. I want to tell her all of this but I don't. What she does on her terrace is none of my business.

She sees me sitting on a white plastic chair on my own terrace, a leftover from my old garden set, drinking my morning coffee and lighting up a cigarette. The white tiles in my own tiny strip of space are shiny but strewn with wayward ashes and some squiggles of hair that the wind has plucked from my scalp. The scraggly black strands look forlorn without my dog's golden hair tangled along with them. Her own ashes now sleep in a small wooden box on top of my bookshelf, and beside it, a tuft of her fur rests undisturbed by the wind under the gleam of a glass dome keepsake. The woman on my left looks over at me dolefully with an almost imperceptible shake of her head. I can practically see the gears in her brain kicking alive, churning and wheeling over *why, in this day and age, would somebody still choose to smoke, why not just jump over the railing of the terrace down to the ground twenty-nine floors below and be done with it,* to which my own gears quickly churn back, *well, we all self-destruct somehow—we just do it in different ways. You shouldn't fret. What I do on my terrace is none of your business.*

I almost say the last words out loud, but just then a flock of gray doves flies over us, and my head snaps up. A few seconds later, another one. This goes on for about five times before I realize that it's the same flock circling round the building. They are shaped like an arrow, the alpha bird at the tip and his six minions divided into two slants of three. They look like cadets on a morning jog, warming up before the commander releases them to their designated posts for the day. In the space between the fifth and the sixth round, I look over to the woman on my left and see her hand still holding the watering can aloft, water dribbling down her hapless hibiscus, making them nod like somnolent bobbleheads, her face upturned and waiting for the doves like I am, grasping at the harmony in the gray and the order in the middle of random things like the dying and flying of the things we hold dear, and sharing in the same pockets of grace that happen when one remembers to look up.

9

Loyalty

Peter Grandbois

Characters

Peter Grandbois—a forty-nine-year-old professor of creative writing at a small liberal arts college. He is married and has three children, two dogs, two cats, and an aquarium full of fish. For him, the year is 2014, the year he is granted tenure.

Alexander (Sasha) Romankov—Five-time world champion foil fencer from the former Soviet Union, considered by many to be the greatest fencer in history. As a member of the Soviet military, he prides himself on precision and discipline in everything. For him it is 1983, the year before the Olympics in which he is favored to win, the year before the Soviet Union will boycott those same Olympics. He is thirty years old and has just won his fifth world championship title.

Kobo Abe—Japanese novelist and playwright, most famous for his novel *Woman in the Dunes*. The quintessential artist, he is married to a painter, and has established his own theatre company. He is known for his surreal, almost nightmarish explorations of individuals trapped in contemporary society. For him, it is 1993, the year of his death. He is sixty-nine years old. He has been several times nominated for a Nobel Prize but never won.

Setting: A café at a small town in the Midwest. It is early morning.

(The scene opens with KOBO and SASHA siting on opposite sides of a table in the corner of the café. They've finished their espressos and are now turned away from each other and staring in opposite directions. Sasha checks his watch while Kobo doodles on a napkin. PETER arrives flustered with his mug of tea.)

Sasha: You're half an hour late

Peter: (sitting) Sorry. One of the dogs had diarrhea. You wouldn't believe the mess. Then, my son forgot his lunch. I had to drop it by the school.

Kobo: He'll never learn that way.

Sasha: (nodding his head) He's right.

Peter: The dog or the boy?

(Kobo and Sasha simply shake their heads.)

Kobo: My father was strict in all things.

Sasha: Your father wanted you to become a doctor and look what happened.

Peter: Listen. Before we start, I need to know. Did either of you have children?

Kobo: You brought us here to ask us that?

Peter: I've been searching the Internet all morning in preparation for this meeting, and I can't find out anything.

Sasha: I thought this breakfast meeting was to discuss your subpar footwork. Aren't you trying to get back into fencing?

Peter: Well, yeah … I'd love any pointers you have for …

Kobo: I thought you wanted to talk about playwriting. A life in theatre.

Peter: That, too. I feel so lonely as a novelist. What's it like to collaborate with …

Sasha: You don't know what you want, do you? I should have known. Stupid American!

Kobo: Wait a second. He has a lot of interests. Maybe it's a sign of brilliance.

Sasha: Brilliance is a perfectly executed direct attack. It's something demonstrated. Proven. You know it when you see it.

Kobo: The simple mindedness of the military man!

Sasha: Nothing worth knowing can be understood with the mind. Truth lies in the body.

Kobo: On that we might agree. Though the body can also lead us astray.

Sasha: Nonsense!

Peter: Look! It wasn't easy getting you two here. I had to pull a lot of strings in the space/time continuum. So, can we please not argue!

Sasha: You've got to pick your loyalties. You say you want the life of an artist. You also want to be a great fencer, and you want a family.

Kobo: Jack of all trades, master of none.

Sasha: Exactly.

Peter: I don't understand.

Sasha: Of course you don't. You think like an American. You think you can have it all, think all you have to do is try and the world will lie down at your feet.

Peter: How did *you* do it? How did you stay so dedicated to your craft?

Kobo: Sacrifice.

Sasha: Da. You have to kill what you love.

Kobo: Dedication is a harsh mistress.

Sasha: Anything gets in your way, stab the fucker!

Kobo: I don't know if I'd go that far.

Sasha: Because you're soft.

Kobo: You try living in Japan after the war, much less trying to write!

Sasha: You're almost as bad as him. (He nods to Peter) With your medical degree. All that wasted time!

Kobo: I won't even dignify that with an answer. (Kobo takes another napkin and begins drawing something furiously.)

Peter: You didn't answer my earlier question. Do either of you have children? Do you have a family?

(Kobo continues drawing. Sasha crosses his arms and stares at Peter, shaking his head.)

Peter: See, if you're talking about killing your hobbies, or your girlfriends—I'm being metaphorical of course—or the job you hate, your TV habit, the friendships that suck up your time, I think I understand, but if it's your family ... well, that's what I want to know. What if it's your family?

Sasha: Life is messy.

(Kobo holds up his napkin. We see a drawing of two men fencing, one with a pen, the other with a sword. The man with the pen has just stabbed the man with the sword. Blood spurts from the wound.)

Sasha: Very funny.

Kobo: The artist is loyal to his art. There is nothing else.

Peter: Bullshit! What about life? What about the fact that the artist has to live life, to experience it if he's ever going to write about it?

Kobo: You've been reading too much Hemingway. He "lived" life and look where it got him. Three marriages. A drunk. Dead.

Sasha: Don't forget the Nobel Prize.

Kobo: What's that supposed to mean?

Sasha: Nothing. It's just that you've been nominated so often … and you're not getting any younger.

Kobo: How dare you!

Peter: Can we please stay focused? I don't want to talk about Hemingway, or Nobel Prizes, or …

Sasha: Are you going to be loyal to yourself or to others?

Kobo: That's really the only question.

Peter: Can't I be both?

Sasha: You really are stupid, aren't you?

Kobo: Don't be so hard on him, Sasha. Let the kid try.

Sasha: There's one good thing about the Soviet system. It eliminates choice. I knew from the moment I could walk that I would be a fencer. My first memories are of holding a sword in my hand.

Kobo: Doesn't lack of choice also eliminate passion?

Peter: Yes … If you're going to have real passion, it's got to be because it's something you choose to do.

Sasha: More American brainwashing. (Shaking his head at Kobo) I'm surprised at you. You should know better than anyone that devotion creates passion. Time and discipline are passion's muses. Haven't you heard of the ten thousand hour rule?

Kobo: I don't think I could have ever become passionate about medical school.

Sasha: (laughing) You flunked out three times!

Kobo: That choice was made for me by my father.

Sasha: Had you stayed, had you put in the time, devoted yourself to it, you would have found the passion.

Kobo: (almost to himself) I'm not so sure.

Peter: There's a big difference between choosing to do something and being forced to do something.

Sasha: But let's be honest, Peter, no one forced you to have a family. No parent told you to raise children or you'd be disinherited.

Peter: I know. I know. I don't mean that.

Kobo: Are you sure?

Sasha: Because it sounds like you're making excuses.

Peter: What I mean is that there's a gray area between choosing and being forced … and sometimes that gray area gets …

Kobo: Messy?

Peter: Yes!

Sasha: Gray areas are just another American contrivance. A convenient excuse. They allow you to overthink. The truth is you want it all, Peter. You're not willing to sacrifice. To kill what gets in the way. No wonder you were only a mediocre fencer.

Peter: Wait a second! That's not fair. And besides, I was pretty good.

Sasha: Mediocre.

Peter: You don't know! You can't know because you never had children.

Sasha: How do you know I don't have children?

Kobo: Yes, how do you know?

Peter: I mean … do you or don't you?

Kobo: Why is it so important? You have to live for yourself.

Sasha: Find out for yourself. You can't live another person's life.

Kobo: You can't look for models.

Sasha: I could be the best father, the best husband alive, but that's not what it's about. That's not your story.

Kobo: Or maybe I ignored my children. They all grew up unhappy, and now they hate me. That's not the point.

Peter: Then what is?

Sasha: The point is that you so desperately need it to matter. The point is that you're trying to live like everyone else instead of listening to yourself.

Peter: I don't get it. I thought we were going to meet here to talk about what it means to loyal to your craft, to others.

Kobo: You have to be loyal to yourself.

Peter: But what if I don't like myself? What if this self is not who I want to be?

Sasha: Grow up! Nobody likes themselves.

Kobo: Why do you think we do what we do? We're all trying to escape who we are.

Peter: Really? I didn't know.

Kobo: When I first started my own theatre, many people told me that my writing would suffer. They told me if I didn't dedicate myself completely to my craft, I wouldn't become the great writer I was supposed to be. But who is this great writer? He's a creation of others. He's not me.

Peter: So you're okay with the fact that you might never win the Nobel Prize?

Kobo: (He ponders this for a moment) Our first loyalty is to ourselves, to recognizing the demands of our own ego, and to knowing those demands are separate from us. They do not come from us

Sasha: More intellectual nonsense! Where do they come from then? My desire to be the best drives me. It allows me to shut out everything else.

Kobo: Yes, and where will you be next year when you don't have an Olympic gold medal?

Sasha: Shut up! I don't have to listen to that! I'm number one in the world. No one trains harder than me. The gold is mine to take.

Kobo: (to Peter) He doesn't know, does he?

(Peter shakes his head.)

Sasha: Know what?

Peter: The Soviet Union will boycott the 1984 Olympics. You'll miss your chance at a gold medal.

Sasha: What are you talking about? That's impossible … There's no way …

Kobo: It's true.

Sasha: Fine. If next year doesn't work, there will be the next Olympics or the next.

(Kobo and Peter shake their heads.)

Sasha: What? You're saying I'll never win an Olympic gold?

Kobo: How does it feel now? Still sure about all those sacrifices?

Sasha: Fuck you! You're not getting the Nobel either!

(Kobo looks to Peter, and Peter shakes his head "No.")

Kobo: They wouldn't have given it to me anyway. My work is too strange.

(Kobo returns to doodling on his napkin.)

Peter: Isn't it good enough that you stuck with your art regardless of what people thought, regardless of the rewards?

Sasha: I don't want to talk about it anymore.

(Kobo throws his pencil against the wall.)

Peter: But you've got your work! Kobo, you published what, fifteen or sixteen books? How many plays?

Kobo: It doesn't matter.

Peter: It has to matter! (turning to Sasha) And what about those five world championship medals? Not to mention the team titles …

Sasha: Without an Olympic gold, they're nothing.

Peter: I can't believe this. You guys are my role models. Sasha, you told me I couldn't have it all. Kobo, you said it was all about sacrifice.

Kobo: Do as we say, not as we do.

Peter: What's that supposed to mean?

Sasha: It means stop looking to others to find your path. There is no right path! You can do everything. Every god damned thing. You can sacrifice until you bleed. You can work and work and work only to find your own government will betray you.

Kobo: Nobody owes you anything.

Sasha: That's right, kid. The sooner you learn it the better.

Peter: So, the only loyalty is to oneself?

(Both Kobo and Sasha stare at Peter, waiting for him to finish.)

Peter: And it doesn't matter what path I take? It doesn't matter if my life looks like yours? If you had children or not? If you get married or not? Or even who you marry?

Kobo: Why are you phrasing it as if these are all questions?

Peter: And all that matters is that I stick to it, stick to my own messy life?

Sasha: Okay, now you're sounding like one of those self-help books. Can we stop before I get a soft American belly, too?

Kobo: (standing) Yes, I think our time is up here.

(Sasha stands as well. The two make as if to leave.)

Peter: Wait! Don't go! I think I'm just starting to understand.

Kobo: (to Sasha) He's worse off than we thought.

Sasha: (to Kobo) Da. He still thinks the answer lies out there.

Peter: Can you repeat the part about how we can't look for models? I think I need to hear that again. Does it mean the right path is inside us or that there is no path?

Kobo: (to Sasha) All we have is our work.

Sasha: (to Kobo) And it looks like that's all we're ever going to get.

Kobo: (to Sasha) Should we leave him?

Sasha: (to Kobo) There's really nothing we can do. Besides, look at him. He's a mess.

(Peter mumbles to himself, asking himself question after question.
Scratching his head.)

Sasha: (to Kobo) We shouldn't have come.

Kobo: (to Sasha) The most important lessons can't be taught.

Sasha: (to Kobo) True.

Kobo: (to Sasha) It's sad really.

Sasha: (to Kobo) Another reason to get out of here.

(The two exit. Peter stares after them, hands out, imploring.)

10

Mighty Pawns

Major Jackson

If I told you Earl, the toughest kid
on my block in North Philadelphia,
bow-legged and ominous, could beat
any man or woman in ten moves playing white,
or that he traveled to Yugoslavia to frustrate the bearded
masters at the Belgrade Chess Association,
you'd think I was given to hyperbole,
and if, at dinnertime, I took you
into the faint light of his Section 8 home
reeking of onions, liver, and gravy,
his six little brothers fighting on a broken love-seat
for room in front of a cracked flat-screen,
one whose diaper sags it's a wonder
it hasn't fallen to his ankles,
and the walls behind doors exposing sheetrock
the perfect O of a handle, and the slats
of stairs missing where Baby-boy gets stuck
trying to ascend to a dominion foreign to you and me
with its loud timbales and drums blasting down
from the closed room of his cousin whose mother
stands on a corner on the other side of town
all times of day and night, except when her relief
check arrives at the beginning of the month,
you'd get a better picture of Earl's ferocity
after-school on the board in Mr. Sherman's class,
but not necessarily when he stands near you
at a downtown bus-stop in a jacket a size too
small, hunching his shoulders around his ears,
as you imagine the checkered squares of his poverty
and anger, and pray he does not turn his precise gaze
too long in your direction for fear he blames
you and proceeds to take your Queen.

11

A Log Cabin Square

Sarah Minor

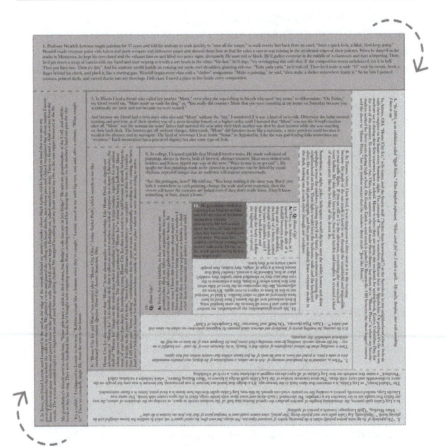

12

When You Were a Boy in Maine

Jessica Hendry Nelson

You took your red-striped fishing rod out into the yard—neon yellow bobber electric against the opaque gray sky—and cast into a puddle of snowmelt and waited. Brown fields, early spring, early morning. No one around for miles, except your mother in the kitchen window smiling to herself, and the dog, Bob, who one day soon, at twenty-years old, will lay down on the driveway for a nap and die, accidentally run over by your father in his haste and big truck, the dog's tail thrashing wildly against the gravel, reflex and not joy, while you watched stricken from the patio.

I envision you, small, six-year-old boy, as you slowly reel in your line through clumps of dead grass, because a body of water, a puddle broken overnight even, surely must contain fish. Water-blue eyes, sandy-bottom hair, your pants overlarge yet too short, barefoot boy in April. You fish until dusk, then slump over your spaghetti dinner, dreaming storks scooping bass from nearby ponds and dropping them into swimming pools in distant, wealthier neighborhoods—a story you'd heard once from you-can't-remember-who and taken to heart. You won't accept your empty fishing creel by your feet, and keep lifting its woven hatch to check, while old Bob curls around your ankles, weightless as blown grass.

And yet, to this day, I'm not sure you fully understand the stranglehold of story. Once, you were a superstitious boy. You believed in the magic of storks and wearing the same pair of socks to every basketball game. Of putting on your clothes in a certain order, pants always last. But you never caught that fish, you lost games, and by the time we met in college, you were convinced we'd ruin our friendship by trying for something more. And this has been your approach to most everything ever since. *If I expect the worst, I can only be pleasantly surprised.*

When I try to understand why you changed your mind about us having kids three months before our wedding—*I can't*, you'd said finally, *I'm not meant to be a father*—I think about the stories we tell ourselves about ourselves; if this sort of storytelling manifests the future. I've never considered an alternative narrative to motherhood. And so you've erased two souls from the banks of my horizon—the child I'd hoped to have and the mother I was always becoming. I keep lifting the hatch of my mind, searching for a story that might contain a happy and childless ending.

But all story is magical thinking. The only difference between your superstitions and my faith in story is nothing much.

———

I think of another story.

This one takes place 457 miles and fifteen years south of here and goes I was in love with a different boy I'll call S.

S. was sad most all of the time. We were going to get married and have children and I would make him whole and well. (Already, you can predict how this story will end.) But then he left me and the neighborhood for the army at age eighteen, two weeks before his mother killed herself and no one was surprised. The note had read like a job resignation. ("My circumstances have changed," I remember him quoting.) In her place, she had appointed her youngest son, S., to care for his siblings. And oh how I've always loved the solemn boys, the ones in long blue overcoats who visit every day for ten years, toeing the gravel driveway in silence, and never share their love or grief or rage, and then one day fail to show up altogether, only circle my dreams still (years after I also left the neighborhood for good, and met you, and we married)—S.'s hands on my face inside the rooms in which we took the same drugs together as teenagers—and I wake up thrashing, and you open the curtains to the sun and say, *Look*.

You wouldn't understand that it's the story, and not the boy, that haunts me. The real boy—a man now living in New York City—is not, has never been, who I wanted him to be. Just a character in my story, and me in his, until we found one another again a few years ago and he finally told me what I'd always wanted to hear, inside that dark bar in our old neighborhood— *I love you, I've always loved you*—tall and tattooed and army-strong, and I knew suddenly it was not me he loved but the story of us: childhood sweethearts reunited on the other side of years and war. Broken halves who together make a whole. *You were meant to be,* the story insists. *You were always in the process of becoming.*

When I watched that truth bear down on him in the seconds that followed, it was as crushing to both of us, I think, as any death.

What happens when an angry boy goes to war?

You wouldn't want to see me un-medicated, S. warned.

We sipped our beers in silence, the bartender shouting up the stairs, *last call,* and we toasted.

———

I wish I could say the story ended there.

That we finished our beers inside that silence and left.

That he hadn't told me then—

in the dark bar in our old neighborhood, gazing down at my knees, a sudden source of wonder, while all the old narratives began to reassemble in the space between his lips and my thighs

—about leaving basic training all those years ago to collect his mother's ashes and carry out her final wish: her feather-light urn to the shores of the Atlantic, bearing it aloft and alone into the wind and waves and letting fly her flaked ashes, food for the fishes, into the roiling and indifferent sea.

But here's the thing about wishes: they can only come true, and are not inherently so.

Later he learned the unthinkable, that his uncle, her brother, had secretly buried his sister—*We're Catholics for Christ sake!* the uncle later argued—and the ashes S. had scattered just his uncle's old dog.

How I wish I could release him from that fact; un-see his face when it told it to me in the bar that night.

———

Inside the hatch of my mind, I slip a fish into the puddle while your back is turned, before you toddle away crestfallen for dinner.

How I wish those tiny tugs on your line had been real and not just hope for a happy ending, a hook tangled in grass.

I can't help but hold this story up as the last vestige of your optimism, feeble as it might seem, except I know the power of story. How ten thousand years ago, hyenas stacked human bones by the bushel. But then we invented language, heroes, stories. We told lies about men defeating saber-toothed tigers until they really could. We imagined surviving and then we survived.

You imagined loving me until you did.

I know that story fails us half of the time. There is no viable story to make sense out of the senselessness of war, for example, or the rewriting of a woman's final chapter. I cannot write S. into wellness, just as I cannot will a child alive. I know this now.

But when I ask you, time and again, *Are you sure ... ?* I am asking you not to give up on the miraculous. I am raging against the inevitability of entropy; the uselessness of faith.

I am saying: *I do not accept it.* The mechanics of salvation *are* salvation.

I am telling you he was happy, your old haggard dog. In those final moments, cast out from the confines of a body, he was ecstatic.

13

Buying a House

Sean Prentiss

As Chad the Realtor slows his car onto quiet Lockwood Avenue, he says, *This is 626 Lockwood. Tell me what you think.*

Chad and I are searching for my first home to buy. I've just gotten a new job as tenure-track professor in western Michigan. I guess I'm ready to settle down. I guess after a life moving town to town, fifteen states in the last twenty years, it's time to plant roots.

We're on the fifth house today. The first house we checked had a huge front porch and sat in an upscale neighborhood. *You can make fifty grand off this house*, Chad said. Inside, the house had a gutted kitchen, sagging floors, ruined sheetrock. *A fixer-upper, for sure*, Chad said. I thought of the time needed to put the house back together, how I'd rather write or travel than drywall and spackle. We moved on.

The second and third houses had moldy basements and cracked foundations. Chad just nodded back toward the front door. We left without seeing the upstairs. The fourth house had such a cute kitchen that it felt like I'd need a trophy wife and a cooing baby before I moved into the house to live happily ever after ...

As we stop at this Lockwood house, the first thing (the very first thing) I notice is the front porch. Chad must know what I'm thinking because he says, *Look at that screened-in porch.* I'm a sucker for sitting outside. For watching the world go by.

I walk onto the porch, turn around, listen to the screen door slap shut, and stare back at the quiet street. A basketball net on rollers. A beat-up pickup. A tricycle tipped over on the sidewalk. Chalk drawings in front of a neighbor's house.

I imagine early autumn, my feet up on a table, a Pabst. Maybe grading student essays in the afternoon sun or reading a book of poetry. (Hugo. No, no, Wright! *Suddenly I realize/that if I stepped out of my body I would break/into blossom.*) I think, *This could be my street. My porch. Mine.*

Then the scene changes and I am no longer reading James Wright. Instead, my next lover (a girl I have yet to meet—but I can see her perfectly—rounded cheeks, face in a grin, thin lips, long brown hair, curly) is standing on this porch. It is our first date (a date we laughed through, at a restaurant, later the long walk home) and it is latest dusk—nearing dark. Lockwood is quiet. The air cold (nearly freezing). The air still. Standing on my porch, I lean toward her.

***

Chad unlocks the front door and holds it open. I walk into a tiny foyer as Chad says, *Nineteen hundred square feet. A house to grow into.*

I barely hear Chad. Instead I see my father visiting from three states away. As he walks in the front door, I reach for his leather coat. As I see my dad's future visit, I think about how most of my adult years, I've felt like I wasn't living up to what my father expected. I felt that I wasn't being successful (though he's always been supportive of every one of my harebrained ideas). But I have always felt that, sure, I was skiing and traveling and even earning my terminal degree, but I wasn't successful in the ways that I thought he'd care about. But now I'm tenure-track. A real job. A real life.

Standing in the foyer, I almost mumble those words, *A real job. A real life.*

I imagine my father talking to his friends over glasses of merlot, saying, *My youngest son, Sean—remember him?—just got a tenure track job in Michigan. Teaching creative writing. He's buying a house in Michigan. An old Craftsman.*

***

As Chad leads me into an older kitchen, he says, *This kitchen needs work, but it's an easy redo.*

I think about how I'll never redo the kitchen. No stainless steel appliances. No tile floors. No fresh paint on the walls. I'll just put a wooden table—old and worn and scratched and found in a house I rented in Idaho—in the corner. I'll buy two thrift store chairs.

As Chad points out the dishwasher, the gas stove, the cabinets, I find myself in the future—god, this house has a way of transporting me—to nights eating alone, crockpots made during long weekends, the smell of stew blanketing the house. I'll read a magazine while eating a quick meal. The second chair at the table unmoved for weeks (months?)—waiting.

Waiting for that next lover (Or has she already left?). I'll wash the few dishes, leaving the kitchen as clean as I find it today.

***

In the master bedroom (whenever I hear *master bedroom* I imagine a canopied bed, pink walls, doilies on the bureaus), Chad pulls up the blinds. The afternoon sun blinds me with its dazzling light, illuminating the dust in the air. I twist from the sun as Chad moves to the living room—giving me time. Time. I need time.

With the bedroom empty of furniture, I turn a slow circle, arms outstretched—touching empty space. Empty space. *Empty space.*

I imagine this bedroom after I move in. A single bed with poorly fitted sheets (They come undone every night I toss and turn.), a nightstand for my book of the week (a mediocre collection of essays, later a novel by Abbey), a dresser full of wrinkled clothes. What else? What else? My cell phone. What else? House keys. What else? Sneakers and dress shirts in the closet. What else? Nothing. What else? Nothing. A room to fill with nothing.

But maybe in a year (or in two, or three), my next lover—the one I kissed on the porch—will move in. In another year, she'll become my wife. And I question (alone in this bedroom) how is it possible that after twenty years of not getting married (dodging three marriage proposals) that now I can no longer stop thinking about marriage. It's not that I want to get married. It's just friends married. Friends and family expecting me married. My mother asking, *Have you met any nice girls in Michigan.*

Not yet, Mom, not yet.

I think to my future lover and how once she becomes my wife, the small bed will be replaced with a queen. She will hang new blinds on these windows (though we'll never shut them—let the sun flood us). The old furniture moved out, donated. And my keys, they'll end up in a clay dish that my wife will buy at a flea market (just for my keys). When I toss my keys in the dish, the clanging will remind me of something—though I'll never figure out exactly what.

***

In the living room, I run my hands along hardwood floors. Chad says, *Oak. I have the same wood in my house.*

In five years (Or ten, fifteen?) if I buy this house (this very house) will these floors only feel the slow steps of my feet quietly moving room to room? The lonely steps of me coming home day after day from work at the university? Or will—some distant year—there be the patter of a child (A daughter? A little girl in pigtails?) running over these slick floors (her giggles bouncing off the walls)?

I've never wanted kids (or a wife, or even in these last few years a serious girlfriend). But now I'm studying the creaking of these floors (like an Indian in a 1960s Western with his ear pressed to the tracks listening for the sound of a coming train) for the pattering of a child's steps. I don't want 4 a.m. wakeups. I don't want to change diapers. I don't want to have her burp on my shoulder. I don't want to teach her to throw (Okay, okay, maybe I want to teach her to throw—first an awkward sidearm throw, later a laser. *Good job, girl!*).

But in this living room—warm with its yellow walls—it feels that if I buy this house (this very house, this Lockwood house), I'll need a child. Not just because I'll own the house, but because if I own the house, this house will need a child (Is this just me telling lies? Trying to pretend it's not my wants?)—her voice bouncing off walls, her cries from her bedroom calling to me—to me (only me) during the middle of her nights (she has such cute nightmares—monsters in the closet, a dream where she couldn't find me.)

As I envision all of this, I cannot find her mother. I cannot find her at all. I grow desperate. Where is she? The yellow walls blind me, it seems.

***

Chad asks, *Do you need more time?*

I want to say, *Just a minute. One minute* (though I mean a lifetime or two).

I want to say, *I can see all the world.*

I want to say, *Hold me. Someone. Please?*

I want to say, *Every story is true and every story is a lie.*

Instead I nod. Chad moves to the front porch. I hear the clicking of the door.

In the living room, I stare at the ceiling until it is forty years into the future (the mortgage paid off, the water heater and furnace twice replaced). I am seventy-seven with a beard of gray. I lie in the queen bed as a chest-rattling cough runs through my body. Then another. In a hallucination, I call to that future wife, wanting her by my side (holding my hand through this)—never realizing (this is for the best, the best) that she's been gone years and years (maybe exactly a thousand years). The divorce papers in a filing cabinet in the basement (mildewed, brittle). Or did she die young, cancer?

Such a sad story, the neighbors will whisper as they watch my daughter play on the sidewalk.

When the coughing subsides, a live-in nurse (or is it my daughter, home for her father) feeds me ice chips, takes my pulse. When the days (now the minutes) are done and it is latest dusk (the same time of day as when I first kissed that girl), I use my last energy to lift my arm. The nurse, the girl?, hurriedly stands from her seat. She rests her hand on my forehead, but she struggles to understand this final moment. Am I calling to her? Am I pointing to a western sun?

This house echoes, *Stay down, champion, stay down.*

***

As Chad locks the front door tight—

—as the sun sets over 626 Lockwood, as the trees stand bare (still earliest spring), as the grass lays down (from long winter), as a grandfather wheels in his grandson's basketball net, as three children play army (*Bang, bang, bang, you're dead.*)—

—I stand on the front porch and think, *I can own this house. I can own it all.*

14

The Funambulists

Jonathan Rovner

Conjure up two people—let's say one man and one woman—and place them in a nondescript room. Don't slap them down like stamps in an album; people are fragile, after all. Fill the room with tension. The problem, of course, is that tension doesn't look like anything. You might have to use your imagination. Maybe floodwaters are filling the room with a sluggish inevitability, or else a ticking bomb is sitting on the coffee table you just invented to have somewhere for the bomb to sit. Wait, scrap all that. Put them instead on a wire high above the earth. They can't see to the bottom, and neither can you. Now you've got something. Two tightrope walkers—one man, one woman—face to face and not touching. Each watches the other. The man is thinking (because you make him) that if they fall, at least they will fall together. But the woman, who is wiser, knows that there are some places you can only go alone. Each watches the other in fear, but also anticipation. Because they know something is about to happen. Keep them there, balancing. As long as nothing moves they still have a chance. Try not to invent wind.

* * *

The following screenplay, never to be performed, is called *An Uneventful Night in the Lives of Two People, One of Whom is the Author*[1]. In the interests of full disclosure, please be aware of the following emendations and substitutions:

- My crippling fear of rejection is represented by stale vaudeville-style jokes in the manner of the late Henny "Take My Wife … Please!" Youngman.

---

[1] Title is tentative and subject to change.

- My girlfriend's frustration is expressed by the blowing of bubbles from one of those cheap bottles with its accompanying plastic wand that you can buy at the dollar store.
- My paralyzing inability to make a decision—large or small, personal or professional—is represented by the eating of waffles.
- Poetry will henceforth be rendered as "*Star Trek: The Next Generation Fan Fiction.*"
- My girlfriend's dog, a lovable but needy and enormous Great Dane, is represented by an eighteen month old baby named ~~Snuggles~~ Ralph.
- My girlfriend's cramped one-bedroom apartment with the prostitute next door who sits on her front porch watching her pimp across the street near the park where no children play, with the liquor store two doors down where someone got shot last month, with the dealers on the corner every night, with its decrepit fixtures, blown sockets, raccoons under the floorboards, black mold, poor insulation, and hardwood floors (and isn't there something especially unforgiving about hardwood floors?) that, scrub as you might, will never come clean, has been transplanted into a comfy and spacious country cottage with a wide fireplace (plenty of chopped wood out back), deep shag carpet, and the plaintive sounds of rural night: owls, cicadas, the occasional coyote. Not wolves though. Let's keep wolves out of it.
- My anxiety is represented by the cuckoo clock I wear on a string around my neck (yes, almost *exactly* like Flava Flav).
- Night terrors will be referred to as the iconic 1980s children's game Lite-Brite.
- My hands, marked by their softness as those of an academic who has not done hard labor in nearly a decade, are, at a pivotal point in our narrative, replaced by the hands of a clown—chalk-white, unyielding, obdurate.
- The clown's hands are a transposition of the hands of a middle-aged male neighbor who babysat my girlfriend many years ago while her parents were at work.
- As a tribute to the yearning for specificity—for the nailing of things down in their rightful places—that we as sad-sack pilgrims cling to desperately on this all-too-often fetid earth, the names of television programs and peanut butter cups have not been altered.

The repeated childhood sexual abuse that warped and perforated my girlfriend's ability to trust is represented by a large pink elephant, which stands patiently in the corner, unremarked upon but insistently present. It does not speak and does not leave.

FADE IN:

INT. COTTAGE--EVENING

DOLORES WOEBEGONE, a slim, lovely woman of early middle age, with hard brown eyes and wearing threadbare jogging pants and a loose-fitting sweatshirt, lies supine on a pleather loveseat with a MacBook open on her lap and her bare feet in the lap of TOM FOOL[2], a balding, nervous man with slumped shoulders who seems to have difficulty sitting still. On the floor, near the foot of the couch, RALPH stares dolefully at the television, which is playing a syndicated episode of the oft-vulgar animated show *Family Guy*.

> DOLORES
> Tell me if you think this can work.

Tom mutes the television. He makes a show of cocking his head, a silent actor overemphasizing the action of "listening." This hackneyed attempt to elicit a chuckle goes unacknowledged.

> DOLORES
> (reading)
> "The third time Captain Jean Luc
> Picard traveled back in time, he was
> surprised to find himself at 221B
> Baker Street, face to face with the
> one and only Sherlock Holmes."
> (beat)
> Well?

> TOM
> I like it.

---

[2]I'm aware that it's unnecessary to give myself a pseudonym, but it feels right.

                    DOLORES
          You don't like it.

                    TOM
          I've been in love with the same
          woman for twenty years. Don't tell
          my wife, but I wish I'd've married
          her!
               (beat)
          It's resonant, evocative. The
          repetition of "time" and "time"
          serves, I think, as a kind of
          anaphora that beckons the reader
          deeper into the euphonic
          juxtaposition of "Sherlock" and
          "Holmes."

                    DOLORES
          You really like it?

                    TOM
          Of course I do.

                    DOLORES
          Thank you!

Tom smiles and returns the television to full volume.
Onscreen, the town's lovable elderly pedophile is on
a ladder, his face pressed to a window, watching an
obese teenage boy dance shirtless around a bathroom.
Tom quickly changes the channel to MSNBC.

                    DOLORES
          Have you looked at any of those PhD
          programs?

Tom produces a plate of stacked waffles and a knife and
fork. He cuts the stack and indelicately shoves a dry
forkful into his mouth.

                    TOM
                 (chewing)

I love you...³

Dolores, her jaw rigid, unscrews the plastic cap from
a plastic bottle of bubbles, dips the wand in, and
blows out. A steady stream of bubbles fills the air.
The tiny door on the clock around Tom's neck springs
open. A pastel-colored jaybird thrusts itself into
the open air.

                    JAYBIRD
          Cuckoo.

The jaybird withdraws. One particularly large bubble
breaks against Tom's nose.

                    DOLORES
               (shrugging)
          Brad and Annie asked if we could
          babysit the girls on Saturday. I
          said of course we would.

                    TOM
          I love you...

                    DOLORES
          Oh, I love you! If you don't want
          to, just say so!

                    TOM
          My wife won't go anywhere without
          her Discover card, but I'm the one
          who ends up discovering the bill!
               (beat)
          Happy to. Really.

                    DOLORES
          I'm sorry. I didn't mean to yell.

---

³This phrase of endearment, common currency of lovers the world over, serves in this text as proxy
for the filler sound "Um..." as well as the exclamation "For Godsakes!"

She scoots closer to him on the loveseat, hesitates, and moves back to her original position. Ralph, still lazed out on the lush shag carpet, begins to whine.

              DOLORES (CONT'D)
        He wants to be up here with us.

              TOM
        He's a baby.
          (addressing Ralph lovingly)
        Aren't you? Who's a good boy? Don't
        you like the floor?

Dolores stiffens.

              DOLORES
        Please don't talk to him that way.

              TOM
        Babies don't understand English. All
        he hears is the tone of my voice.
          (beat[4])
        I'm sorry.

Dolores blows a small trail of bubbles, but clearly her heart is not in it.

              DOLORES
        It's fine. It's fine. What do you
        want for dinner?

              TOM
        Whatever you want is fine.

              DOLORES
        Thai?

---

[4] I probably should have mentioned this earlier, but these beats, or pauses, can, at the discretion of the reader, be interpreted one of two ways: either pregnant, in the sense of a Christmas morning wake-up call (the expectation of joyful recompense just around the corner), or else teeming with a stockingful of nothing—think of wind in the high desert, or mausoleums, or a recently-emptied womb.

Tom notices that Al Sharpton has begun discussing the Penn State pink elephant scandal. He quickly clicks the remote control, pausing just long enough on *CSI: Miami* to see a young woman's pale corpse atop the morgue table and to hear the words, "Assuming he's the killer, why didn't we find any semen in her?" He settles on a QVC program attempting to hawk (for three easy payments of $29.95, plus S&H) a gaudy amethyst necklace in the shape of a heart.

> TOM
> Thai works.

> DOLORES
> Or we could get a pizza.

Tom sets down the remote control and with crumbs stuck to his fingers stuffs an entire waffle into his mouth.

> TOM
> (chewing, swallowing with
> difficulty)
> What'ver 'ou want.

> SHE
> Or maybe we'll just eat our feet.

[Author's Note: Though it is unnecessary—and often the mark of a rank amateur—to include specific camera directions, I think it's long past time for an extreme zooming out. Start slowly, then pull back faster. Here are our characters as viewed from the top of the nearest sweetgum tree; here they are as viewed from a ten-story building; here they are from a supersonic jet that hangs suspended in the air, neither moving forward nor—yet—falling. From the right height, any place will seem so small against the landscape that it's nearly impossible to imagine the people there are anything but perfectly all right. It's a game you can play. Conjure up a world that makes sense, where the people who need you are never disappointed. Where you are never woefully inadequate.

Convince yourself that everything is going to be all right. As you've done since you were a small child, use your imagination to escape. There's a ten-foot concrete wall in front of you? Just imagine a door, lower your head, and charge. Sometimes, logic be damned, you'll make it through. But sometimes the wall will not yield. And as you lie in the dirt at the foot of it holding your bruised and concussed head, the wall will coldly explain that there is a kind of pain you cannot comprehend, let alone remedy. If a man exists who could heal this pain (a real man, the kind you've read about in books), you are clearly not him. You—by not being him—are making it worse.]

            DOLORES (CONT'D)
        (furiously blowing bubbles)
    Just tell me what you want!

            TOM
    My wife went to one of those fancy
    spas and got a seaweed mask facial.
    You look great, I said, but when are
    they taking it off?
        (beat)
    You're right. I'm sorry. Thai sounds
    delicious.

He sets down his plate of waffles. She sets down her bubbles and moves closer to him. They look at each other, at first almost skittishly. He smiles. She smiles. They are safe again, and together. He reaches out his hand to touch her leg, just above the knee. But it's a cold and bloodless ivory hand that clamps itself down on her leg.

Somewhere deep inside, ignorant of the passing of years or the maturation of the body or a lifetime of kindnesses heaped up like sandbags to safeguard the ramshackle flood walls, her hypothalamus activates the sympathetic nervous system, mobilizing the nerves into a sort of fist, and the adrenal-cortical system springs into action, dumping dozens of separate hormones into the bloodstream to prepare for the coming danger.

The leg stiffens.

As though stung, the hand withdraws.

                    TOM
               (barely audible)
          Read me some more.

She shakes her head softly. Across the room, watchful
of all that transpires and with the unflagging vigilance
of a sentinel, the pink elephant says nothing.

                    TOM (CONT'D)
          Please.

                    DOLORES
               (rotely)
          Geordi La Forge, his leg snared and
          hooked by the bear trap, tore his
          gaze away from wicked Moriarty and
          sought out the reassuring face of
          his noble Captain--

Onscreen, a poof-haired saleswoman is explaining that
the origin of the heart symbol can be traced directly
to the Gospel of John.

                    TOM
               (scowling)
          That's wrong.

She purses her lips tightly and closes the laptop.

                    DOLORES
          Hmm?

                    TOM
          I was just reading about this. They
          think it comes from a plant called
          silphium.

                    DOLORES
          What does?

                    TOM
          The heart symbol.
               (beat)

It was a big deal like three
thousand years ago. In Minoan Crete.
Where the minotaur comes from.

She shudders. He mumbles a curse at himself and adds
"minotaur" to the ever-evolving list of triggers[5] to
avoid at all costs.

> DOLORES
> And it's a big deal that you know
> that?

> TOM
> *My wife wanted a BMW for Christmas,*
> *and I said: Whaddya trying to do,*
> *Break My Wallet?!*

> DOLORES
> And it's important that I know you
> know that? Right now, while I'm
> reading?

He takes a bite of waffles, starts to stand, and
reconsiders. Then he stands and strides purposefully
across the shag carpet into the clean and roomy kitchen.
Outside, an owl gives a mighty hoot. It sounds like a
gunshot. He removes two individually-wrapped Reece's
Peanut Butter Cups from the freezer, unwraps them on
the counter, sweeps the bits of stray chocolate into
the sink, and returns to his place on the sofa. He
hands them both to her and she eats slowly.

> DOLORES
> I'm so tired.
>   (sniffling)
> I was up till dawn playing *Lite-Brite*.

Then like a gunslinger she unsheathes the flimsy plastic
wand from its bottle and begins to blow. Bubbles surge

---

[5]These include, but are not limited to: broken instruments, unwashed sheets, socks, dramatized violence—actual or implied—against humans, animals, or property, and the music of Gordon Lightfoot, Jim Croce, and Jackson Browne. And sometimes me.

forth in a frenzy. They float up to the ceiling, sink down to the carpet, and fill the empty spaces between them. She dips and re-dips the wand; she pants with the effort. It's almost beautiful, these thin liquid shells of iridescence that glance off one another or merge, that collect the flickering colors from the television screen and rebroadcast them in wobbly miniature. A world of bubbles, like something out of Willy Wonka. And then they begin to burst, one by one, into splashes of soap that disappear in bright gleaming shivers.

Trembling, Tom collects the last crumbs of waffle from his plate. Ralph, his nose twitching with the smell of chocolate, begins to whine.

> TOM
> (dismissively)
> Shh. Quiet, dingus.

> DOLORES
> Don't talk to him like that.

She beckons Ralph to join them. In order to make room, she slides half onto Tom's lap, still holding her laptop. The baby leaps to the loveseat and sinks into the cushions with a contented sigh. Dolores has gone rigid. Tom feels the tensed dead-weight of her against him, a mannequin carved from oak. They sit for a long beat, as though frozen, and then she opens her computer again. Ralph licks his lips and blinks happily at the television, which has landed finally on Lawrence Welk. The orchestra, full of staid white men in suits, is in the throes of its own magnificent blandness. Trumpets toot politely; drums knock like an invited guest; the piano is a balm of warm notes. Elderly couples dance arm in arm.

> DOLORES
> (staring dully at the computer
> screen)
> Tell me if you think this can work.

> FADE OUT

15

Memoir

Vijay Seshadri

Orwell says somewhere that no one ever writes the real story of their life.
The real story of a life is the story of its humiliations.
If I wrote that story now—
radioactive to the end of time—
people, I swear, your eyes would fall out, you couldn't peel
the gloves fast enough
from your hands scorched by the firestorms of that shame.
Your poor hands. Your poor eyes
to see me weeping in my room
or boring the tall blonde to death.
Once I accused the innocent.
Once I bowed and prayed to the guilty.
I still wince at what I once said to the devastated widow.
And one October afternoon, under a locust tree
whose blackened pods were falling and making
illuminating patterns on the pathway,
I was seized by joy,
and someone saw me there,
and that was the worst of all,
lacerating and unforgettable.

16

Trisha

Vivek Shraya

My story has always been bound to your prayer to have two boys. Maybe it was because of the ways you felt weighed down as a young girl, or the ways you felt you weighed down your mother by being a girl. Maybe it was because of the ways being a wife changed you. Maybe it was all the above, and also just being a girl in a world that is intent on crushing women. So you prayed to a god you can't remember for two sons and you got me. I was your first and I was soft. Did this ever disappoint you?

You had also prayed for me to look like Dad, but you forgot to pray for the rest of me. It is strange that you would overlook this, as you have always said "Be careful what you pray for." When I take off my clothes and look in the mirror, I see Dad's body, as you wished. But the rest of me has always wished to be you.

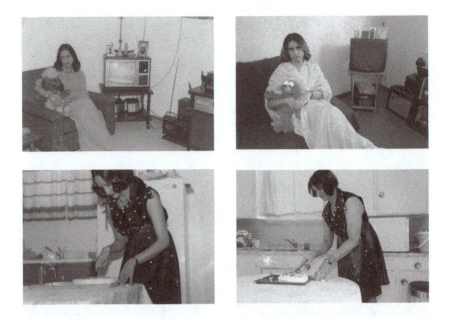

I modelled myself—my gestures, my futures, how I love and rage—all after you. Did this worry you and Dad? Did you have the kinds of conversations in bed that parents of genderqueer children on TV have, where the Dad scolds the Mom—"This is your fault"? No one is to blame. Not you, not the god you prayed to. I was right to worship you. You worked full-time, went to school part-time, managed a home, raised two children who complained about frozen food and made fun of your accent, and cared for your family in India. Most days in my adult life, I can barely care for myself.

I remember finding these photos of you three years ago and being astonished, even hurt, by your joyfulness, your playfulness. I wish I had known this side of you, before Canada, marriage and motherhood stripped it from you, and us.

I learned to pray too. My earliest prayers were to be released from my body, believing that this desire was devotion, this was about wanting to be closer to god. I don't believe in god anymore, but sometimes I still have the same prayer. Then I remind myself that the discomfort I feel is less about my body and more about what it means to be feminine in a world that is intent on crushing femininity in any form. Maybe I got my wish to be you after all.

You used to say that if you had a girl, you would have named her Trisha.
  -VS

17

Call It Rape

Margot Singer

Still life with man and gun

Three girls are smoking on the back porch of their high school dorm. It's near midnight on a Saturday in early autumn, the leaves not yet fallen, the darkness thick. A man steps out of the woods. He is wearing a black ski mask, a hooded jacket, leather gloves. He has a gun. He tells the girls to follow him, that if they make a noise or run he'll shoot. He makes them lie face down on the ground. He rapes first one and then the others. He walks away.

It is September, 1978. Two of the girls are my classmates; the third is a friend of theirs, visiting for the weekend. As a day student, I hear the news on Monday morning. I am fifteen and, like most of us—good girls at an all-girls boarding school—my experience of sex so far consists of sweaty slow dances and a few nights of awkward groping and beery kisses with boys I never see again. At the special all-school meeting convened that morning, the headmistress informs us of the security guard that has been hired, the safety lights that soon will be installed. Another woman, a cop or counselor, steps up to the microphone. "Rape is a crime of violence, not sex," she says. She repeats it, like a mantra, to make sure we understand.

I try to picture the girls out there in that ravine behind the dorm, dead leaves and pine needles and dirt cold against their skin. The porch light shining dimly through the trees. The man, the mask and gloves and gun. But there the tableau freezes. I simply can't imagine it: the logistics of it, the lying there, the terrible anticipation, and then. Wasn't there *something* they could have done, I can't help thinking, three-on-one like that?

Still, the incident does not make me fearful. I'm not afraid to be home alone in my parents' house, just a few miles down the road. I'm not afraid to walk home from my music lessons along the wooded path that winds around the pond behind my house or to take the T into Boston by myself. I don't believe that what happened to those girls could happen to me. More precisely, it doesn't even occur to me that it could. I can't make any of it touch me: the powerlessness, the fear, the shame.

A few weeks after the rapes, a man is arrested, a tennis pro from a respected local family. Everyone is shocked, relieved. The girls stay in school. They get over it, or so we all believe.

The word rape comes from

The word "rape" comes from the Latin verb *rapere*: to seize, to take by force, to carry off. Rape, in its original sense, was a property crime, a form of theft. The early Romans famously seized and carried off the Sabine women, being short on wives. Poussin depicts the Sabine women flung over the Romans' shoulders, abandoned infants wailing on the ground, fathers wrestling the soldiers to get their daughters back. But in the center of the canvas, in the midst of all the chaos, a slender, blue-gowned woman can be seen strolling off arm-in-arm with her assailant, her head tilted amorously toward his. The Roman historian Livy records that the Sabine women were advised to "cool their anger and give their hearts to the men who had already taken their bodies." A happy ending for an imperial foundation-myth.

Other words come from the same Latin root as "rape": *rapture, ravage, rapt, ravenous, rapacious, ravishing.* Ovid's *Metamorphoses* is filled with stories of ravishing nymphs seized and carried off by rapacious gods: Io, Daphne, Callisto, Europa, Andromeda, Leda, Persephone. (There are more than fifty sexual attacks in Ovid, by one scholar's count.) Correggio paints Io in an erotic swoon, her head tipped back, her lips parted, her body one long, sensuous curve of flesh. You might be forgiven for forgetting that Jupiter has just chased her into the woods, whereupon, in Ovid's words, "he hid the wide earth in a covering of fog, caught the fleeing girl, and raped her." Titian pictures Europa in a similar state of rapture, sprawled blowsily across the back of a muscular white bull (Jupiter), her fleshy thighs parted, her translucent gown in disarray, a milky breast exposed. Inspired by Titian, Rubens depicts the abduction of the daughters of Leucippus by the twins Castor and Pollux as a Baroque spiral of rearing horses, gleaming armor, flowing golden hair, creamy female skin. The daughters, languidly reaching out for help, do not look exactly happy, but neither do they seem especially distressed.

I read Ovid and study Roman history in high school. For a fine arts course in college, I go to the Isabella Stewart Gardner Museum and study Titian's *Rape of Europa* and Botticelli's *Tragedy of Lucretia*. I write essays on the aesthetic qualities and cultural contexts of the art. But as far as I can remember, I never consider the fact that these scenes are all depicted from the perspective of a man. It doesn't occur to me to ask what it means to glorify sexual violence, to conflate *rapture* and *ravishment* and *rape*.

Cossacks

My mother stands before the bathroom mirror, putting on lipstick, brushing her hair. I am watching her get ready to go out, as I have done since I was a little girl—my beautiful mother, with her slender wrists and ankles and thick dark hair. She sprays on her perfume, Hermès's "Calèche," its blend of rose and iris, oak moss, and woods, even now the essence of my mother, a luxuriant, sexy smell. My father brings her gifts of perfume when he travels abroad for work.

My mother has hazel eyes, high cheekbones. She brushes rouge onto her cheeks, tilting her face before the mirror. They are a good-looking couple, my parents, romantic, although often enough, they fight. My father mutters curses under his breath when he is angry, hissed first syllables hinting at awful names: "*fu—- cu-*," "*stu— sh-*." He makes all the money and has all the power, my mother complains. She urges me to pursue a career, to be independent, not to marry young the way she did.

My mother inherited her high cheekbones from her mother, she tells me, whose parents emigrated from Czarist Russia at the turn of the century, fleeing the pogroms. My image of pogroms comes from *Fiddler on the Roof's* horseback-riding, vodka-swilling Cossacks in their leather boots and belted tunics. Who squat and kick their heels out as they dance, their arms folded across their chests. Who rip their spears through Motel and Tzeitel's down pillows and wedding quilts.

My mother takes a tissue and blots her lips, leaving a coral lip-print kiss. "The Cossacks had high cheekbones," she says. "There must have been some Cossack blood back there, somewhere."

Somehow I understand that she is talking about rape. About the vestiges of that history of violence, helixed like a secret in the DNA of every cell inside her body, and in mine.

Lois Lane

The summer after my first year in college, I get a job working as a reporter for a suburban Massachusetts newspaper, *The Middlesex News*. I am assigned to the Waltham bureau, a dingy storefront office on Moody Street. The editors and reporters sit at metal desks along one side of the room. The opposite side belongs to circulation, and every morning the delivery people (not boys on bikes, but shuffling adults in beat-up cars) file in to deposit their collections, interrupting the buzz and clack of our electric typewriters with the jangle of the coin-sorting machine. I write features on a diner-turned-Chinese restaurant, on neighborhood objections over a cut-down tree, on a museum of industry, on a summer camp for gifted kids. After a few weeks, I am promoted to editorial assistant and assigned the police and court beats.

I have never had a real job before. In the mornings, I sleep too late and arrive at the police station with my hair dripping down the back of my skimpy tee shirt or the summer dress my mother probably should have advised me not to wear to work. The cops hoot when I approach to read the blotter. When they learn my name is Margot, they call me Lois Lane.

"Hey, Lois! Howya doin'?" they shout when I walk in, their Boston accents thick. "Where's Clark?"

On Monday mornings, they say, "Hey, Lois, you get married yet?"

I am embarrassed and a little offended but mostly flattered by the teasing. I squirm as I copy into my reporter's notebook the previous days' offenses: vandalized mailboxes, minor drug busts, stolen bikes, toilet-papered trees. Then in August there's a rape. The victim, a single woman in her twenties, is awakened at five a.m. by an intruder ("a stocky, powerful man with an Italian accent," I improbably report) who climbs in through her ground floor bedroom window with a white sack over his head. He holds a knife to her throat and threatens to kill her if she makes a sound or tries to run for help. It's an August heat wave: oppressive, muggy, East Coast heat. Fans whir in the windows of the station house. Sweat trickles down my chest as I stand in the police chief's office, pen in hand, the cover of my notebook flipped back.

Deputy Chief Rooney leans back in his desk chair and sighs. He is a heavy man, his collar tight around his ruddy neck. He says, "It's hot. People get crazy, you know, when it's hot."

I know only enough to roll my eyes, afterward, when I tell people what he said. I do not know that this was the third rape in less than three weeks in Waltham. That the only female rape counselor on the Waltham force was laid off in the last round of budget cuts. That an average of 1.5 women are sexually assaulted in Boston every day. At seventeen, I consider myself a feminist, but I have not read Susan Brownmiller's 1975 book, *Against Our Will*. I have not heard of the slogan "Take Back the Night."

I am Lois Lane. "Wednesday I had a big story—rape!" I write in my journal at the end of the week. "My story made the front page on Thursday. It was all very exciting. Went out to dinner with Mom and Dad."

Denial

Not long ago I read a memoir, *Denial*, written by a terrorism expert named Jessica Stern. Stern was fifteen in 1973 when she was raped, along with her fourteen-year-old sister, at gunpoint in her Concord, Massachusetts, home. In 2006, at Stern's request, the Concord police reopened the case files and connected her assault to forty-four other similar rapes in the Boston area. Eighteen of the rapes occurred within an eight-block radius in Harvard Square; victims included the thirteen-year-old daughter of Harvard Law School's dean. Other rapes occurred at nearby boarding schools. Two girls were raped in their dorm at Concord Academy. Two girls were raped at a private school in Natick. Two girls were raped at my high school, Dana Hall.

Whoa, I think. I know this story. That guy— the tennis pro?—raped forty-something other girls as well? But the details do not add up. I remember three girls being raped, not two. Moreover, the man who police say assaulted Stern and her sister was arrested in 1973 and spent the next eighteen years in jail. In 1973, I was ten, not in high school. Have I misremembered what happened? Or did the police make a mistake? Finally, searching the *Boston Globe* archives, I find an article detailing the rapes that I remember, dated November 1978. It opens with this lead:

Lt. Victor Maccini has been a Wellesley policeman for 32 years. His memory faltered the other day when he was asked when his department had conducted its last intensive rape investigation. He gazed out of his office window and shook his head slowly before answering. "Gee ... a rape case? I don't remember," he said. "We've had them, though, but they've always been on the outskirts, like Needham or Newton."

But buried a dozen paragraphs down, the same article states:

Police concede, however, that the case is almost identical to a case in 1971 in which two Dana Hall students reported that they were raped at gunpoint by a masked gunman. That case was never solved.

It takes a minute before I comprehend that we are talking about two different incidents, both at my high school, just seven years apart. Until now, I'd never heard of the 1971 rapes. I can't find a single mention of them in the press. Thirty-three years later, I am stunned. So many girls, raped, not "on the outskirts," not in the crazy heat of August, but in their homes and dorms, in the tony Boston suburbs where I grew up. I was right there, but I had no idea.

In an op-ed piece published in the *Boston Globe* in 2010, Amy Vorenberg reveals that she is the girl Stern refers to in her book as "Lucy," the daughter of the Harvard Law School dean, raped in 1971 by a masked gunman in an upstairs bathroom of her mother's house while her family and friends talked and laughed downstairs. The police issued no warning. The next night, the same man raped two more girls just down the street. No one said a thing. "I have been silent long enough," Vorenberg writes. "Although 40 years have passed, respected institutions still suppress information about sexual assault, and rape remains the most underreported of violent crimes."

The tennis pro, as it turns out, was not the rapist. He was acquitted after a short trial at the end of November, 1978. The case was never solved.

Red running shorts

It is the end of exam period of my senior year in college. I am finishing a thirty-five-page paper, and I have stretched it right to the end. I sit at my desk, chewing on my pencil, riffling through my stacks of notes, the scribbled pages of my draft. The paper is due at five p.m., and it is already mid-afternoon, and I have not yet finished writing, have not yet begun to type.

I phone my professor to ask for an extension. Just until the morning, I plead. Just for time to type. I expect him to be sympathetic. I'm a senior, a good student, a hard worker. I've already turned in my honors thesis, passed my orals, won a prestigious scholarship to graduate school. There is a faint buzzing on the line. I wait.

He says, "If that paper is not at my house by nine o'clock tomorrow morning, I'm giving you an F."

Right.

I pull an all-nighter finishing the paper. In the morning, I walk across Harvard Square to the address the professor has given me. It's a long walk;

I don't have a car. I haven't showered or changed my clothes. My eyes are gritty, my hair greasy. People are strolling along the sidewalks, new leaves fluttering on the trees, but in my fatigue, nothing feels quite real. I climb the steps and ring the bell.

He comes to the door wearing bright red running shorts and nothing else. He is bare-chested, barelegged, barefoot, practically naked, except for those red shorts. He is square-jawed and blond-bearded and runner-thin. He motions for me to come in.

I step into the living room. He picks up a telephone that is lying on the table off the hook and, cradling the receiver between his shoulder and his cheek, continues whatever conversation he was having before my arrival. He flips rapidly through the pages of my paper, the one I've worked so hard on, the one I stayed up all night to type. He is skimming, making a show of disinterest, I think. He flips the pages, murmuring into the phone. I perch on the edge of the couch and wait. A clock ticks in the kitchen, which I can see through an open door. There is no one else in the house, as near as I can tell. After a little while, he hangs up the phone and fixes me with a look.

"I would have given you an A," he says, "but the paper is late. So I'm giving you a B instead." He comes around the table to me. My heart is beating hard. I'd like to protest—I wrote a thirty-five-page paper, after all, and it's good!— but I do not, cannot, speak.

He writes something on a card, slides it into an envelope. He holds it out to me. "I want you to go over to University Hall now," he says, "and turn in my grades."

Grades are not due for several days, I am quite sure. He has no right to make me run his errands for him. But he is giving me an order, not an option. He stands there in his red running shorts, bare-chested, practically naked, holding out that envelope. It's clear that he would have no compunction about ripping it open and changing the B to an F if I refuse. It's clear he could do anything he wants.

He could, for example, push my head down to those red running shorts and make me suck his dick.

He does not do it, but he could.

I take the envelope and walk back across the square and turn it in.

Oleanna

Anita Hill is on the radio, promoting her new book. It has been twenty years since the 1991 Senate confirmation hearings in which Hill accused Judge

Clarence Thomas of sexual harassment. People are calling in to thank her: women and men who admire her bravery, mothers whose daughters have grown up taking it for granted that it's not okay to tell lewd jokes in the workplace, to touch a woman without asking, to hold out rewards in exchange for sex. I'm thinking of my teenage daughter, what she will encounter soon at school or work. How much has changed?

David Mamet's play, *Oleanna*—which I saw at its Harvard Square premiere in 1992, just seven months after the Thomas hearings— dramatizes a power struggle between a college student, Carol, and a young professor, John. Carol is on the verge of failing and desperate to pass John's course. John patronizes Carol's lack of understanding, interrupts their conversation to talk to his wife on the phone, then tells Carol that if she comes to his office for private tutorials, he'll give her an "A."

In a gesture that might or might not be paternal, John reaches out to touch her shoulder. Carol files a sexual harassment complaint. John's tenure bid is put on hold. When John tries to talk Carol into dropping the charges, he grows angry and grabs her arm, and she raises the charges to attempted rape. In the play's final scene, John loses control and beats Carol with a chair. "Oh, my God," he says, realizing what he has done. From where she cowers on the floor, Carol looks up at him and says slowly, "Yes, that's right."

Mamet complicates the narrative of sexual harassment, giving Carol the power to destroy John, making John both a monster and a dupe. Watching the play, I find that I am shocked that Carol has such power. It has not dawned on me until now that in my own run-in with my red-running-shorts-clad professor, six years earlier, I had power, too. (Like John, my professor did not have tenure. All I would have had to do was file a complaint!) Yet I can't help feeling that John, for all his smugness and paternalistic hypocrisy—or, for that matter, my professor—does not deserve to be destroyed. Does power necessarily corrupt? Or are we more complicit in protecting privilege than we'd like to think?

Campus watch

I am now a college professor, the one with power (such as it is) over deadlines, extensions, grades. Since the eighties, of course, things have changed. I keep my office door open during student conferences, watch my gestures and my language, encourage students to engage with questions of power, privilege, race, gender, class. College is no longer a boys' club. These days, in the classroom, the women outperform the men. They raise their hands and voice opinions. They are diligent, articulate, and bright.

At the college where I teach, as elsewhere, kids drink, hook up. Here, as elsewhere, girls get drunk at parties, black out, and wake up to discover they've been raped. Girls are assaulted walking across campus and in their dorms, by strangers and by friends. A study funded by the U.S. Department of Justice estimates that one in five female students will be raped during their college years. But over eighty percent of victims do not report the crime.

A former student of mine is one of the few who does speak up. Almost nothing about her case is clear. She says she did shots before going to a party and can't remember anything that happened after that. The boy in question says she came on to him aggressively at a party and clearly wanted sex. She says she only discovered she'd gone back to his room when she heard the gossip the next day. People who were at the party confirm they saw her grinding with him on the dance floor. After a disciplinary hearing, the boy is suspended for the year. She receives vicious messages, calling her a slut, accusing her of ruining his life.

I don't know what to think. My mother says, "Why should the boy take all the blame? In my day, as a girl, you knew you had to take responsibility for yourself." My husband says, "It's not that complicated. You just don't mess around with a girl who's drunk."

When we meet for coffee, my student says her parents are planning to appeal the verdict; his parents have filed suit. She's looking into transferring to a different college, although so far this semester, her grades are not so great. "It's been pretty rough," she says. She shakes back her long hair and fiddles with her coffee cup. "You are not a victim," I want to tell her, but we both know it is too late. You become a victim once you call it rape.

The morning after

In the late 1980s, after graduate school, I go to work for a consulting firm in New York. It's the kind of job that, not even a generation ago, was the sole domain of men. But the group of associates I am hired with is nearly forty percent women, and we're sure the senior ranks—scarcely four percent women—will catch up soon enough. We're well educated, well paid, and young enough to believe that you can have a high-powered job like this and still get married and have kids. *I want it all and I want it now*, reads a button I've tacked up on my bulletin board.

Office romance is officially against the rules but common nonetheless. At an off-site meeting in Arizona during a business trip, one of the partners—

I'll call him Rick—approaches me after dinner on the final night. He invites me to skip the party and go out for a drink with him instead. He is a few years older than me and more senior in the firm, but I don't work with him directly, and he's not my boss. He is single and athletic and not bad looking and has a reputation for being really smart. I say sure.

The bellman calls us a taxi. As soon as we leave the irrigated grounds of our hotel, the Sonoran Desert opens up, a bleak expanse of sand and scrub grass cooling beneath the evening sun. The cab driver takes us to a bar on the outskirts of Scottsdale, a converted bunkhouse with a row of dusty Harleys parked out front. We settle at a picnic table, and Rick fetches himself a nonalcoholic beer and me an Amstel Light. He is fun to talk with, and I like his blue eyes and his smile. The possibility, even the likelihood, of sex flares between us like the distant heat lightning forking over the ridge of the McDowells.

I go back with Rick to his hotel room of my own free will. I am not drunk. I let him take off my clothes and lead me to the bed, filled with the strange attraction of a stranger's body touching mine. We enter such situations with certain expectations. We expect intelligent people to behave intelligently, colleagues to behave collegially, people with whom we have a lot in common to think the way we think. So when I ask if he has a condom, I don't expect him to laugh and say, "Oh, I don't do condoms." I don't expect that he won't stop. We are two bodies in motion, and momentum exerts its force. My mind whirls, but no words come out.

Very quickly, it is over. He sighs and rolls away. I phone my doctor the next day and ask for the morning-after pill. I hear only what I take for disapproval in her voice as she gives me instructions, her tone clinical and clipped. I don't remember if she asks me about what happened. I'm pretty sure she doesn't use the word *consent*. Anyway, I consented, didn't I? I could have said no, could have tried to stopped him, but I didn't. I fill the prescription, swallow the pills, and for the next twenty-four hours, I throw up. I don't talk to Rick. I tell my friends I must have caught a stomach bug. The wretchedness of my secret feels like the punishment I deserve.

What is it about no means no

Jury duty, Salt Lake City, 2004. At the courthouse, people wait in rows of plastic chairs, mumbling into cell phones, as a film plays overhead about the civic importance and personal rewards of jury service. Finally, a few of us are called up to the courtroom for the voir dire. We stand in turn and answer questions printed on a laminated sheet. One of the questions asks what kinds of things we read. A number of people say "only religious material." I'm an East Coast liberal, working toward an English Ph.D.; I tell them: *The New Yorker*, literary fiction, Derrida. I'm thinking that I'll be dismissed.

After the questioning, the judge informs us that the criminal trial we're being selected for is a rape case. The defendant, who is married to the victim, is being tried on five counts of rape. The judge asks if anyone feels they cannot be objective in this kind of case. She asks if anyone has a problem with the concept that the defendant is innocent until proven guilty. Several people raise their hands and are excused. I'm in.

Spousal rape has been against the law in Utah, as in most states, since 1991, but the concept is still not so easy to digest. The wife and husband in this case are young and poor and have two small kids. She works in a gas station convenience store. He is out of work. We're told they fight over child care and who gets to use the car. We watch a video of him being interrogated by a detective who appears to be coercing him to confess. We watch as the wife takes the stand and starts to cry, her waist-length brown hair hanging in her face, as she says she loves her husband, has always loved him, loves him still.

We understand that the law says you don't have to kick and scream or struggle for an unwanted sexual act to be considered rape. That you don't have to be physically threatened or forcibly pinned down. That you have to be capable of consent, and that you can withdraw that consent at any point. That rape is not the victim's fault. We understand all this and yet. We struggle, listening to the testimony, with the fact that this man did not use force, that his wife did not fight back. We sit around the table in the jury room and argue for hours, conflicted and confused:

"What bothers me is that she didn't *do* anything to stop him."

"Come on, what could she have done? She said she knew she *couldn't* stop him no matter what she did."

"She told him, 'Stop, you'll wake the kids.'"

"But was she like, 'Oh, we really should stop, honey,' or like, 'You need to stop right this minute?' How can you tell?"

"Look, it's not as if he hurt her. Bad sex isn't a crime."

"It doesn't make any difference whether or not he hurt her. She didn't want to do it. That's her right."

"Haven't we all done things we didn't want to do? That's called life."

"She got up there on the stand and said she loves him."

In the end, we can't agree to call it rape. They're both young and foolish, we rationalize. None of us wants to be responsible for ruining a young man's life.

After we deliver our not-guilty verdict, the prosecutor comes storming back. She is furious, her red hair ablaze.

She says, "What is it about 'no means no' that you all don't understand?"

Antipodes

Traveling in New Zealand, I strike up a conversation with an American in a Queenstown café. He's thirty-something, my age as well, a high school science teacher who, like me, has taken a leave of absence from work. His accent is appealingly familiar. He seems like any number of the fellow travelers I've met while on the road alone: friendly, companionable, polite. After we finish eating, he invites me to walk back with him to his hostel to watch a movie on the common room TV. It's a pleasant, early autumn evening—March in the antipodes—and I have nothing else to do, so I agree. We meander across town, chatting about Wanaka and the Milford Sound, our hikes along the Franz Josef Glacier, the sea-eroded rocks at Hokitika, the seals basking on the beach at Jackson Bay.

At the hostel, the common room is deserted and nothing good is playing on TV. I look around for the proprietor of the hostel, other guests, but there's no one else in sight. The fluorescent lights buzz overhead. Sitting beside him on the couch as he clicks through the channels, I feel the energy between us shift. After a bit, he puts his arm around me and pulls me to him. He tries to kiss me, but I shake my head, pull back. "I'm sorry," I say, feeling like a jerk. I didn't mean to lead him on. It really didn't occur to me this is what he had in mind.

He stiffens, but instead of backing off, he presses closer, fumbling with the zipper of his pants with one hand, pushing my head down with the other, angling his pelvis toward my face. He does not hurt me, but there is nothing but aggression in his actions. For a moment, I consider giving in. It's just a blow job, after all. But instead I pull free, stand up. His anger radiates toward me, hard and petulant, like a child's, only he is no child.

"I'd better go," I say.

He says, "You fucking bitch."

I leave him sitting on the couch. Outside in the darkness, fear catches me by the throat. It is quite a long distance back to where I'm staying, and I'm not sure I know the way. I walk as quickly as I can without running, scanning the dark streets for a taxi, for attackers, my room keys threaded through my fingers, adrenaline vibrating through my limbs. I am less angry with him than with myself.

I thought I knew how to take care of myself, but I fucked up.

In my journal, I write only: "Met F. at dinner. Took a walk back to his hostel." I edit out the details but not the shame, which lingers, even after all these years.

Rape is rape

Rape happens behind closed doors, between the sheets, in locker rooms, in prisons, in churches, in refugee camps, in dorms, in back alleys, in three-thousand-dollars per night luxury hotel suites. It happens between the powerful and the weak, between men and women, men and boys, husbands and wives, adults and children, strangers and lovers, between ordinary people like you and me. You might say you're just having a little fun, horsing around, hooking up. Sometimes there's a knife or gun. Sometimes there's a kiss. It isn't so easy to tell lie from truth, intention from mistake.

After a Toronto cop tells a group of college women that they shouldn't dress provocatively if they don't want to get raped, women around the world take to the streets dressed in bras and camisoles and fishnet tights, the word *SLUT* scrawled in Sharpie across their bare arms and backs. Bloggers rail against rape culture. Activists wage campaigns for better information and awareness, trumpeting the slogan "rape is rape." All this talk gives me a bit of hope. I'd like to think my children will grow up to a world where girls are not attacked at gunpoint in their homes or dorms or taken advantage of when drunk, where threats or accusations of rape are not used to gain political advantage, where women can express their sexuality without being shamed as sluts, where men and women understand that no means no and yes means yes. But I'm not so sure.

Maybe anatomy is destiny; maybe Freud was right. The language of desire is the language of violence, after all. Sexy women are knockouts, bombshells, stunning, dressed to kill, femmes fatales. Love is an abduction: your heart is stolen. You're smitten, hooked, swept off your feet. Cupid's weapon is an arrow. Sex and violence, violence and sex, twine together in a knot that cannot be undone.

18

Invisible Partners

Ira Sukrungruang

On my mother's refrigerator in Chiang Mai, Thailand, are pictures from my high school dances in Chicago, when we lived in a bi-level as a happy immigrant family—Homecoming, the Sweetheart's Dance, Prom. There are so many photos of me you can barely see the surface of the fridge, just a hundred smiling Ira's with various forms of facial hair. But those dance photos—someone is missing in every one of them.

My mother has cut out my dates.

It is me, in suspenders and hunter green slacks, an arm around No One. It is me, wearing contacts for the one and only time, and my hand is on the hip of No One's waist. It is me, in a tux, cheek-to-cheek with No One.

"Why did you cut my dates?" I ask.

My mother sews together the pants I ripped earlier in the day when I was kowtowing to Buddha at a temple in the center of town. She laughed so hard her dentures popped out.

"I save what I want to remember," my mother says. "Those girls, I don't want to remember."

"Do you do this with other pictures?"

My mother shrugs. She does not lift an eye off of the needle. "Sometimes."

"Who else?"

"I cut your father out all the pictures, too," she says.

"Why?"

My mother's glasses are thick. When she looks up, they enlarge her eyes, like a bug. "I want to remember what I remember."

*

They have been relegated to oblivion—my dates—that void where all halved pictures go. I imagine a planet of them. So many lost partners, so many severed parts. Anniversary photos, family vacations, too-close selfies. All disunited. There they mingle, in a two-dimensional world. There they try to find a fit to complete the photo. But no cut fits flawlessly, an imperfect puzzle.

Those dates—Becky, Sharon, Vicky—find a table in the corner of a coffee shop. They are beautiful in their dresses, their hair primped and pampered, their nails painted vivid red. Vicky's banana straps made boys in that coffee shop look with envy. Becky's lips stood out from the pale of her skin. Sharon's blonde hair fell soft over her shoulders, like strands of fine yarn. In this world, they are best friends, though in walking and talking world they occupied different circles. In this world they play one role, and it is the one role they share: Ira's date.

The night comes early here, but the sky never darkens. Lights swirl like a perpetual disco ball. They tell each other stories of the dance.

"Ira, he can move, can't he?"

"I didn't know a Thai guy can James Brown like that."

"Did he do the running man for you?"

"I love how his face gets puffed and red."

They comment on how he was the perfect gentleman, except for Becky, who found him dancing with Tanya Tallon, his senior year crush; they went as friends anyway, so it didn't matter.

"And when a slow dance came on, he'd pull you close and you can feel the warmth of his torso."

"He had shoulders you can rest your head on."

"You felt other things, too."

And they laughed and laughed and laughed. There was so much about Ira that was entertaining, how he went to the bathroom every fifteen minutes to check on his hair, how he was always paranoid a booger was hanging out of his nose, how he kept asking whether they were having fun. They agreed he was such a boy, but different from the others, respectful, always thinking about them before anything else. They said he was the perfect gentleman, never going for a grope or fondle without permission.

"He let me wear his jacket when we were on an after dance cruise on Lake Michigan."

"It rained hard afterwards, so he gave me his umbrella and carried me to the car, so my dress wouldn't drag."

"He was so shy when he kissed me."

A melancholy settled in among them then, those three dressed up girls. This happens a lot in the world of halved pictures. They wished their other half was there, their versions of Ira, asking them to the dance floor, holding them tight, singing in their ear how beautiful they were, how this song was theirs, how this night was theirs, how they did not have to fear anything, not even a pair of scissors come to down to sever them.

19

The Professor of Longing

Jill Talbot

243: The Professor of Longing

Dr. Jill Talbot

Contact: talbot1@boisestate.edu | 426–7060

Office: LA 102 C (a room I share with a broken shelf and three people I never see)

Office Hours: Before and After Class and once in a booth in the Hyde Park Bar & Grill

Course Description: This course is about failed attempts. It's about me standing in an office two states and two months ago handing over a letter declaring that I was leaving academia indefinitely. It's about being on the road—Utah, Idaho, Montana—climbing north before having to turn around, scramble south. It's about the trying months of summer and ending up in a circumstance not on any map. It's about Boise instead of Missoula, about adjustments instead of adventure, about impediments edging out impulse, bi-monthly paychecks that can't cover rent and daycare, my last cigarette. It will be writing in a cramped corner on a plastic tv tray in a foldout chair bought at a thrift store. By the end of the semester, the focus will be two am phone calls and bad checks. For the final, look for a bookcase and a loveseat in a living room with the front door left wide open, my four-year-old daughter's favorite polka-dotted vest forgotten on the kitchen counter.

Texts: We're not going to read anything beyond my own proclivities. We'll discuss stories, essays, and poems that remind me of my most recent misgivings, the lingerings I'm unable to yield, the words underlining my past. Our study will include recurring images, my own, of course, as well as the themes of my disposition. The text in this class is me.

Attendance: It's strange to think I'm even here. Years from now, I will feel as these weeks were nothing more than an interruption, a curve in the story's road.

Disclaimer: While these aren't the texts I really used that semester, they most accurately reflect who I was during those weeks when I kept my eyes to the sidewalk.

August 22	Walt Whitman and Emily Dickinson, Selections
	Whitman has many famous lines about celebrating himself and containing multitudes and taking to the open road, sounding his barbaric yawp, yet stylistically, he used a device called "cataloging." A long list. Write that down. It's important, because we all catalog, make long lists of lovers, of things to pack, pros and cons, items at the drugstore. Some catalogs come with details, like wine lists. Some in a shorthand no one but us can read, and if enough time goes by, neither can we, as we pull a forgotten slip of paper from the bottom of a purse or a pocket and stare at a mystery.
	Dickinson used dashes in her lines, random capitalization, difficult to decipher punctuation. She wasn't consistent in her usage, and often her poems were in unfinished forms. But it's the dashes that draw me, so we'll focus on those. Sometimes they appear at the end of a line, others in the middle, interruptions. Still, other poems are words alone, no dashes at all. Emphasis? A writer's pen carrying over to the next word, down the line? Never intended as part of the prosody at all, like a pause in a conversation misinterpreted as silence or disagreement when it's only search for the right words? Or are they like bridges crossing a question?
	We'll be seeing these elements throughout the semester: catalogs of loss, of what lies between or is left to the end, the choices too difficult to decipher.
	I'll tell you up front: he left. So let's look at an opening line of Dickinson's: "You left me, sweet, two legacies—"
	And he did, one, the legacy of our years together that began with the Eagle River and a half moon. The other, the sweetest legacy, our daughter, who, I suppose, he never saw as part of his prosody. That dash—his disappearance. And so, to the Whitmanesque open road he went, "afoot and lighthearted," while, me? My lines are a bit further down: "I carry my old delicious burdens .... I carry them with me where I go/I swear it is impossible for me to get rid of them."
	The delicious burdens I bear because no state, not this one or the last three I've lived in can trace a line underneath Kenny and make him pay child support. He's the dash that keeps dashing, a catalogue of unanswered phone calls.

August 29	**Kate Chopin, "The Story of an Hour"**
	A "storm of grief" I know well. And that feeling of being locked in a room alone and looking out of it, fearing the feeling that's coming and not being able to beat it back. For years I wanted to be free, and yet, I had "loved him–sometimes." Here is the conflict in—the balance of—maintaining individuality while sharing a life with someone. I'll tell you I've always wanted to share a duplex with a man, him on one side, me on the other, so we have our separate spaces together, but I will not divulge that sharing a life with someone is not a thing I've ever been able to sustain, that I have repeatedly chosen "self-assertion" over "possession," that I can discuss love within the context of a work of literature, but surviving it, for me, is an "unsolved mystery."
	If you need to see me before class, check outside the double doors on the East side of the building. I'll be huddled near a trash can, smoking like a stranger outside a convenience store.
September 5	**Charlotte Perkins Gilman, "The Yellow Wallpaper"**
	I am trapped inside my own yellow walls. The apartment I rented on Dewey Street, about a ten minute drive from the University, is the middle unit in a three unit structure, and mine is undoubtedly the smallest, crammed between the other two. The landlord who met me at the property in late July on my drive back from Montana opened the door to a hideous site: yellow walls with accents of a deep red, a clash so revolting I almost didn't step inside. Gilman's description resonates: "The color is repellent, almost revolting; a smoldering unclean yellow." But there were only two weeks before classes began, the other apartments I had seen not livable or in questionable neighborhoods, and I still had to drive back to southern Utah to pick up Indie, who had stayed with friends while I found a job and a place in Missoula, now Boise.
	The apartment has a bathroom off of the kitchen, a proximity that bothers me, a stand-only shower, a tiny bedroom, one closet. This is the smallest place I have ever lived, including graduate school. Indie and I share a bed, one we found in the storage shed, and we sit side by side on a loveseat, the only size that still only barely fits along the wall. The state tells me I make thirty dollars over the limit to qualify for assistance. I think that's about what I spend on smokes a month.
	Gilman admitted to altering her experience in her story, using "embellishments and additions, to carry out the ideal." The ideal, she felt, was to keep women from going crazy. Later this semester, I will sit on the loveseat in the middle of the night, cutting my arms with nail scissors, assume this is what is happening to me.

September 12	**Willa Cather, "Paul's Case"**
	Paul is what is considered a fragmented character. He embodies two worlds but doesn't really live in either. My mother on voice mail, asks, "Where are you living?" And I'm not really sure. I'm not even sure I'd call what I'm doing here living.
	Indie's daycare costs four hundred dollars a month. Every two weeks, I make just two hundred over that. Then there's the rent, the groceries at Albertson's and the wine I can't stop drinking, not to mention the quarters for pool where I teach Indie to play while we share a hamburger at the Hyde Park Bar & Grill. I am a fragmented character: I stand before you confident, poised, engaged. I stand inside myself a wreck.
September 19	**Sherwood Anderson, "Mother"**
	Another window watching woman. This is a story that uses where a character lives as a metaphor for how he lives: "The hotel in which he had begun life so hopefully was now a mere ghost of what a hotel should be." I think of my apartment, how it stands for the way there's not enough room here, a suffocation.
September 26	**John Steinbeck, *The Wandering Bus***
	I love how the woman in this chapter tells her whiskey glass, "Now you just stay here and wait for me." Alice Chicoy stands inside the screen door of the lunchroom, watching the bus drive away before setting out the CLOSED sign and taking a day to herself. In these her hours of rare isolation, she waits on herself, downs a glass of whiskey, then beer, suddenly realizing that "the way you drink changes the taste." At some point, she goes into her bedroom (attached to the diner) and grabs a mirror, sets it down in front of her and serves her selves. I've done this many times, sipping Chardonnay in front of a mirror, keeping myself company. Like Alice, I too have become frightened, worried that I will run out. Of time, of wine, of cities in which to start over. When I get really worried, I start dialing and in the mornings, I have to check my phone to see who I talked to and for how long.
October 3	**F. Scott Fitzgerald, "Babylon Revisited"**
	In the spring semesters, I teach this on or around my daughter's birthday. In the fall semesters, I teach it in October, the month five years ago when I wrote to Kenny: "Jack Kerouac wrote that 'everyone goes home in October.' It's October, and the last leaves are falling from the tree outside our bedroom. Come home." Unlike Charlie Wales, he never came back for his little girl. At least Charlie Wales tried.
	I love Indie enough for two parents. This part, at least, I get right.

October 10	**Ernest Hemingway, "A Clean, Well-Lighted Place"**
	This story is a memory of an afternoon outside a basement apartment in Fort Collins, me in the green chair, him on the porch step, discussing the old man and the two waiters. During class, I draw the peak of a triangle drawn on the board with a line across the very tip of it, the fractions 1/8 above, 7/8 below. When I shade in the depths below the surface, I think how the story of us exists so far down I'm at a level where I can't even see what was there and what never was anymore.
	He and I used to smoke on the back porch of our last apartment. Here I smoke on the tiny step outside our apartment. Yesterday, Indie asked me to quit. I said yes. I'm one bad habit down from a pile that's stacked like unwashed dishes in the sink.
October 17	**John Cheever, "The Swimmer"**
	Choosing a Cheever story is like choosing a wine. I consider the concentration, the clarification, the finish I want to persist and not be short-lived. This story is about a man who drinks his way home only to find an empty house, all the doors locked. Here we discuss the way a character can look "in at the windows, [see] that the place [is] empty." An inversion of all those other characters who look out, wish to leave.
	How can I explain that I'm not even near halfway home, and it's getting darker with every week here, the muddy waters of my life churning, and I'm about to drown.
October 24	**Tennessee Williams, *A Streetcar Named Desire***
	Class cancelled.
October 31	~~**Jack Kerouac, On the Road Part I**~~
	Sherman Alexie, "The Lone Ranger and Tonto Fistfight in Heaven"
	I just read this last week while sitting at the Hyde Park Bar & Grill in the middle of the afternoon. Alexie writes about anger and imagination being the key to survival, and I can admit, I don't get angry enough, so maybe I balance my survival with what I imagine. I underlined this: "I knew there was plenty of places I wanted to be, but none where I was supposed to be." A recurring theme in literature, the search for a place where one belongs. But it's these questions I'd like to raise, to hear your thoughts: "How do you talk to the real person whose ghost has haunted you? How do you tell the difference between the two?" Because I can't figure that part out.
November 7	**Joan Didion, "The White Album"**
	Didion, similar to Anderson, discusses the house she lived in as being indicative of the times and her own state of mind. Things were fucked up. The world no longer made sense. The center was not holding. She told herself stories in order to live. I've become very good at telling myself stories.

Essay Due. Assignment: Discuss the significance of a character's house and his/her relationship to it by focusing on three of the works we have read and discussed. You are also required to discuss two texts (poems, essays, films, stories, novels) that do not appear on this syllabus.

The check I wrote last week at the Hyde Park Bar & Grill bounced. I knew it would.

November 14	**Raymond Carver, "The Ashtray" | "Why Don't You Dance?"**

A stanza from the poem:

> Then walks back to the table and sits
>
> down with a sigh. He drops the match in the ashtray.
>
> She reaches for his hand, and he lets her
>
> take it. Why not? Where's the harm?
>
> Let her. His mind's made up. She covers his
>
> fingers with kisses, tears fall on to his wrist.

A line from the story:

> His side, her side.

Class adjourned.

November 21	**Amy Hempel, "Memoir"**

An interesting story with only one sentence—enough to tell the story of a life. The three hours of class not enough to explain what that means. I'm unraveling. Can you tell?

November 28	**Pam Houston, "Cowboys are My Weakness"**

Discussion: "This is not my happy ending. This is not my story."

While you discuss, I've got to go in the hallway to return a phone call. A friend called to say I left a scary message on her voice mail at two o'clock in the morning. I'm going to tell her I'm fine, that I'm in class going over a story with an unnamed narrator. It won't be a lie. This is my story.

December 5	**Tim O'Brien, "The Things They Carried"**

We will close our study by examining the effect of Whitmanesque cataloging in prose form and how Lt. Jimmy Cross carries the letters of a girl he hopes loves him, even though the narrator shows us it isn't so. The young lieutenant reads her words again and again, as if he can change their meaning. When her words distract him from the war, he burns them. I tell my students it doesn't matter, he'll read those letters for the rest of life.

Those misinterpreted letters like the checks I keep writing, and for some reason, I pretend it doesn't matter. My balance already overdrawn past anything I can catch up with in time for the check to clear. Two years from now, I'll send one hundred and sixty dollars a month to pay down the damage I'm doing here, but for now, I'll keep writing false words and fake numbers on a small slip of paper, convincing everyone but myself they mean anything.

	We'll cut the last meeting short, because another night turned into some version of the darkest part of Alice Chicoy's afternoon once I decided there was no way I could stretch my severe salary across another semester, so I've been cataloging my choices for the next city and am in a bit of a panic.
Final	Your final is a representation of what you have learned in this class that may not be measured by exam or essay. I'm bringing a stack of parking tickets I have accrued over the course of the semester, the manifestation of the fines owed to me, the fines I own.

20

Nostalgia

Abigail Thomas

It's a man and a woman and they've climbed to the top of a mountain and it's evening and from where they stand they can see whole worlds and tiny bright cities and since he had coaxed her up this high, because he wanted to show her everything, he had his arms around her tightly because she was afraid of falling. And the sun actually did go down on their right at the exact moment the moon rose on their left, and this would have happened anyway, they both knew that, still they were glad to have seen it together. Whether they lay down and made love or did not make love under a billion stars is if no real interest to anyone (there being no small boys present) and who they were, and whether he knew the names of every tree and flower and if she loved lavender, or it rained, all these details will vanish like everything else. It happens all the time, you know, the sun goes up and comes down, it rains, we button and unbutton our clothes and turn on our sides to make love because all warm animals need other warm animals right from the beginning, or they go crazy and die. So if he had green eyes and she had blue and if they loved or did not love each other for good reasons or bad, and if they used the old words and did or did not make promises nobody keeps, no matter, let's let it go.

21

First

Ryan Van Meter

Ben and I are sitting side by side in the very back of his mother's station wagon. We face glowing white headlights of cars following us, our sneakers pressed against the back hatch door. This is our joy—his and mine—to sit turned away from our moms and dads in this place that feels like a secret, as though they are not even in the car with us. They have just taken us out to dinner, and now we are driving home. Years from this evening, I won't actually be sure that this boy sitting beside me is named Ben. But that doesn't matter tonight. What I know for certain right now is that I love him, and I need to tell him this fact before we return to our separate houses, next door to each other. We are both five.

Ben is the first brown-eyed boy I will fall for but will not be the last. His hair is also brown and always needs scraping off his forehead, which he does about every five minutes. All his jeans have dark squares stuck over the knees where he has worn through the denim. His shoelaces are perpetually undone, and he has a magic way of tying them with a quick, weird loop that I study and try myself, but can never match. His fingernails are ragged because he rips them off with his teeth and spits out the pieces when our moms aren't watching. Somebody always has to fix his shirt collars.

Our parents face the other direction, talking about something, and it is raining. My eyes trace the lines of water as they draw down the glass. Coiled beside my legs are the thick black and red cords of a pair of jumper cables. Ben's T-ball bat is also back here, rolling around and clunking as the long car wends its way through town. Ben's dad is driving, and my dad sits next to him, with our mothers in the back seat; I have recently observed that when mothers and fathers are in the car together, the dad always drives. My dad has also insisted on checking the score of the Cardinals game, so the radio is tuned to a staticky AM station, and the announcer's rich voice buzzes out of the speakers up front.

The week before this particular night, I asked my mother, "Why do people get married?" I don't recall the impulse behind my curiosity, but I will forever remember every word of her answer—she stated it simply after only a moment or two of thinking—because it seemed that important: "Two people get married when they love each other."

I had that hunch. I am a kindergartener, but the summer just before this rainy night, I learned most of what I know about love from watching soap operas with my mother. She is a gym teacher and during her months off, she catches up on the shows she has watched since college. Every summer weekday, I couldn't wait until they came on at two o'clock. My father didn't think I should be watching them—boys should be outside, playing—but he was rarely home early enough to know the difference, and according to my mother, I was too young to really understand what was going on anyway.

What I enjoyed most about soap opera was how exciting and beautiful life was. Every lady was pretty and had wonderful hair, and all the men had dark eyes and big teeth and faces as strong as bricks, and every week, there was a wedding or a manhunt or a birth. The people had grand fights where they threw vases at walls and slammed doors and chased each other in cars. There were villains locking up the wonderfully-haired heroines and suspending them in gold cages above enormous acid vats. And, of course, it was love that inspired every one of these stories and made life on the screen as thrilling as it was. That was what my mother would say from the sofa when I turned from my spot on the carpet in front of her and faced her, asking, "Why is he spying on that lady?"

"Because he loves her."

In the car, Ben and I hold hands. There is something sticky on his fingers, probably the strawberry syrup from the ice cream sundaes we ate for dessert. We have never held hands before; I have simply reached for his in the dark and held him while he holds me. I want to see our hands on the rough floor, but they are only visible every block or so when the car passes beneath a streetlight, and then, for only a flash. Ben is my closest friend because he lives next door, we are the same age, and we both have little brothers who are babies. I wish he were in the same kindergarten class as me, but he goes to a different school—one where he has to wear a uniform all day and for which there is no school bus.

"I love you," I say. We are idling, waiting for a red light to be green; a shining car has stopped right behind us, so Ben's face is pale and brilliant.

"I love you too," he says.

The car becomes quiet as the voice of the baseball game shrinks smaller and smaller.

"Will you marry me?" I ask him. His hand is still in mine; on the soap opera, you are supposed to have a ring, but I don't have one.

He begins to nod, and suddenly my mother feels very close. I look over my shoulder, my eyes peeking over the back of the last row of seats that we are leaning against. She has turned around, facing me. Permed hair, laugh lines not laughing.

"What did you just say?" she asks.

"I asked Ben to marry me."

The car starts moving forward again, and none of the parents are talking loud enough for us to hear them back here. I brace myself against the raised carpeted hump of the wheel well as Ben's father turns left onto the street before the turn onto our street. Sitting beside my mom is Ben's mother, who keeps staring forward, but I notice that one of her ears keeps swiveling back here, a little more each time. I am still facing my mother, who is still facing me, and for one last second, we look at each other without anything wrong between us.

"You shouldn't have said that," she says. "Boys don't marry other boys. Only boys and girls get married to each other."

She can't see our hands, but Ben pulls his away. I close my fingers into a loose fist and rub my palm to feel, and keep feeling, how strange his skin has made mine.

"Okay?" she asks.

"Yes," I say, but by accident my throat whispers the words.

She asks again. "Okay? Did you hear me?"

"Yes!" this time nearly shouting, and I wish we were already home so I could jump out and run to my bedroom. To be back here in the dark, private tail of the car suddenly feels wrong, so Ben and I each scoot off to our separate sides. "Yes," I say again, almost normally, turning away to face the rainy window. I feel her turn too as the radio baseball voice comes back up out of the quiet. The car starts to dip as we head down the hill of our street; our house is at the bottom. No one speaks for the rest of the ride. We all just sit and wait and watch our own views of the road—the parents see what is ahead of us while the only thing I can look at is what we have just left behind.

22

Incompressible Flow

Elissa Washuta

Big whirls have little whirls that feed on their velocity,
And little whirls have lesser whirls and so on to viscosity.

—*Lewis Fry Richardson*[1]

When my boyfriend asked me whether I was afraid of him, I told him I was not. When he told me I should be, I told him I was not. We hadn't been dating long but I already loved him. He worked on the boat motor in the sun while I sat on the dock, memorizing his biceps and reading one of his engineering textbooks I pulled from his bookcase. "You don't need to read that," he said, but I wouldn't accept that there were any books whose meaning I couldn't break. "It's too beautiful not to make sense to me," I said. "Too poetic." He said, just like the time he told me he loved me while he was sleeping and I was awake all night, "It doesn't mean what you want it to mean."

The science of fluid dynamics describes the motions of liquids and gases and their interactions with solid bodies. There are many ways to further subdivide fluid dynamics into special subjects. The plan of this book is to make the division into compressible and incompressible flows. Compressible flows are those in which changes in the fluid density [are]

impossible to predict: some days, love's viscosity was high, shown to me by his trust in my hands on the wheel of his boat. Love drove my slender biceps to scrub and wax fiberglass for days while he took to the uncovered, aging motor like a surgeon on an open heart. On the water, I studied his movement as he flipped his body upside-down, every muscle a hard cord

---

[1]All italicized passages from the textbook Incompressible Flow by Ronald Lee Panton. Edition unknown. The copy I used is in my ex-boyfriend's apartment, and I will never go back there.

when his wakeboard hit the lake. Other days, we fought. I was mad because he wouldn't say he loved me; he was mad because I was an idiot.

Incompressible flows, of either gases or liquids, are flows where density changes in the fluid are not an important part of the

fights we had. Whether I was having fun. Whether I was being bipolar. Whether I could help it. "We're more alike than you think," he said when I told him there was a thing inside me that I couldn't control. We never fought about the boat or the water. The only safe subject, eventually, was the one I couldn't understand.

The wing moves in a straight path, while the ship's propeller blades are rotating. The propeller operates in water, a nearly incompressible liquid, whereas the wing operates in air, a very compressible gas. The densities of these two fluids differ by a factor of

whether you believe what went on in my head or what came from his mouth the night I woke up with my nose between his finger and thumb, my mouth under his pressed palm. The water kicked at the beam that suspended the bed above the lake. The white moon stared hard. My boyfriend said, "You were snoring," and released me.

In spite of these obvious differences, these two flows are governed by the same laws, and their fluid dynamics are very similar. The purpose of the wing is to lift the airplane, while the purpose of the propeller is to

produce the thrust on the boat. I begged us forward, into our second winter, into seriousness as our friends put on suits and gowns and got serious adult marriages. He poured water on my cat and picked her up by her neck. In secret, I started smoking again.

The interface between a solid and a fluid is imagined to be a surface where the density jumps from one

brand of magic to the next, swelling and shrinking under the weight of my boyfriend and his board. He made the water seem like pavement. I tried the board, but the water flowed everywhere, never yielding to me as it did for him.

It is hard to give a precise description of a fundamental concept *such as mass, energy, or force. They are hazy ideas. We can describe their characteristics, tell how they act, express their relation to other ideas, but when it comes to saying what they are, we must resort to*

lying to ourselves. I don't remember whether I was afraid of him. I remember the way I would scream at him, drunk on beer gone hot in the sun that anointed the lake, but I've forgotten the topic and remember only the subtext. I don't even remember the words he used to convince me I should submit to being fucked in ways that hurt me. Years later, my psychiatrist told me my outbursts had probably been PTSD episodes. I didn't remember being afraid. I remembered feeling like I was in love. I can't make the division because I still don't understand the terms.

After he broke up with me, I chain-smoked for years. Water is nearly incompressible. Air is compressible. I still wonder whether I really did love him right up to the moment he started to smother me, whether I loved him in the second I thought I was going to die.

23

The Limit

Christian Wiman

*I don't understand anything… and I no longer want
to understand anything. I want to stick to the fact… If I
wanted to understand something, I would immediately
have to betray the fact, but I've made up my mind to
stick to the fact.*

—Dostoevsky, *The Brothers Karamazov*

I

I was fifteen when my best friend John shot his father in the face. It was
an accident, I'm certain, and but for the fact that I'd dropped a couple of
shotgun shells as I was fumbling to reload, the shot could have been mine. I
sometimes wonder what difference that might have made.

We were dove-hunting, catching them as they cleared the edge of the
small tank on John's family's property outside of town. Surrounding the tank
was a slight rise of brush before the fields, and John's father, a country doctor
who shared a small practice with my father, had wandered off through the
brush behind us to check the fenceline. I was close to my limit that afternoon,
which I'd never gotten, wearing one of those hunting vests with pockets big
enough to hold a dozen or so birds. I remember the full feel of it, reaching in
every so often to touch the little feathery lumps as they cooled. It was nearly
dusk, my favorite time in west Texas, the light like steeping tea, shadows
sliding out of things.

I'd been hunting for a couple of years. It seems odd to me now that I was
allowed to have a gun, as my family's history was not a placid one, and I
myself was prone to sudden destructive angers and what my grandmother
would call "the sulls." I have more than one vivid memory of being in my

bedroom as one of these angers subsides, books and clothes scattered on the floor, a chair and dresser overturned. I take the shotgun from under my bed and pump a shell into the chamber—roughly, so everyone in the house is sure to hear. No one comes. No one ever comes. I set the stock on the floor, lean my chin on the top of the barrel, stretch my arm down toward the trigger I can't quite touch, and wonder if this is something I'll grow into.

Theatrics, that gun aimed at my parents more than myself, with a kind of calculated malice that, twenty years later, makes me wince. My mother was terrified of guns. That my brother and I weren't allowed to have toy guns as we were growing up, yet both got shotguns as gifts in our early teens, is ironic, I suppose, though in that flat world of work and blunt fundamentalism in which I was raised, where in grade school county history lessons I learned the virtues of a man who'd slaughtered three of the seven white buffaloes known to exist, where one branch of my family had spent their happiest years in a town called "Dunn," it has only a sad sort of retroactive irony.

My mother's repellance of guns was something more than the expression of a delicate feminine sensibility. Her own mother had been murdered in front of her and her two brothers when she was fourteen. The killer was her father, about whom I know only that he was compulsively itinerant, almost certainly manic-depressive, and for the month or so prior to the act had been living apart from his family. He walked in the back door one evening and killed his wife as she was cooking dinner, waited while his children ran out into the fields, then laid down beside her in some simulacrum of spent desire and shot himself in the head.

This was just a story to me, less than that, really, since it wasn't so much told as breathed, a sort of steady pressure in the air. I don't remember it ever being mentioned, and yet I also don't remember a time when I didn't know about it. It had more reality for me than the night in my infancy when my father, who was also given to the sulls, went into his room and didn't come out for several months, for I have no memory of this and didn't learn of it until after I'd left home; but less reality than the aunt, Opal, who'd committed suicide before I was born. Supposedly, the whole extended family had conspired for a time to create their own private climate of calm, eradicating all hints of darkness from their lives like a country rigidly purging its past, steering conversations toward church and children, hiding the knives. It was hunting, as one might imagine, that proved most difficult in this regard, though Opal's husband was very careful to make sure their two sons kept their guns "hidden" under the beds, the shells all locked up in a little chest to which he had the only key. It seems not to have occurred to anyone that they might simply stop hunting and get rid of their guns. It was Texas. They were boys.

My family was so quiet about these matters that I thought they were something we were supposed to be embarrassed about. I learned early and no doubt too well that only certain kinds of violence were acceptable, both as topics of conversation and as actions. I loved the story of the uncle who, frustrated by a particularly recalcitrant cow, slammed his fist into its skull so hard that the cow dropped immediately to its knees like some ruined supplicant. I loved my immense, onomatopoetic uncles, Harley and Burley, who'd storm into town after months on offshore oil rigs, the nimbus of gentleness around each of them made more vivid and strange by their scars and hard talk, the wads of cash they pulled from their pockets like plunder.

And though I was mildly, reflexively disciplined by my father after the one truly serious fight I had growing up, when I was consumed with an anger that still unnerves me and continued to beat a cowboy I'll call Tom even after I'd broken bones in my hand and every blow was doing me a lot more damage than it was doing him, I was alert to the tacit masculine pride. Even the principal who meted out our corporal punishment for fighting on school grounds whipped our backsides with a kind of jocular aggressiveness that amounted to approval.

But anything that suggested madness rather than control, illness rather than health, feminine interiority rather than masculine action, was off-limits. Or perhaps not so much off-limits as simply outside of the realm of experience for which we had words, for I don't remember *resisting* discussing these things, really, or having them deflected by adults. Later, when I would begin to meet other young writers, who like myself generally had more imagination than available experience, the events of my family's history would acquire a kind of show-and-tell exoticism, little trinkets of authenticity brought back from the real world. That it wasn't a real world, not yet, that it had no more reality for me than what I read in books, didn't seem to matter too much at the time.

Now it does. At some point I stopped talking about my family's past and began re-inventing it, occasionally in what I wrote, but mostly just for myself, accumulating facts like little stones which I would smoothe and polish with the waters of imagination. I chose them very carefully, I realize now, nothing so big that it might dam up the flow, nothing too ugly and jagged to be worn down into the form I had in mind. Psychoanalysis is "creating a story that you can live with," I have been told, and perhaps that's what I was doing, though in truth I think I wanted less a story I could live with than one I could live without, less a past to inhabit than some re-created place I could walk finally, definitively away from.

The bullet hole between my grandmother's shoulder blades, then, and the way she crumples faster than a heartshot deer. I can see my grandfather stepping away from the door, can see the look in his eyes which, I know, is meant to assure his children as they back slowly out of the room that he is as baffled and saddened by this as they are, that they needn't be afraid, that he would never, never hurt *them*. He walks heavily across the room, steps over his wife, and, in some last gasp of that hopeless hardscrabble sanity his children will inherit and pass on, turns off the stove so the dinner won't burn, then lies down beside her on the floor

I can see my Aunt Opal, too, gathering the laundry, humming something, deciding at the last minute to wash the coats. She is not beautiful but there is something of the landscape's stark simplicity about her face, a sense of pure horizon, as if what you saw were merely the limit of your own vision, not the end of what is there. As she shakes out her husband's coat, a single forgotten shotgun shell falls out of the pocket onto the floor. I can see the dull copper where the light dies, the little puckered end of the red casing.

Lately, though, more and more, it's John I see, standing stolid and almost actual in his boots and hunting vest, lifting his shotgun to his shoulder and laughing as I fumble to load mine. He is physically very similar to me but at ease in his body in a way I'll never be. He does not yet inhabit that continuous present that precludes remorse, but already he is all impulse and action, whereas I am increasingly deliberate, increasingly interior. There is some inner, inarticulate anger we share, though, and recognize in each other. When John's begins to slip out of control, the results for the people around him will be immediate, palpable, and utterly disastrous. My own implosion will be no more noticeable to the people around me than something I've imagined.

The gun that goes off in my ear now is a fact. It is muted by all the intervening years, by all that has happened, both internally and externally. Still, the authority of its report surprises me, as does the strangely muffled shout that seems to occur at almost exactly the same time, as if the dove, which once again John has not missed, which as I look up is plunging downward, had a human cry.

II

I don't want to kill myself. I never have, though for a time not too long ago the act emerged in me like an instinct, abstractly at first, and with a sort of voluptuous, essentially literary pleasure (Nietzche: "The thought of suicide is a powerful solace; it enables a man to get through many a bad night.'"). Gradually the thought became more painful as it became more concrete, more dangerous as it became more familiar, more alienating as it became more my own. I thought of it as a kind of cancer in my mind, because eventually no matter what I was doing—teaching a class, sitting at a dinner party, trying to write, waking every hour of every night to check the clock— *that* was what I was doing, attending to that slowly clarifying imperative that beat itself out inside me as steadily and ineluctably as my own pulse.

I told no one. I couldn't. On the couple of occasions when I'd made up my mind that I would tell friends what was happening, my heart began to race, I had difficulty breathing, and I simply had no language for what I needed to say. Also, even during the worst of it, I always doubted the validity of the feeling, suspected that, like the impersonal stories I used to tell about my distant familial history, it might just be a bit of disingenuous self-dramatization. Despite the fact that I've had relatives on both sides of my family commit suicide; despite my knowledge that my father has resisted the impulse all his life, and my sister has twice attempted the act, I suspected I might be faking, using the thought of suicide as a way of avoiding the more mundane failures of my life. I wasn't going to tell anyone until I was *sure*. But how does one prove such terror is real except by committing the act itself?

My father knew, not definitively, perhaps, but with something like that visceral sense by which an artist comes to recognize the flaws in anything he's made. Our relationship is as fitful as ever—we go months without talking to each other—but there is more ease between us now, more forthright affection and trust. I think this has more to do with him than me. During the fifteen years or so when our relationship consisted of little more than holiday exchanges of information, he endured a divorce, bankruptcy, the loss of his medical practice, the death of his second wife, divorce again, back surgery, an almost fatal rattlesnake bite, a heart attack (from the volume of serum given to counter the snakebite), cancer, a plane crash, alcoholism, the estrangement and self-destruction of his children, and no doubt several other calamities which he's managed to keep secret. It was a run of luck that would have mellowed Caligula.

During the approximately six months that I was—what to call it?— thinking, sinking, we talked on the phone twice. On both occasions he asked me, out of the blue, and with a sort of mumbling quietude that I've begun to recognize in my own voice at emotional encroachments, "Do you ever think of doing away with yourself?" That's just the way he said it, "doing away with yourself," which led me to make a snide, annihilating comment about the linguistic imprecision and general uselessness of psychiatry, because in his late forties that's what my father had become, a psychiatrist living on the grounds of a state hospital, where suicide was as ubiquitous and predictable an impulse as hunger, where even the doctor whose place my father had taken, whose office he used and whose bedroom he slept in, had "done away with himself."

Some families accumulate self-consciousness in the way that others accumulate wealth (and perhaps one precludes the other). A man who eats and works and copulates all with same bland animal efficiency somehow sires a son who, maddeningly to the father, pauses occasionally in the midst of plowing to marvel at the shapes in the clouds, or who sometimes thinks fleetingly that perhaps there is an altogether different order of feeling than the mild kindliness he feels toward his wife. He in turn has a son who has the impulse to be elsewhere—geographically, sexually, spiritually—but not the wherewithal to wholly do so, who lives the impulsive, appetitive lives of his own children in the fixed world of his parents, and destroys both. A person emerging from the wreckage of this—and many simply don't—is likely to be quite solitary, given to winnowings and adept at departures, so absurdly self-aware that he can hardly make love without having an "experience." He might even be, maddeningly to all concerned, a poet.

That I should have turned out to be a poet seems strange to me for all sorts of reasons—I don't relish poverty or obscurity, to name just two—but my background has never seemed one of them. Bookless though it was, my childhood, with its nameless angers and solitudes, its intimate, inexplicable violence, seems to me "the very forge and working-house" of poetry. Tellingly, my father, though he certainly never read poetry, is the one member of my family for whom my becoming a poet never seemed at all odd or surprising. I begin to understand this now. He knew—he taught me—love's necessary severities, how it will work itself into, even be most intense within, forms of such austere and circumscribed dimensions that, to the uninitiated, it might not seem like love at all.

I am eight years old. My mother has been scratched by the kitten we've had for a month or so, and there has been a flurry of panic and activity as she has had the beginnings of a severe allergic reaction and been rushed to the hospital. I don't know where my brother and sister are, or why I've come home with my father, or if my mother is all right. I'm sitting on the couch, staring at the television, though it's not on. My father is looking for something in a kitchen drawer, now he's back in the bedroom looking for something else. My face is boneless, ghostly on the black screen. I'm hardly there. He walks past me with the kitten in one hand and a hammer in the other, opens the sliding glass door to the porch, closes it behind him. I shut my eyes, will myself away.

It's eight years later. My father is having an affair. He and my mother are at the edge of what will be a nasty, protracted, ruinous divorce in which their children will be used as weapons. It's the middle of the afternoon on a schoolday and I'm stoned, maybe on speed as well, I forget. Some little argument cracks the surface of civil estrangement we've tacitly agreed upon, and out of that rift all the old anger rises. I begin to curse at my mother in a way I've never done before or since, now I break something, now something else, and she's scared enough to call my father at the hospital and leave the house until he rushes home.

They come in together. I am sitting in the living room, seething, waiting. My father stands over me and quietly—guiltily, I realize, the first flaw in his hitherto adamantine authority—asks me what is going on. I tell him I'm ashamed of him. I call him a liar. I curse him in the harshest and most profane terms I can muster. He hits me open-handed across the face—hard, but with a last-minute hesitation in it, a pause of consciousness that seems to spread like a shadow across his face and, as he sinks into a chair, is to this day the purest sadness I have ever seen.

I stand up slowly. I am vaguely aware of my mother yelling at my father, of my sister in the doorway weeping. I am vaguely aware that our roles have suddenly and irrevocably reversed, that he is looking up at me, waiting for what I'll do. I hit him squarely between the eyes, much harder than he hit me. He does nothing but cover his head with his hands, doesn't say a word as I hit him again, and again, and again, expending my anger upon a silence that absorbs it, and gradually neutralizes it, until the last blow is closer to a caress.

That was the end of my childhood. My father moved out within a month or so, and in the same time I gave up drugs (well, close enough), began the exercise regimen that I've maintained for twenty years, and started assiduously saving for the tuition for my first year of college, to which I was suddenly determined to go, and which I would choose entirely on the basis of its distance from Texas. Once there I sometimes went months without talking to any member of my family, whose lives seemed to me as dangerously aimless and out of control as mine was safely ordered and purposeful. I began to read poetry, which I loved most of all for the contained force of its forms, the release of its music, and for the fact that, as far as I could tell, it had absolutely nothing to do with the world I was from.

And then one night John killed a man outside of a bar. I'd kept up with him somewhat, had been forced to, in fact, since in a final assertion of physical superiority he'd ended my lingering relationship with my high school girlfriend by impregnating her. I knew that he'd gone to work in the oilfields, and that he was deep into drugs. Our friendship had fallen apart before this, though, a slow, sad disintegration that culminated in a halfhearted, inconclusive fistfight on a dirt road outside of town. I forget the reason for the fight itself, and anyway it wouldn't be relevant. What we were trying to do, I think, was to formalize the end of something that had meant a great deal to both of us, to attach an act we understood to a demise we didn't.

My mother called to tell me about it. John had gotten in an argument with a stranger that escalated into blows. They had been thrown out of the bar by bouncers and continued the fight in the street. In front of some thirty or forty people John had slowly and with great difficulty won the fight, beating the man until he lay on his back gasping for air. And whether the pause I've imagined over and over at this point is something that came out in the trial, or whether it's merely some residual effect of my friendship with John, my memory of a decent and sensitive person to whom some glimmer of consciousness must surely have come, what happened in the end is a fact. At nineteen years old, with his bare hands, in front of a crowd of people who did nothing, and with a final fury that must have amazed that man who was only its incidental object, John destroyed him.

Hanging up the phone, sitting there in my dorm room of that preposterously preppy college fifteen hundred miles away from my home, it all came back, the guns and the fights, the wreckage of my family, my friendship with John, the wonderment in his voice in the hours after that hunting accident when he kept saying, *I shot my father, I shot my own father,* as if he were trying out the thought, trying to accomodate it in his consciousness.

I did what I always do: I went for a run, thirteen miles through the hills of Virginia, much farther than I usually ran, but without difficulty, my heart a steady thump-thump-thump in my chest. It was not release. It was the same thing as my precipitous decision to get out of Texas, no different from what poetry would be for me for years, until I would finally find myself back home one day, living on the grounds of that state hospital, collecting facts. It was what suicide would have been the final expression of: flight.

III

Dr. Miller's face was obliterated. He walked out of the brush across from us and around the edge of the tank with the hesitant precision of someone making his way across a familiar room in the dark. Amid the blood and loose bits of skin there were clumps of pellets cauliflowering his cheeks and the sockets of his eyes, distorting his forehead and throat like a sudden, hideous disease, his dark shirt darker down his chest. His lips, too, were so misshapen that it was hard at first to understand the directives he was giving us, though he spoke calmly, deliberately, with the same west Texas mix of practical necessity and existential futility that no crisis could ever shock my own father out of.

He drove. I don't remember there being even a moment of discussion, though both John and I had our licences by then, and though Dr. Miller had to lean over the steering wheel to see, wincing as the pickup jolted over the ruts and stones. I was sitting in the middle of the seat, John at the door. I kept trying not to look at Dr. Miller, kept thinking that his breaths were shorter than they should have been, that I could hear blood in his lungs.

There were two gates before we got to the road. At the first one, John simply leapt back in the truck as it was still moving, leaving the gate unlatched. Dr. Miller stopped, turned his head like some sentient piece of meat toward us, and said, "Close the gate, John."

At the second gate, after John had gotten out of the truck, Dr. Miller said without looking toward me, "You didn't fire that shot, did you?"

Could it be, in life as well as in writing, that our deepest regrets will not be for our lies, but for the truths we should not have told?

"He didn't mean to," I said, the words spilling out me, "it was an accident, we thought you were in the south pasture, we didn't hear you, we … "

"It's my fault," Dr. Miller said peremptorily, putting his hand on my knee. "I know that."

About halfway through the ride John began to weep. He was leaning over against the door, and as his shoulders trembled up and down, it seemed years were falling away from him, that if he were to reach out it would be with a hand from which all the strength was gone, if he were to speak it would be in the voice of a child. I looked out at the fields that had almost vanished, darkness knitting together the limbs of mesquite trees, accumulating to itself the crows and telephone poles, the black relentless pumpjacks which, when John and I spent the night out here, beat into our sleep like the earth's heart.

Dr. Miller drove himself straight to my father, who was still at the office. My father registered no more alarm for Dr. Miller's injuries than Dr. Miller himself had done, though my father did, I noticed, immediately and carefully touch my face, my shoulders and arms, as if to ensure himself that I wasn't the one hurt.

John and I waited in my father's office. I sat in my father's chair behind the desk, John in the chair across from me, looking out the window. This is when I remember him saying, "I shot my father, I shot my own father," not to me, and almost as if it were a question, one that neither I nor anyone else could answer. Not another word was said. I sat there watching the clock on the wall across from me, willing it to go faster, faster.

To be a writer is to betray the facts. It's one of the more ruthless things about being a writer, finally, in that to cast an experience into words is in some way to lose the reality of the experience itself, to sacrifice the fact of it to whatever imaginative pattern one's wound requires. A great deal is gained, I suppose, a kind of control, the sort of factitious understanding that Ivan Karamazov renounces in my epigraph, *form*. When I began to spiral into myself and into my family's history, it was just this sort of willful understanding that I needed. I knew the facts well enough.

But I don't understand, not really. Not my family's history and not my childhood, neither my father's actions nor his absence. I don't understand how John could kill someone, or by what logic or luck the courses of our lives, which had such similar origins, could be so different. I don't understand, when there is so much I love about my life, how I could have such a strong impulse to end it, nor by what dispensation or accident of chemistry that impulse could go away, recede so far into my consciousness that I could almost believe it never happened.

It did happen, though. It marked me. I don't believe in "laying to rest" the past. There are wounds we won't get over. There are things that happen to us that, no matter how hard we try to forget, no matter with what fortitude we face them, what mix of religion and therapy we swallow, what finished and durable forms of art we turn them into, are going to go on happening inside of us for as long as our brains are alive.

And yet I've come to believe, and in rare moments can almost feel, that like an illness some vestige of which the body keeps to protect itself, pain may be its own reprieve; that the violence that is latent within us may be, if never altogether dispelled or tamed, at least acknowledged, defined, and perhaps by dint of the love we feel for our lives, for the people in them and for our work, rendered into an energy that need not be inflicted on others or ourselves, an energy we may even be able to use; and that for those of us who have gone to war with our own minds there is yet hope for what Freud called "normal unhappiness," wherein we might remember the dead without being haunted by them, give to our lives a coherence that is not "closure," and learn to live with our memories, our families, and ourselves amid a truce that is not peace.

I hear my father calling me from what seems a great distance. I walk down the hall of the office that has long ago been cleared out and turned into something else. But here are my family's pictures on the walls, here is the receptionist's window where my sister and I would play a game in which one of us had some dire illness which the other, with a cup of water, or with some inscrutable rune written on a prescription pad, always had the remedy for. And here is John, small and terrified, walking beside me.

Dr. Miller is sitting up on an examining table, his face swathed in gauze, his shirt off, revealing a sallow, soft, middle-aged body. Its whiteness shocks me like a camera's flash and will be the first thing I'll think of when, within months, John tells me that his father has left for another woman. We stop just inside the door, side by side. My heart seems almost audible.

"Well now," my father says, smiling slightly as he looks to the table then back to us, "did you boys get your limits?"

Dr. Miller laughs, and John moves toward him.

He is all right. Everything is going to be all right. I stick my hand in my pocket full of cold birds to feel how close I've come.

24

Self Erasure

Brooke Juliet Wonders

Words cannot possibly describe

sorry

I'm afraid

I'm afraid

I am so sorry

I'm afraid

I am so very sorry

I fear

I'm really really

truly deeply sorry

Rob

██ how
████████████████████████████████ I could not be there for you
████████████████████████████████ I'm ██████████████████
██ only so strong and █████████████████████████████ I just no
longer knew how. ███████████████████████████████████
████████████████████ the good in the world █████████████
███
███████████████████████████████████████ caused me
the most hurt ████████████████ I am ██████████████████
███████████████████████████████ here for myself. Please
remember █████████████████████ to be █████████████████
content, █████████████████████████████████ living ██
███████████████████████████ people ██████████████
████ Family, loves, friends, acquaintances. █████████ a choice like this is
████████████████████████████████████ selfish █████
███
███
███
███
███
███████████████ TAKE CARE OF YOURSELF████████████████
███
███
███
███
███
████████████████████████ before you forget how.

Oh my god I love you so much.

Rob

cannot

not

difficult,

no

I just haven't been

Haven't been able to

hurt   I couldn't

if that no longer holds true   you're no longer living

I've reached that point

not fair

no longer hold any allure.

now I   can't bare [sic] the pain.

it's   hurt too much for too long.

For far too long

you lose track of what in life is truly you.   you no longer know what to do with yourself and then noone [sic] else knows what to do with you either.

Rob

███████ love ██████████████████████████████
████████ have meant ██████ am █████████ could not be ██████
██████████████████ have been █████████ afraid ██████
was █████████████ found ██████████████ give ██
█████████████ afraid ████████████ haven't been ████
Haven't been able to find ███████████████████ been
██████████ seeking out and holding on to. ███ have always been ████
███ love ██████████████████████████ caused ██
█████████ feel ██████ am █████████ couldn't be ████
█████████ been ████████ been able to be ███████
remember █████████████ have to be ████████████
████████████████████ holds █████████████ living. ██
afraid ██ reached █████████ affecting ████████████ love ██
██████████ loves, ████████████ know ████ choice █████
█████████ to deal with ██ know ███████████ gesture
███ am █████████ seen ███████████████████
████████████████ fear ███████████████
gotten ████████████████████████████████ bare
██████████ think ██ to say is ███████████████
████████████████████ take care ████████████
███████ TAKE CARE ████████████████████
thought ██████████████████████████████ lose
████████████████████████ know ████████████
██████ know █████████████████████ knows ████ to
do ████████ Find ████████ Cling ████████████ are
████████████ is █████████████████████ Give
████████████████████████ forget ███.

████████ love ████████

Rob

I

am

content, because

I am

now

noone

Rob

██████████████████████████████ Words ████████████ describe ██████
███

███████████████ later years ████████████████████████████ my heart
████████ strong and █ just found ██████████████████████████████████

████████████████████████████ the good in the world ████████████████
████████ seeking █████████████████████████████████ the person
███ I love most in the world and and the person that ██████████████
████████████████████████████████ I could █ be ███ for
you ██
████████ first and foremost ████████████████████████████████████
██ living. ███
██████████████████████ It's affecting ████████████████████████
███████████████████████████████████ a choice like this is
██ fair to ██
███

████████████████████ this world ████████████████████████████████
███████ All I can think of to say is I██ really really ████████████
███████████████████████████████████████ care ██████████████
████████████████████████████████████ For ██████████████████
██ you ███
███
███

███████████████████████ your family███████████████████████ are
wonderful people. ███ there is not a sweeter soul around than ████████
█████████████████████████████ you ████████████

Oh my god I love you so much.

Rob

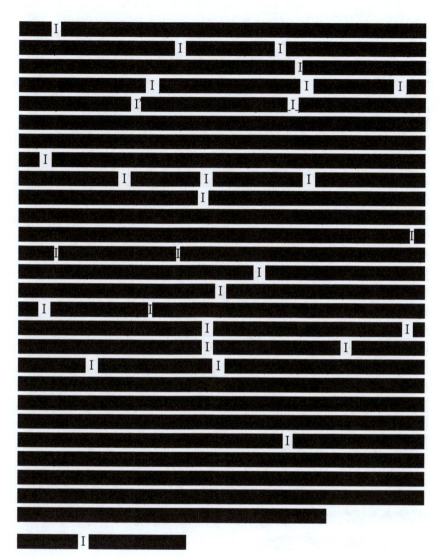

Rob

██
██
██
██
██
██
██
██
██
██
██
██
██
██
██
██

████████████████████ I've seen many beautiful sunsets and more than my
share of breathtaking sunrises ██████████████████████

██
██
██
██
██
██
██
██
██
██
████████████████████████████████

Oh my god ██████████████

Rob

My boyfriend ▮ took his ▮ life ▮▮▮ on August 21, 2005. ▮ years later, I still can't ▮▮▮▮ read this letter without ▮▮▮.

25

Godspeed

Xu Xi

The day our cook threatened to quit, I witnessed my first layoff.

The victim was Ah Siu. Hers was a no-name name, without clear demarcation for a family or first name. Back when my father still had money in the sixties, she was hired to look after the four children. "Nanny" would be too classy, "domestic helper" too modern and politically correct. Back then she was a "servant," along with our cook and washerwoman.

When she first arrived, I was around seven or eight and promptly fell in love. She was everything my mother could not be: lenient, undemanding, tolerant of my childishness. Most of all, she seemed to favor me, or so I imagined, the unworthy eldest child whose only job in the family was to serve as an "example" for the younger ones. I despised my exemplary role, even as I guarded it with fierce pride, relishing the privilege of being told that *Mummy must take care of brother because he's sickly, or sister who's still small, or sister who's not as good a girl as you.* I didn't always trust that praise, wondering if perhaps Mummy actually didn't want to take care of me. Ah Siu gave me all her time, listening to my stories, paying me undivided attention, treating me like her own girl.

All three servants boarded with us, sharing a bedroom in the rear two-bedroom guest flat we owned, and only had one day off. They were expected to start work at sunrise and retire at night, often quite late. My parents did not like us spending time in their quarters, but I hung out in the rear apartment, curious and lovestruck, my excuse being the piano which I practiced in that living room. I thought of the servants as part of our family because, despite everything my parents said to the contrary, I saw no difference between them and us, especially not Ah Siu.

It was a shock, then, when she told me she had a home in the New Territories and a little girl, a daughter she saw once a week, on Sundays, her day off. How could she belong to someone else? She was my Ah Siu, mine! Yet

I quickly swallowed that thought, overwhelmed instead with sorrow that Ah Siu couldn't live with her family, and turned my anger towards my parents, Mum especially, that such employment injustice existed. However, this did not translate into *my* not having Ah Siu. I was a pragmatic, if melodramatic child.

After that, I treated Ah Siu with a little distance, except when the desire to be babied overwhelmed. If my report card was less than stellar, Ah Siu gave me a never-mind smile. If Ah Yee, the cook, yelled, as she often did, I could flee to Ah Siu's tenderness. I was not a sissy child, and in fact, resisted tears to win the "good girl" accolade from Mum. But what I recall of Ah Siu was a sweet refuge in the raucous household of my childhood, where my father was often overseas on business, my mother overwhelmed and exhausted by the household and servants, where guests needed "to be waited on hand and foot" as Mum said of our numerous Indonesian relations, especially those of my father's, because the servants and my mother had to work twice as hard for these folks, accustomed to legions of servants in their large Indonesian homes, in contrast to our puny three.

Then came the big fight, the details of which I never knew, between Ah Yee and Ah Siu. Shouts and tears. Mum intervening. Loud threats by our cook that she would quit, right now, if Mum didn't fire *that woman*. Before I knew it, Mum said Ah Siu was leaving. Not a single objection I raised was heard; a good cook, however temperamental, was harder to find.

Ah Siu packed her things and prepared to leave.

I sulked. I refused to leave my bedroom. So what, I told myself, *she's only a servant*, echoing my mother's words.

At the last possible moment, I snatched my favorite thing of the time—a tiny statue of Mercury with his quicksilver wings—and ran to the front door. *Here,* I said, *this is for you,* and tried to tell her about the Greek messenger god. But I was inarticulate, unable to tell a story, unable to arrive at catharsis.

She took the statue, smiled a never-mind smile, hugged me, and we cried in each other's arms.

And now I am grown up, or at least pretend to be, and to date have not perpetuated the indentured servitude of a "domestic helper" for myself. Once, back in the eighties in New York City, I hired a part time cleaning woman from Columbia. Watching her work, I felt slightly ashamed, because after all, I should be capable of cleaning up my own mess. Throughout my adult life in Hong Kong, I have cleaned and cooked for myself. Of course, unlike many friends and acquaintances, I do not have children as well as a career, so I don't have to balance that equation. Yet I cannot help feeling there is something wrong with the equation, that it is fundamentally unsound, even if it is the basis of the global economy of the servant class.

Why is it Hong Kong's well being depends on perpetuating the servant class?

Today's Ah Siu's are Filipino. Her day off is usually Sunday, and in some households, she works the long, absurd hours of my family's servants back in the sixties. I know all the arguments: Hong Kong provides employment for a nation of people whose economy needs help; our city has laws and does not tolerate abuse or unfair treatment of the servant class; this is just the way of the world, isn't it, that some rule and others serve? The subtext is clear: in the end, they are "only servants," democracy be damned.

Yet what is it about our culture that this upstairs-downstairs practice thrives so long and well, this wholly intolerable thing?

This year, my sister and I became employers, for the first time in both our lives, of two domestic helpers from the Philippines. They do not clean, cook or care for either of our households, because their jobs are to live with and look after our elderly mother who has Alzheimer's, and who needs round-the-clock monitoring. One woman is a qualified nurse, the other an excellent cook. Both of them are educated and intelligent professionals, as well as wives and mothers, hardly "servants." We call them employees, and though I live at my mother's address, my space is separate and I clean it myself. The only concession is to have them do my laundry, as there is only one washing machine on location. But the ironing is my job since I am fussy about my clothes. This is not something I need to employ someone to do for me.

For my mother however, as her memory fades, she has her "girls" at home to simulate the noise and chatter of family, since none of her real family live with her. My mother, as she grows more frail slips in and out of the life she once knew, ordering the "servants" around as a salve to pride, even though they know better than to pay attention. It is unenviable, the way we age today.

And I am merely a messenger, the fleet-of-foot god, with the story of a privileged history I cannot revise. All I can do is try to live a life that does not perpetuate the wholly intolerable, to avoid what strikes me as childish practices, the ones my city seems so unable to eliminate.

26

A Few Thoughts while Shaving

Kristen Millares Young

It's getting harder and harder to shave my pussy, let alone the tight star of my asshole. At this point in my pregnancy, a leg up and lifelong sense of my own topography are required to circumnavigate the globe of my belly. A hand mirror would be good, but this isn't the 70s, though it might as well be, since in a proverbial sense I just took off my panties in a room full of like-minded people.

My husband shaves his beard with my razor every morning. The blades are dulled by the time they get to me, but I don't mind. He's worth it. He thinks I can make it as a novelist, a belief I have not been able to shake, despite the odds.

We're planning on two kids, and as this boy burgeons within me, I'm considering whether to ask my doctor to harvest my tubes moments after birth, if it happens that I deliver by Caesarian after a full day of unmedicated back labor, like the first time, last year.

Disaster looms. Murphy's Law and all. I can't even write what I'm afraid might happen. It's smart to keep a generator. That's what I learned growing up in hurricane country. That, and get a ring on your finger before it's too late. The good ones get gone, and what's left is damaged beyond repair. Or maybe that's me.

Will I have time to write, or won't I? That's not a question that kids answer for you. It's a discipline, like joy, and I'm working on it.

I didn't think I'd get to make these decisions. Twelve years ago, I woke shaking from anesthesia to a nurse who told me they took my right ovary while I was out. Didn't ask, slipped a sack around its bulk and began chopping, working with a camera and a knife and a noose tightened around the mouth of the bag.

My hospital room filled with bouquets. I shocked a college friend by tossing the carnations. He didn't know I was capable of such ruthlessness. He should have seen what I did to the drafts of my first novel, but by then, we were no longer speaking.

After weeks of healing up, I shuffled to the stationary store, wincing with the pull of each stitch, taking the sidewalk so slow that people parted and coursed around me, and for the first time, I felt true kinship with the old.

I had to rest on a bench halfway down the block. Hand on my swollen stomach, I stared into a café. At its door, a starched waitress looked me over. You should eat, she said. Think about the baby. I smiled, the smell of warm garbage rising around us. Dumpsters still make me nostalgic for New York.

The point is, I was given time to develop nostalgia and have children. Ovarian cancer is deadliest in the young. By what must be called a miracle, no small mercy but a goddamned miracle, a cyst grew on my left ovary to sound the warning bell with painful farts and bloat while, unbeknownst to the many scans that preceded my surgery, a tumor grew over my right ovary like a second skin, a shroud.

Turns out my surgeon was the curious sort. Once she cut out the cyst, she turned her camera on my other ovary—took a tour through the neighborhood, so to speak—and I can only imagine the shock and dread of seeing what slipped past the tests, and perhaps a moment of self-congratulations before she readied another bag to pass through the hole she'd opened at my bellybutton.

She didn't save the tumor for me to inspect. She said it looked like cauliflower, but gray.

I was given time.

During my first pregnancy, dark patches of skin surfaced on my forehead and upper lip, where they bob like kelp in the sea. Lines have moved in around my mouth and eyes. My first birth scar healed red. It smiles, eclipsed by my planetary torso.

My bout with cancer was over quick. No chemo, no radiation. The tumor was borderline, not quite benign, but not yet on the attack. I think of it as a dandelion head teeming with fluff, cupped slow and careful before the gust.

After the swelling subsided, everyone thought I looked great, by which they meant skinny, and I was. Released from my post-grad internship by editors who sent a card but no job offer, I booked a colonoscopy and an unpaid reporting assignment in Buenos Aires. I coasted on the savings from my first internship, that cushy cul de sac, having learned frugality from both sides of my family, the military line and the immigrants. My forebears knew how to duck a dictator and surface in a new country. Like them, I was eager to work.

Soon after, I became a beat reporter at a daily paper. Business, then politics. Which was exhausting, as one might imagine, deadlines rolling in without cease, the stress candied with exhilaration I chose for myself as though my body had not already warned me. Even now, years after the newspaper closed, my eyes are shadowed. I drive myself hard, draft after draft. In the dark hours, my elder son cries and reaches for me, his sobs echoing to his brother through thick fluid. I haven't slept the night since he was born.

I am learning to accept myself. I hear that's the first step toward love. And I need, so desperately, to love these boys right. If only for that reason, I will do this thing that I once found unfathomable.

Besides, my face looks like it's fixing to stay this way.

My dad ignored the lump in his throat for months. The tumor's shadow cuts across his neck in a picture of him on the boat in the Everglades, his head to one side. Just before the diagnosis, he was swarthy and powerful. He emerged from chemo pale and thinned. Radiation burned his throat so bad he toted a thermos of milk for years.

He's strong again. We're fighters in this clan. My kin have a habit of leaving trauma behind. By which I mean moving on. But of course, you always carry it with you.

When I was fourteen, my mother sent me back across the country to my dad's home in Florida. Just for the summer, to spend some time with him since the big move. When I got back to California, her hair was different. Coiffed, with shiny bangs. She was bony, and in the dimmed light of her bedroom, her smoky eyeliner made her look like a movie star.

Of course, she'd had a double mastectomy and started chemo while I was gone.

At first, I didn't want anyone at school to know she was sick. I hate being pitied. When the news got around, I felt weak and went to lie down in the bleachers during volleyball practice. I told no one about the papery space suits we were made to wear for visits after her bone marrow transplant. Someone accused me of using her surgeries to delay turning in papers, which was true. Nothing sharpens the mind like a deadline.

That may be why I'm so productive while pregnant. I will not give up on this manuscript despite fatigue that settles over me like fog. I have to sit down midway through my showers. Good thing there's a bench. I move on to my legs, what I can reach of them, while my toddler plays with plastic dinosaurs, sponge letters, a yellow bucket he fills and empties, again and again.

I know. How can I shave with him in the shower? When else?

I weaned him when he was fourteen months old, and I deep into my second trimester. Nearing birth again, my breasts have readied for the suckle, heavy with golden drops that well onto my thighs. To transcribe my family history of treacherous insides feels like begging questions I can ill afford to pose.

Submitting to one's own potential demands constant parley with the loss of control. Labor taught me that. My first inkling was when I pooped on the body pillow my sister lent me. Oh, I said. Okay.

I threw up dozens of times in the hours that followed.

To catch the wave of pain and stay above it. To breathe it down. To rock back and forth, standing, kneeling, in the bathtub, on the bed, down the hall, arms round the neck of the nearest person who can bear such weight. To fill the room with sound. To recognize there will be no end to pain until life is brought forth, slick and wriggling, from a slit of some kind.

For this sole purpose, I would have given of myself unto death. If there comes a choice, save the baby, I told my husband. Don't say that, he replied. You're both coming home with me.

Nothing worth doing comes easy. I have plumbed my whole being for the hope needed to bring these treasures into the world. They are teaching me to yield to joy.

I tap my razor onto the wall. Our son spreads the foam across the tile and draws a sun in the bristles.

Over time, I have come to understand that there is no deserving of happiness, only the great fortune of receiving it. By this measure, I am rich, given a vocation and years to see it through, granted one son and pledged another, gifted promise that lives within, kicking and kicking and kicking.

Contributors

Austin Bunn is the author of *The Brink* and his writing has been published in *The New York Times Magazine*, *The Atlantic*, *Best American Science and Nature Writing*, *Best American Fantasy*, and the *Pushcart Prize*. He wrote the screenplay to the film *Kill Your Darlings*, starring Daniel Radcliffe. "Basement Story" won the *Missouri Review* Audio Essay prize and has been broadcast on WBEZ, Australian Radio 360, and at the *Third Coast* Audio Festival.

Amy Butcher is the author of the forthcoming *Mothertrucker*. Her first book, *Visiting Hours*, earned starred reviews and praise from *The New York Times Sunday Review of Books*, *NPR*, and others. Additional essays have earned notable distinctions in the 2015, 2016, 2017, and 2018 editions of the *Best American Essays* series. She is an Associate Professor of English at Ohio Wesleyan University and lives in Columbus, Ohio, with her two rescue dogs.

Seo-Young Chu is an associate professor in the English Department at Queens College, CUNY. Her publications include *Do Metaphors Dream of Literal Sleep? A Science-Fictional Theory of Representation*, "I, Stereotype: Detained in the Uncanny Valley," "Chogakpo Fantasia," "Free Indirect Suicide," and "A Refuge for Jae-in Doe: Fugues in the Key of English Major."

Melissa Febos is the author of *Girlhood*, *Whip Smart*, and *Abandon Me*. She is the winner of the Jeanne Córdova Nonfiction Award from LAMBDA Literary and the recipient of fellowships from the MacDowell Colony, Bread Loaf Writer's Conference, Virginia Center for Creative Arts, The BAU Institute, The Barbara Deming Memorial Foundation, Vermont Studio Center, and others. Her work has recently appeared in *Tin House*, *Granta*, *The Believer*, *The Sewanee Review*, and *The New York Times*.

Kathy Fish has published five collections of short fiction, most recently *Wild Life: Collected Works from 2003-2018*. Her work has been anthologized in *Best Small Fictions*, *Best American Nonrequired Reading*, and a forthcoming *Norton Reader*. She is a core faculty member for the Mile High MFA at Regis University in Denver, Colorado, and teaches her own intensive online flash fiction workshop.

Harrison Candelaria Fletcher in the author of the award-winning *Descanso for My Father: Fragments of a Life* and *Presentimiento: A Life in Dreams*. His lyric essays, personal essays and prose poems have appeared in such venues as *New Letters, TriQuarterly, Fourth Genre* and *Brevity*. A native New Mexican, he teaches in the MFA Programs at Vermont College of Fine Arts and Colorado State University.

Ross Gay is the author of three books of poetry: *Against Which; Bringing the Shovel Down;* and *Catalog of Unabashed Gratitude,* winner of the National Book Critics Circle Award and the Kingsley Tufts Poetry Award. He is the author of the essay collection, *The Book of Delights*. Ross is co-author of the chapbook "Lace and Pyrite: Letters from Two Gardens," in addition to being co-author of the chapbook, "River." He has received fellowships from Cave Canem, the Bread Loaf Writer's Conference, and the Guggenheim Foundation. Ross teaches at Indiana University.

Och Gonzalez is a writer, artist, and teacher from Manila, Philippines. Her work in nonfiction has earned her a Palanca Award for Literature in the Philippines, and her writing has appeared in *Esquire, Brevity Journal of Literary Nonfiction, Panorama Journal of Intelligent Travel, Flash Fiction Magazine, Microfiction Mondays,* and elsewhere. She is currently at work on her first collection of flash nonfiction.

Peter Grandbois is the author of ten books, the most recent of which is *half-burnt*. His poems, stories, and essays have appeared in over one hundred journals. His plays have been performed in St. Louis, Columbus, Los Angeles, and New York. He is the poetry editor for *Boulevard* and teaches at Denison University in Ohio.

Major Jackson is the author of five books of poetry, including *The Absurd Man, Roll Deep, Holding Company, Hoops* and *Leaving Saturn*. His edited volumes include: *Best American Poetry 2019, Renga for Obama,* and Library of America's *Countee Cullen: Collected Poems*. A recipient of fellowships from Guggenheim Foundation and the National Endowment for the Arts, Major Jackson is the Gertrude Conaway Vanderbilt Chair in the Humanities at Vanderbilt University.

Sarah Minor is the author of *Slim Confessions, History of the Interior* and *The Persistence of the Bonyleg: Annotated,* a digital chapbook. Minor is the recipient of a Research Fellowship to Iceland from the American-Scandinavian

Foundation and was awarded the *Gulf Coast* Barthelme Prize in Short Prose. She teaches creative writing at the Cleveland Institute of Art.

Jonathan Rovner recently finished a three-year stint teaching English in Sulaymaniyah, Iraq. His work has appeared in *The Indiana Review, The Normal School*, and *Willow Springs*, among others. He lives in northwest Nebraska with his wife and daughter.

Vijay Seshadri the author of the poetry books *Wild Kingdom, The Long Meadow, The Disappearances*, and *3 Sections*, as well as many essays, reviews, and memoir fragments. His work has been widely published and anthologized and recognized with many honors, most recently the 2014 Pulitzer Prize for Poetry and, in 2015, the Literature Award of the American Academy of Arts and Letters. He currently teaches at Sarah Lawrence College.

Vivek Shraya is an artist whose body of work crosses the boundaries of music, literature, visual art, theatre, and film. Her best-selling book *I'm Afraid of Men* was heralded by *Vanity Fair* as "cultural rocket fuel." A five-time Lambda Literary Award finalist, Vivek was a 2016 Pride Toronto Grand Marshal and has received honors from the Writers' Trust of Canada and the Publishing Triangle. She is a director on the board of the Tegan and Sara Foundation and Assistant Professor of Creative Writing at the University of Calgary.

Margot Singer is the author of a novel, *Underground Fugue*, and a collection of linked short stories, *The Pale of Settlement*. She is also the co-editor, with Nicole Walker, of *Bending Genre: Essays on Creative Nonfiction*. Her work has received a number of awards, including Edward Lewis Wallant Award for Jewish-American Fiction and the Flannery O'Connor Award for Short Fiction. She is a Professor at Denison University, in Granville, Ohio, where she directs the creative writing program.

Ira Sukrungruang is the author of three nonfiction books: *Buddha's Dog & Other Mediations, Southside Buddhist*, and *Talk Thai: The Adventures of Buddhist Boy*; the short story collection *The Melting Season*; and the poetry collection *In Thailand It Is Night*. He is the president of *Sweet: A Literary Confection* and the Richard L. Thomas Professor of Creative Writing at Kenyon College.

Jill Talbot is the author of *The Way We Weren't: A Memoir* and *Loaded: Women and Addiction*. She's also the editor of *Metawritings: Toward a Theory of Nonfiction*. Her essays have appeared in *AGNI, Colorado Review,*

Diagram, Ecotone, Hotel Amerika, Longreads, The Normal School, and *The Paris Review Daily,* among others.

Abigail Thomas is the author of *Safekeeping, A Three Dog Life,* and *What Comes Next and How to Like It.* She lives in Woodstock, New York, with her dogs. She has four children, twelve grandchildren, one great-grandchild, and a high school education.

Ryan Van Meter is the author of the essay collection *If You Knew Then What I Know Now.* His essays have been selected for anthologies including *Best American Essays.* He lives in California and teaches at the University of San Francisco.

Elissa Washuta is a member of the Cowlitz Indian Tribe and a nonfiction writer. She is the author of *White Magic, Starvation Mode,* and *My Body Is a Book of Rules* and co-editor of *Shapes of Native Nonfiction: Collected Essays by Contemporary Writers.* She has received fellowships and awards from the National Endowment for the Arts, Creative Capital, Artist Trust, 4Culture, and Potlatch Fund. Elissa is an assistant professor of creative writing at the Ohio State University.

Christian Wiman is the author of numerous books of poetry and non-fiction. He has been editor of *Poetry* magazine and currently teaches at Yale.

Brooke Juliet Wonders is an assistant professor at the University of Northern Iowa. Her work has appeared in the *Collagist, Cutbank,* and *Black Warrior Review,* among others. She serves as nonfiction editor at *The North American Review* and is also a founding editor of *Grimoire Magazine.*

Xu Xi 許素細 is author of fourteen books of fiction and nonfiction, most recently *This Fish is Fowl: Essays of Being.* An Indonesian-Chinese-American diehard transnational, she splits her life, unevenly, between the state of New York and the rest of the world.

Kristen Millares Young is the author of the novel *Subduction.* The current Prose Writer-in-Residence at Hugo House, Kristen is a prize-winning journalist, book critic, and essayist. Her work appears in the *Washington Post, The Guardian, The New York Times, Poetry Northwest, Crosscut, Hobart, Proximity, Moss, Pie & Whiskey,* and *Latina Outsiders: Remaking Latina Identity.* Kristen was the researcher for the *New York Times* team that produced "Snow Fall," which won a Pulitzer.

Index